LECTURES ON SOCIAL MORALITY.

SOCIAL MORALITY.

TWENTY-ONE LECTURES

DELIVERED IN

The University of Cambridge.

BY

F. D. MAURICE,
PROFESSOR OF CASUISTRY AND MORAL PHILOSOPHY.

WIPF & STOCK · Eugene, Oregon

Wipf and Stock Publishers
199 W 8th Ave, Suite 3
Eugene, OR 97401

Social Morality
Twenty-one Lectures Delivered in
The University of Cambridge
By Maurice, Frederick D.
ISBN 13: 978-1-60899-714-5
Publication date 5/12/2010
Previously published by Macmillan and Co., 1893

THESE LECTURES,

ADDRESSED TO YOUNG MEN

AND DESIGNED SPECIALLY FOR THEIR USE,

ARE DEDICATED

TO TWO WHO DID NOT HEAR THEM,

FOR WHOSE WELL BEING AND WELL DOING,

DOMESTIC, NATIONAL, HUMAN,

THE LECTURER

HAS THE DEEPEST RESPONSIBILITY,

THROUGH WHOM HE HAS LEARNT TO FEEL

FOR ALL THAT ARE ENGAGED IN THE CONFLICTS OF THEIR AGE,

WHO HAVE TAUGHT HIM

HOW POOR, HELPLESS, AND USELESS

THE LIFE OF A FATHER ON EARTH WOULD BE

IF THERE WERE NOT A FATHER IN HEAVEN.

PREFACE.

THESE Lectures, since they are in a great measure historical, will inevitably suggest to the reader the elaborate work on *The History of European Morals*, which has obtained so much and such deserved celebrity during the last year. Much as I might have learned from Mr Lecky's volumes I determined not to look at them till I had completed my own task. I might have been tempted to borrow unlawfully from them; I might have confused my method by frequent attempts to shew wherein it differed from his. I can now read what he has written without either of these dangers, and therefore with all the interest which an author so wise and serious must inspire. I can, however I may dread the comparison, encourage my readers to consider carefully his statements and arguments even when they are most at variance with mine.

With regard to *Statements*, it will be seen that I am not likely to complain of Mr Lecky for being too severe on practices and notions which have been grafted on Christian Morality and have been supposed to form a part of it. The value of such exposures—the duty of making them and of not confining them to those from whose opinions we dissent—I have recognized throughout these Lectures. Some will think that I have gone further than Mr Lecky, that I have exhibited the failure of Greek, of Latin, of Teutonic Christianity more conspicuously, if in less detail and with far less learning, than he has done. I felt myself bound to do so, because I was asserting a Theological basis for Morality, and because the tendency, it seems to me, in all these 'Christianities' has been to devise another basis for it. Mr Lecky not proposing this object to himself could afford to be more tolerant of our offences than I have been.

Tolerance is not what I think any Christian ought to crave for himself or of the Society to which he belongs. But looking at the lives of those whom he reverences most as examples of a Christian life, he may ask that they should be allowed to explain what they meant. Such men as Chrysostom, Bernard, Leighton, believed in Christ, not in their Christianity. They complained of their own Christianity and of the Christianity of their times, *because* they believed in Christ. It seems to me that if I apply this distinction to the case about which I am most interested, I may arrive at a method of treating all opinions which will do greater justice to them and to those who hold them. Mr Lecky claims a right to test Utilitarianism, and all other isms, by their moral effects. At the same time he makes large allowances for the influence of the surrounding atmosphere, and of opinions not included in the *ism*, in determining the characters of men and their action upon their contemporaries. Unquestionably I think we ought to reverence a man much more than any System which he boasts of as his, and which cuts him off from other men. But he cannot accept the compliment that he is better than his System. He feels that it has taught him that which makes him more a man than he would otherwise be, he feels that he is below the standard which it sets before him. Is it not possible to justify this belief of his; to ask what it is that has made each man's system dear to him, what connects it with his human life, and not with the narrow, selfish tendencies in him, which are inhuman? May not Epictetus and Marcus Aurelius have perceived something much higher than the word Stoicism can express—an actual governing principle for the life, not a congeries of opinions to be maintained against all challengers? May not the Humanity which the Comtist dreams of be much more to him than all his Positivism, than all the volumes which set it forth? Believing that the true centre of Humanity is He whom all Christian teachers and Societies have professed to acknowledge, I must feel their delinquencies more than those of other men, in so far as they have fallen into Inhumanity. In the object of their belief I find the reconciliation of the principles which have been discovered to all the seekers after some maxim for their guidance and the guidance of mankind.

I do not pretend that I have given an example in this volume of the method which I perceive to be the right one. But I have aimed at it and so have been prevented from adopting the classification of opinions which Mr Lecky deems satisfactory. I cannot regard the Utilitarian merely or chiefly as the antagonist of 'independent Morality.' He may often speak as if he were so; the younger champions of the Sect whose main desire is to trample out every belief which existed in the world before Bentham was born into it, may gladly accept this negative representation of their office. But older defenders of Utility, to whom years have brought the philosophic mind—the philosophic mind being I suppose the equitable one—would perhaps be more ready to die for the conviction which they embraced in their childhood than their more passionate allies, because they entertain it as a conviction and because they have learnt to reverence the convictions of their neighbours as well as their own. If I had no youthful recollections which gave me a regard and affection for some of these I should feel simply as a student that I was bound to recognize their contribution as well as that of 'the independent Moralist' to Moral Science and Moral Practice.

The watchword 'independent Morality,' though I recognize its worth, and accept it as an heirloom from Dr. Whewell, I could never inscribe on my banner. It must always be an awkward one for a writer on Social Morality. His subject must continually remind him of dependencies. According to me it begins from fixed relations; we only learn by degrees in what sense and under what great limitations independence is possible. I appreciate the importance of the stage in our existence when this word acquires significance. But I cannot separate it from the obligations to the Nation or from the affections of the Family out of which the Nation is developed. A thoroughly independent Moralist would I conceive be most immoral.

I should be very ungrateful if I did not confess how much I owe to Mr. Maine's work on *Ancient Law*—not exactly for suggesting to me the method of this book, but for assuring me that in adopting it I should not depart from the most considerate judgment of men aiming at different objects from mine, and possessing a much wider culture. I can scarcely express how great is my delight that an eminent lawyer should find himself obliged simply by his legal studies to abandon the atomic theory of Society and to accept the fact of Family Existence as its starting-point. I am bound to acquit Mr Maine of all responsibility for the consequences which I have deduced from his doctrine; I am equally bound to say how much he has taught me by his own inferences from it.

I ought to explain some omissions which would seem to Mr Lecky very flagrant in the rapid survey of the Moralists from Hobbes to Kant contained in my eighteenth Lecture. He will ask how such names as Hutcheson, Hartley or Reid can have dropped out of the list? Certainly from no disrespect to them or to Descartes, Spinoza, Leibnitz, Condillac, Clarke, Butler, of whom also I have said nothing. I deliberately meant to omit all who could be represented either

(1) as *in any sense* theologians, (2) as *chiefly* psychologists or physiologists. One of these last titles would certainly be given to Hutcheson, Hartley, Reid; their doctrines may have affected Morality, but they are not primarily Social Moralists. Hume earned the name — whatever others may be due to him — when he enunciated his doctrine of Utility. As I intended only to select the most characteristic assertor of each maxim, I should not have spoken of him as well as Bentham if I had not desired to shew how essentially different two opinions may be which a common epithet has confounded. Mr Lecky has also noticed this difference, but he has intimated a preference for the Scotch Sage with which I cannot sympathise. In accordance with the rule which I laid down for myself I have alluded only to Locke as a writer on Government and Toleration; only to Kant's Ethical dogma. To connect morality with Politics and with all social relations has been my wish throughout; I hope that I may hereafter explain where I discover the link between it and Psychology. I should have made my purpose unintelligible if I had entered upon that question in these Lectures.

In an Inaugural Lecture — delivered three years ago at Cambridge — I intimated an intention of delivering separate courses of Lectures on

Casuistry, Moral Philosophy, and Moral Theology. In that design I have persevered to this extent; I have treated of the Conscience which I take to be the subject of Casuistry in one set of Lectures, of Social Morality in the present. But Moral Theology has intruded itself into both; the effort to make that a distinct subject I have found impracticable. It must be so for any one who discovers beneath the Conscience which testifies of our personal existence, beneath all the order of human Society a divine foundation*.

_{* I have been asked by some who attended my Lectures at Cambridge, as well as by friends elsewhere, to state distinctly whether I accept the account of my opinions and objects which was given a week or two ago in a very popular journal, the *Pall Mall Gazette*. I am sure that if the author of that highly flattering criticism does me the honour to glance at the titles of these Lectures—I cannot ask him to take the trouble of reading any one of them—he will perceive that he is bound to denounce me as the most immoral of all writers on Morality, supposing his estimate of me to be the true one. He affirms that I have rendered into a theological dialect the conceptions of humanity which prevail in our age. I have affirmed that those conceptions of humanity when separated from the old foundation, which is simply, broadly, satisfactorily announced in the formularies that are repeated by children and peasants in all parts of Christendom, are narrow, impractical, inhuman. If I am secretly undermining the doctrine which I appear to assert, I hope there is honesty enough in each of my hearers—honesty enough in the critic who has bestowed on me such kindly patronage—to say with the old Homeric hero, 'I hate as the gates of Hell the man who says one thing with his lips and hides another in his heart.'}

CAMBRIDGE,
Nov. 22, 1869.

CONTENTS.

LECTURE I.
SOCIAL MORALITY; WHAT IT IS AND HOW IT SHOULD BE TREATED 1

LECTURE II.
DOMESTIC MORALITY. (1) PARENTS AND CHILDREN . . 24

LECTURE III.
DOMESTIC MORALITY. (2) HUSBANDS AND WIVES . . . 48

LECTURE IV.
DOMESTIC MORALITY. (3) BROTHERS AND SISTERS . . 67

LECTURE V.
DOMESTIC MORALITY. (4) MASTERS AND SERVANTS . . 84

LECTURE VI.
FAMILY WORSHIP 101

LECTURE VII.
NATIONAL MORALITY. (1) THY NEIGHBOUR AND THYSELF . 121

LECTURE VIII.
NATIONAL MORALITY. (2) LAW 137

LECTURE IX.
NATIONAL MORALITY. (3) LANGUAGE 154

LECTURE X.
NATIONAL MORALITY. (4) GOVERNMENT 178

LECTURE XI.

NATIONAL MORALITY. (5) WAR 199

LECTURE XII.

NATIONAL WORSHIP 224

LECTURE XIII.

UNIVERSAL MORALITY. (1) THE UNIVERSAL EMPIRE . 246

LECTURE XIV.

UNIVERSAL MORALITY. (2) THE UNIVERSAL FAMILY . 266

LECTURE XV.

UNIVERSAL MORALITY. (3) THE UNIVERSAL FAMILY SUBJECT TO THE UNIVERSAL EMPIRE (CONSTANTINOPLE) . 294

LECTURE XVI.

UNIVERSAL MORALITY. (4) THE UNIVERSAL FAMILY A LATIN FAMILY (ROME) 316

LECTURE XVII.

UNIVERSAL MORALITY. (5) THE UNIVERSAL AND THE INDIVIDUAL MORALITY IN CONFLICT (15TH AND 16TH CENTURIES) 343

LECTURE XVIII.

UNIVERSAL MORALITY. (6) ATTEMPTS TO DEDUCE THE PRINCIPLES OF HUMAN MORALITY FROM OBSERVATIONS ON HUMAN NATURE (17TH AND 18TH CENTURIES) . 374

LECTURE XIX.

UNIVERSAL MORALITY. (7) THE MODERN CONCEPTION OF HUMANITY (19TH CENTURY) 410

LECTURE XX.

UNIVERSAL MORALITY. (8) DEMAND IN THE NEWEST CIRCUMSTANCES FOR A DIVINE GROUND OF HUMAN LIFE AND HUMAN MORALITY 433

LECTURE XXI.

UNIVERSAL WORSHIP 463

cited and charmed by a set of letters said to be addressed by a native of Ispahan to his friends, which criticized rather freely not only their external acts, but the conviction or want of conviction, the beliefs or unbeliefs, out of which the acts arose. The author of the letters, at first anonymous, proved to be a man of ancient family, the President of a Parliament in the South of France, a learned lawyer as well as an accomplished and vivacious writer. In a later time, after he had visited England, the President Montesquieu exhibited the genius which had produced the Persian letters in a work scarcely less lively, but more akin to the habits of his profession. His *Esprit des Lois* is, or was till lately, on the list of subjects for our Moral Science Tripos. It is, in fact, a Treatise on Social Morality. There was something Montesquieu perceived in every country besides the laws, written on tables or parchments; something besides its different institutions, Monarchical, Aristocratical, Republican. There was a mind which corresponded to these; it was fostered by them; in turn it sustained them; if it was lost they must perish. Whence it came, what accounted for the shapes which it assumed in diverse regions, what influence external circumstances such as climate might have upon it?—these were important questions about which conjectures might be hazarded. But at all events the fact of such differences could not be dissembled; it must be worthy of any attention

LECT. I.

Montesquieu (1689—1755).

Lettres Persanes, 1721.

Esprit des Lois, 1748.

that could be bestowed upon it. Montesquieu was hasty in his generalisations; he often trusted to records which could not endure severe criticism. But the value of his hints to historical enquirers, if they dissent ever so much from his conclusions, cannot be gainsaid. And immensely different as the wide observations of Montesquieu are from those of his friend Chesterfield, there is this likeness between them: they are both occupied with characteristics which are found in men; let them desire ever so much to note the appearances on the surface of society, those appearances point to volcanoes which lie beneath it.

<small>Montesquieu like Chesterfield leads us from the outward to the inward.</small>

Of such volcanoes some countrymen and contemporaries of Montesquieu were beginning to be conscious. The brilliant Parisian circle in which Chesterfield had moved was adorned by wits who declared that the traditions and maxims of the past were perishing; priests hovered about it who were deemed the conservators of those maxims and traditions, and were yet in many ways deepening the impression of their weakness which prevailed in it and had descended to other portions of society. There appeared a man, who stood about equally aloof from the wits and the priests, and who denounced in no measured terms those circles that paid alternate homage to either. He was the son of a watchmaker in Geneva. Though he had led a strange life and done acts which any school or man would have pronounced base—which he felt to be so while he confessed them—yet the old

<small>Jean Jacques Rousseau (1712—1778).</small>

Protestant and Republican traditions of his birthplace had taken a mighty hold upon him. Even while he yielded to the impressions of his senses, he felt an intense and growing horror for what he regarded as the social corruptions of his day. Even while he described scenes which fostered the voluptuousness of cities, he had a passion for the free air of the mountains. Geneva should not, he was resolved, derive its tone from the French capital; it should be a witness against the tastes, manners, the whole social system of France. Rousseau began to be hailed as the champion of natural and savage life against the civilization of Europe. He used language which justified this description. Yet he also used language which might lead us to represent him as an imitator of those old Spartans who trampled upon nature, who sought to subdue it by a rigid education. This contradiction is especially apparent in his *Emile*, a book which has had a very powerful influence in every country of Europe. In it he denounced the schemes of nursery discipline which he thought had destroyed all that was simple and natural in children. He declared that any reformation in society must proceed from a reformation of domestic life. His plans of reformation may often seem to us not less artificial than the practices against which he protests. We may think that a child reared upon his system would have been extremely deficient in the simplicity which he desired to secure for it. Never-

Lect. I.

Nature against Civilization.

Emile.
Education.

Effort after simplicity.

theless, whatever inconsistencies there might be in his conception of the word Nature or in himself, he spoke to a conviction which was deep in the hearts of thoughtful men—nay, of the whole French people. He shewed them that there was something in their Social Morality which needed to be reformed from its root.

Whether this reformation of Social Morality came or not, there did certainly come a dissolution of French Society into its elements. How much Rousseau's "Evangel", especially that contained in his *Contrat Social*, aided in producing this result, Mr Carlyle has told us. The French Revolution was a Social Revolution in the fullest deepest sense of the words. It was not a change of one kind of government for another; it was a decomposition of the whole body governing and governed; a change of feeling respecting the relation of classes in the country to each other; an attempt to overthrow classes altogether. Equality was affirmed to be the basis of Society; of Society in France because of human Society; Frenchmen were equal because men were.

The Revolution therefore by its very terms rejected local divisions; it must embrace the world. All parts of Europe felt the shock of it; there was a vehement delight in the message which it brought; there was a vehement reaction against it. Here in England the delight was felt in many youthful hearts; the reaction was more conspicuous still. The distinction of classes was reverenced as a sacred protest against the levelling doctrine; it was exalted above the distinction of Nations. When the universal Republic became a universal Empire the worth of *that* distinction became evident to many who had sympathized in the first proclamation of Cosmopolitism; the other distinction became less offensive, when orders in the state were contemplated not as an insult to the people but as a defence against tyranny. Nevertheless the Revolution had left its stamp on these early champions as well as on many who had always detested it. Not only such writers as Wordsworth became poets of the poor; witnesses for the sanctity of common life. The novels of Scott, lover of feudalism as he was, shewed a genuine unpatronizing sympathy with human nature in its humblest forms, of which it can scarcely be said that there were any clear traces in our literature since the time of Shakspere. Evidently the doctrine of the illustrious plowman of his land, 'a man's a man for a' that,' had taken possession of his mind; courtly influences might weaken but could not expel it.— There were no doubt fashionable novelists who would gladly have restored the Chesterfield conception of life, and who had admiring readers in the middle class eager for what glimpses they could get about the doings of the highest. Such ambition there will always be in a country like ours, and writers willing, perhaps more or less able, to gratify it. But on the whole the tendency has

The effects of the Revolution upon such men as Wordsworth and Scott.

The fashionable novels.

been in the other direction. Those who have helped us to understand the forms of Society which are found under different conditions in all classes—of which we can in some measure judge for ourselves—have exercised the greatest influence over us. Even a writer like Lord Byron possessed by the feelings of his own order, not much honouring any other, was listened to not chiefly on that account, but because he showed that beneath the artificial surface of his circumstances and of his character, there lay springs of terrible passion which belong to the kind, not the class.

In these instances, different as they are from those I spoke of before, the power of the writer, the interest of the reader, lies in the discovery of a certain character or ἦθος first doubtless in some individual, but in him as connected with a Society smaller or larger, in him as showing what character makes the Society harmonious or discordant, tenable or untenable. And when we examine how this ἦθος becomes known to us, we see that there are certain permanent conditions of Society of which literature has taken account, and which since the French Revolution, more than in the centuries before it, have distinguished themselves from each other. I think you may perceive that Rousseau's hints (1) about domestic life, (2) about civilization, (3) about a more general human Society than those names suggest, have given rise to three kinds of investigations in most respects unlike each other and yet all clearly falling within the sphere of Social Morality.

LECT. I.

1. There has been a vast amount of writing during the last seventy years on the subject of Education, the ends at which it should aim, the persons whom it should benefit, the machinery which is available for it. But no part of these discussions has, on the whole, produced so much effect as that which has followed in Rousseau's line, pointing out the defects in domestic discipline and the way in which it may be reformed. Very able men have given us the fruits of their experience on this topic; it has especially called forth the quicker and more delicate observation of women, whether mothers themselves, or those who like Miss Edgeworth have performed the part of mothers to sisters, brothers, or strangers. However much the hints of such teachers have been directed to methods of intellectual culture, their object has been by one method or another to form a character; their chief skill has been shown in tracing the influence of different members of a family on the characters of each other. The Family, small circle as it must be, has been found large enough for the discovery of innumerable varieties of feeling and disposition, every variety having some tendency to produce another by collision or sympathy. So those who have begun with the most practical purposes of improving household discipline, have also given us clear and vivid pictures of different households which they

First division. Books on Domestic Education.

The Family Character.

have seen or imagined. Historical novels have had a certain attraction for us. Brilliant pictures like those in Ivanhoe when painted by an antiquarian who is also a man of genius, must have an interest even when we suspect them as guides to the true knowledge of an age. But in general the portion of such books which is domestic produces by far the most powerful effect. The strictly domestic story has become characteristic of our times, not in this country only, but, as far as I can make out, in all countries of Europe. The morality may be of one kind or another. The Family may be merely a ground-plot for the display of sensational incidents. Still these incidents are found to be most startling, and therefore most agreeable to those who wish to be startled, when they are associated with outrages of one kind or another upon family order. Those who do not want such stimulants to their own feelings and fancies, and do not hold it an honest trade to mix them for others, have found in the quietest home-life materials for Art. All social harmonies and social contradictions they see may come forth in the relations of fathers and children, husbands and wives, brothers and sisters, masters and servants. There is a certain character they are sure which helps to make a family peaceful or miserable—a home out of which blessings or curses may diffuse themselves over the commonwealth. Even those who are impatient of national boundaries as too narrow, are yet occupy-

Marginal notes: Lect. I. — The Domestic novel more prized than the Historical. — The Sensation novel. — The quiet observer chooses the same field.

ing themselves with theories and controversies about the conditions of the family, some of them denouncing our ordinary conceptions of it as antiquated, some reviving *most* ancient theories respecting it, some maintaining that all the order of Christendom is due to the difference between its domestic forms and that of countries in which polygamy prevails, all its disease and disorders to the loss of the spirit which should quicken these forms. I am entitled therefore to claim the authority of the most thoughtful as well as the most popular writers, of all schools and of both sexes, for the opinion that Domestic Morality is not only an integral portion of Social Morality, but should be the starting point of all discussions respecting it. They are equally agreed that in treating of this topic our business is not chiefly with acts or modes of conduct, but with a character or state of mind from which the acts proceed, by which the conduct must be regulated.

Domestic Morality admitted to be the first stage of Social Morality.

II. The fierce onslaught of Rousseau upon the Civilization which he found in France, and upon the very name of Civilization—his preference for the life of woods—was endorsed in the declaration of Rights which inaugurated the Revolution. For in this declaration maxims determining what Society ought to be were deduced from a state prior to the existence of Society itself. The difficulties and contradictions of that assumption became every day more palpable;

Second division.

The declaration of Rights.

many who embraced Rousseau's doctrine concerning the Sovereignty of the people were industrious in pointing them out. None again have been so much alive to the worth of Civilization, and have been so eager to vindicate it from the charges of Rousseau, as countrymen of his own who have shared in his dislike of the *Ancien Régime*. M. Guizot's work, which is so well known in England, and is so conspicuous for its learning and ability, represents the temper of the time in which it was composed. It is specially occupied in exhibiting Civilization as the antagonist of Feudalism. Strictly, almost sternly, etymological, M. Guizot makes us feel that the word Civilization points specially to that formation of towns, that development of cities, which counteracted the solitary influence of the territorial Proprietor in the midst of his land, the barbarism of those who were, in a great measure, *adscripti glebæ*. With a critical knowledge of history to which Montesquieu could make no pretension, he distinguishes the different agencies, legal, personal, ecclesiastical—derived from the traditions of Rome, from Gothic kings, from the papal authority, from distinguished men—from the co-operation and clashing of these forces—which brought forth a civic life in modern Europe. He has made us perceive the meaning of this process which was working through so many ages. But he does not disguise from us or from himself that it was a mysterious process, which it requires an historical instinct to apprehend, which cannot be reduced under formulas now more than it could when the *Esprit des Lois* was composed. The lights of modern criticism have not tended, he shows us, to make Society, or the Manners of Society, more explicable by mere laws or Systems of Government. On the contrary they have helped greatly to perplex the man who has thought that some one clue would guide him through the labyrinth—that he could determine, for instance, the condition of Europe, by attributing its blessings or its curses to the influence of the Clergy. They have brought with them blesssings and curses which the faithful student of Civilization, according to M. Guizot's notion of it, must equally recognize.

<small>Lect. I.</small>

<small>The co-operation and collision of various forces producing a certain manner or character.</small>

Mr Buckle's work on Civilization is in most respects very unlike Guizot's. At first sight it would seem not to concern my subject, since he has expressed in more than one or two very decisive sentences his opinion, that the further civilization advances, the more will intellectual studies take precedence of moral. Such an opinion is in accordance with one part of the writer's scheme. He had an immense appreciation of statistics; a great confidence that by help of them we may be able to predict in what circumstances certain acts (*e.g.* homicide or suicide) will be frequent or rare. Now the intellect is no doubt chiefly conversant with such calculations as these; they are scarcely applicable to states of mind or feeling; it may

<small>Mr Buckle, History of Civilization in England, Vols. I. and II. 1858.</small>

<small>Reverence for statistics.</small>

LECT. I.

His supposed contempt of Morality more verbal than real.

be difficult to discover how these can be indicated by tables. But Mr Buckle insists strongly on the difference between the nations of the East, which bow before the powers of Nature, and those of the West which defy them. That is a state of mind or feeling. Again he deems it the grand test of a nation's civilization that it loses the disposition to make war and to persecute for religious opinions. He does therefore in fact connect Civilization with the formation of an ἦθος, or Social Morality, however he may trace that ἦθος to certain external conditions or suppose it to be produced by certain exercises of intellect. The Morality which he scorned seems to consist of certain maxims. That he did not suppose these to be of much worth, may be accepted as a proof that he demanded a character which he found they could not of themselves produce. He is not therefore to be set down as an exception to our rule. As much as Montesquieu, or Guizot, he supposes Civilization to consist in a certain social manner; one which cannot be expressed in formal edicts, which must be in the men who compose the society.

Objection to the word Civil or Political as indicating a department in Social Morality.

Here then we have another division of Social Morality. We might call it the Civil or the Political. But useful as both these words are, they are borrowed from countries in which the city had an absorbing importance that does not belong to it in later history. Such cities as Pisa, Milan, Florence, when they first attracted an attention in the Middle Ages seem as if they might represent Italy, as Athens, Sparta, Thebes, often appear to represent ancient Greece. But the Italian of this day will not tolerate that doctrine. He claims to be the member of a nation. London has never stood for England; the most popular writers among contemporary Frenchmen are careful to shew us that we must study the provinces and not merely Paris to know what France is. M. Guizot may be right in opposing Feudalism to Civilisation; but no German or Englishman or Spaniard could possibly refuse to regard feudal institutions as one element in the life of his people. All these considerations seem to shew that the epithet *National* will be more proper to denote the second branch of Morality, than either Civil or Political would be. If we adopt that we shall be in far less danger of missing the link between this portion of our subject and the first; in less danger of confounding it with the one of which I am about to speak. *[Lect. I. Why the epithet National is more convenient.]*

III. The cosmopolitan aspect of the French Revolution has seemed to some its most characteristic aspect. The epithet has survived much of the disgrace which attached to it when it was supposed to indicate a contempt for national distinctions. The title human, or humane (as it used to be spelt), is open to no such objection. Humanity has been accepted as their favourite watchword by a set of philosophers who have devoted themselves most laboriously to the study of the principles of *[Third Division. Human Morality. The Comteist watchword.]*

Society, who even boast that they have founded a new science worthy to be called 'Sociology.' I am not now considering the merits of this somewhat barbarous name. But I wish you to know that if there is any question as to Mr Buckle's opinion about the dignity of Morality, there is none whatever as to M. Comte's. He does not for a moment postpone morality to the intellect; the great work of the positivist philosopher, he says, is to make moral considerations predominant over all other; the normal state of man according to him is that in which the intellect is subordinated to the heart. I may therefore claim him and his disciples as witnesses for that explanation of Social Morality which I have deduced from so many writers of other schools. I am delighted also to have their authority for recognising human morality as the centre in which both the other departments of Social Morality find their purpose and interpretation. Whether that agreement with them implies that Sociology is the highest of all sciences or the ground of all— whether the place I give to Humanity involves me in the Comteist worship of it—we may enquire hereafter. Those questions have no place in a preliminary lecture; that ought only to fix the nature and object of the investigation on which we are entering.

But I cannot leave this distinguished school without saying that I desire on another ground to be a pupil in it. I wish to examine facts—*posi-*

tive facts if that adjective adds any dignity to the substantive—speculations only so far as they may have been offered for the elucidation of facts. If I speak of any theories about the superiority of one form of family life to another—and I shall quote some weighty remarks of M. Comte on that topic—it is only because I find the fact of our existence in families an indisputable one. If I am obliged to dwell on the difference of social forms in different Nations, it will be for the purpose of illustrating the fact that we are members of different Nations, and that one Nation cannot fix the form which is suitable for another. If I examine certain speculations of different philosophers respecting Human Morality, it is that I may shew how each one of these speculations is valuable as bringing into light Facts concerning our position as members of a Universal Human Society, constituted on a certain principle. In one respect, no doubt, I may seem to differ from M. Comte and his disciples. The Family is not lost in the Nation, nor the Nation in Human Society. They are coexistent; instead of giving place, like M. Comte's first theological age, to a metaphysical age, and both being merged in the Positive. But I do not think that I am less adhering to facts, more plunging into speculations, because I am not able to adjust my thoughts to this great theory of succession, and only assume the commonplaces which M. Comte as well as all other persons must recognise.

Marginalia: Theories only to be consulted that we may appreciate Facts more. Coexistence of the different steps of Social Morality.

Here then I might stop; for I have sufficiently set forth the course which I propose to follow, and have justified it by a concurrence of modern authorities and examples. But though I have begun with these, I cannot forget that in this University we confess the dignity of older names and teach you to reverence them. Am I forsaking their guidance in submission to these newer lights? I think the books which we ask you to read may answer that question.

The older authorities.

The purpose of Plato's *Republic* has been variously interpreted. Rousseau, with much plausibility, called it a Treatise on Education. No doubt it contains most interesting discussions respecting the methods by which the mind and character of the members of the Commonwealth are to be formed into harmony with the ends for which it exists. But that the education may be effectual, that we may understand the nature of it, we must learn what the principle of the Commonwealth is. That we may know this we must settle whether Justice is a reality or a fiction, whether it is only an individual principle or also a Social Principle, whether there can be a Society which does not confess it and is not held together by it. We are in fact engaged in the study of Social Morality. We are seeking to find what the ἦθος of a Society—of Society itself— must be, and how that ἦθος can be developed in the citizens of it. The controversies of modern times; the debate between Right and Might,

The Republic.

Justice and Injustice.

which is carried on so fiercely in the schools and in the world; that most difficult of all problems, how the claims of the Individual and of the Society can be reconciled; are all here. The manifold experiences of the Greek Republics, the subtlest wisdom of the greatest Greek thinker, are helping us to unravel threads which are spun about our own lives, which are embarrassing statesmen and common men of the 19th century.

Lect. I. The Society and the Individual.

If you pass to Plato's eminent pupil you encounter an intellect of a very different shape and texture from that with which you have just parted; in some of their leading methods of thought they are so unlike, that the saying has become current, 'The Platonist and the Aristotelian can by no possibility understand each other.' But in the point which I am considering now they are alike. One as much as the other would make Morality—Social Morality—consist in habits, in a character, not in outward acts, still less in formal maxims. The very word ἦθος which I have used as the most convenient to explain this distinction is specially an Aristotelian word. Considering that Aristotle is reckoned so great a dogmatist— that he has composed such an Encyclopædia of studies—it is marvellous how free he is from the temptations of the mere schoolman; how little he trusts in mere formulas; how every virtue of which he speaks is only a virtue as it becomes formed in a man. And if we join the Politics to the Ethics—as he tells us they must be joined—

Aristotle, emphatically the Ethical Philosopher.

22   SOCIAL MORALITY

LECT. I.   we discover that order of Subjects which I am
His ho-   endeavouring to observe. In this respect the com-
mage to
domestic   parison of him with Plato, if it is greatly to his
relations.
advantage, is for us most instructive. The Republic teaches us how the noblest student of Humanity in his eagerness to grasp the Universal is likely to lose sight of the Particular. In Plato's vast Communism the Family is lost. Aristotle acknowledges it as the very basis of political society; the relations of the household are the germs of the different forms of government.

Use of the   Let no one persuade you then that these
past to the
present.   great teachers of former ages must be cast aside in order that you may profit by the wider experiences of your own day. If you despise them, those wider experiences will be no experiences for you; you will carry away a multitude of notions from a multitude of schools; each will trip up the other and make it useless for you. These writers if you use them rightly will shew you the worthlessness of mere notions, the impossibility of separating Morality from Life.

The New   Mr Buckle repeats the words 'As you would
Testament.
that men should do to you do ye also to them likewise,' and asks triumphantly what they have effected for mankind? Speaking according to the lessons of the book in which they occur, I should answer, 'Nothing whatever if they are regarded as mere words in a book; worse than nothing if they are taken as warrants for self-exaltation, as reasons for exalting ourselves as Christians above

other men.' The New Testament I need scarcely tell you is occupied from first to last—specially in the Sermon on the Mount—in shewing that acts are nothing except as they are fruits of a state, except as they indicate what the man is; that words are nothing except as they express a mind or purpose. Nor need I add that it is a Society—a Human Society—in which the preacher of that Sermon assumes that this ἦθος is to be exhibited. It might have sounded a commonplace of Divinity to tell you at the beginning of my Lecture that this is what I hold to be the meaning of Social Morality. We have now seen that no other is found to be satisfactory by any persons who have seriously meditated upon it. I might again seem to be merely following the order of the Scriptures in taking the Family, the Nation, a Society, for all nations and kindreds, as the divisions of my subject. Since upon quite independent grounds that method has recommended itself to us, you will not deem it a less sound or desirable one because it has this sanction.

Its maxim that maxims are nothing except as they point to a character which is manifested in acts.

LECTURE II.

DOMESTIC MORALITY.

(1) *PARENTS AND CHILDREN.*

<small>Lect. II.
The two methods of considering Society.</small> Many writers begin with considering mankind as a multitude of units. They ask, how did any number of these units form themselves into a Society? I cannot adopt that method. At my birth I am already in a Society. I am related, at all events, to a father and mother. This relation is the primary fact of my existence. I can contemplate no other facts apart from it.

Perhaps you will say, 'For each of us separately that no doubt is true. But we want to consider the world at large.' Well! and to what portion of the world at large is this truth not applicable? In what region do you find a man who is not born a son, who is not related to a father and mother? It is a fact for me surely, but it is a fact for you and for every man. And if you determine not to take notice of this fact, not to give it precedence of every other, the effect is, that instead of

contemplating the world at large you will only **Lect. II.**
contemplate yourself. *You* will be the unit about Consequences of
which all events and persons will revolve. Each each method.
man will regard himself as the centre of the
universe. You will at last come to an understanding—a very imperfect understanding—that
each must occupy this place in his own estimation; you will be forced to construct a Society on
that hypothesis.

If, on the other hand, you start from the indisputable commonplace 'We are sons,' such a
way of considering the Universe is from the first
impossible. I cannot be the centre of the circle in
which I find myself, be it as small as it may. I
refer myself to another. There is a root below
me. There is an Author of my existence.

If we adhere steadily to this which would Why the atomic doctrine has prevailed.
strike any one as the true chronological order,
some of the greatest difficulties will be taken out
of our path; instead of being obliged to invent
explanations of social existence, we shall find the
explanations lying at our feet. We shall understand at the same time why men have been led to
crave for such explanations, and to seek them afar
off. The relation exists; there is a manner which
answers to the relation, without which it becomes
untenable, contradictory. But there is a tendency
in each of us to break the relation, to lose the
manner. We strive to be units, though by the
order in which we are placed we cannot be. How
this striving may ultimately become a blessing,

how it may introduce us to other parts of our social order, we shall consider hereafter. At present I must insist that a son cannot be without a father, or a father without a son. To dissolve the relation into its elements is to remake the world.

Authority. As soon as I recognise an Author of my existence, I recognise an *Authority* over me. I do not mean of course that I know anything about the words Author or Authority; that I understand what binds them together. But I mean that in the very fact of Fatherhood Authority is involved, that I learn what it is through my filial relation. I will explain myself by comparing the word Authority with one which lies very near it, which is always in danger of being treated as synonymous with it.

Dominion. I have *dominion*, say over a certain number of acres. There are on those acres dead stock and live stock: ploughs; cattle that are yoked to the ploughs; men that drive the cattle. All these are included in my dominion. Whilst I look upon them *only* as in my dominion I make no distinction between them. Dead stock, live stock, animals, men, they are all regarded as belonging to me, instruments for tilling my land. I begin to see a difference between them. I recognise a bond between me and the men who drive the

Distinction between them. animals. I do not cease to give them orders; but the orders are those of one who has authority, not only of one who has dominion. I may discover that the animals also yield to words rather than

to force; that a certain authority can be exercised Lect. II.
over them. I become *humane* to them. I cease How it affects the
to be a brute possessing brutes; I am a man treatment of men
directing them. I cannot refer either this sense and other creatures.
of fellowship with men or this humane rule over
animals to my separate Nature. Yielding to that,
I shall merely try to assert dominion; whether I
succeed or fail, it will be a battle of physical
forces. But I am related to a Father, he is related to me. I cannot destroy that relation, though
I try. It brings forth a manner in me. If the
separate Nature prevails over this relation, there
will in all cases be dominion, but no authority;
subjection, no obedience, brutality, no manners.

In referring Society and the manners which These principles
make Society possible first to this relation, I am applicable to all times
not, you see, resorting to any grand theory. I and places.
am merely asking you to take account of facts;
of facts which must be wherever men have lived
or do live; of facts which just as much belong to
every English household of this year as to those
of which you read in any records or legends of
the earliest times. Authority and Obedience are
fundamental principles of Society now as they
were in any Saturnian age; the demand for them is
now as much as ever made first in the family; the
seeds of them are there; the interpretation of
them is there. If you try to explain them by the
incidents of a later and more complicated state, you
will be always at a loss. You will find something
which you cannot account for by any arrangements

or conventions: if you seek for it in laws, the laws will drive you back to some primeval order which is implied in them, which they did not create. Proof that this is so I hope to give you before I finish this lecture. First I would make one or two observations which connect what I have said with the lessons of other Moralists.

<small>Can habits exist without Education?</small>

The more you study Aristotle's *Ethics*, the more you will be aware of a difficulty which he, with his customary honesty, takes no pains to hide. He speaks of certain habits which enable men to fulfil their work as men. Are not these habits part of our Nature? What else can they be if they are to be characteristic of our own selves? They cannot come to us from without. They must be internal. And yet they do not spring up in men without education. A most pregnant doubt, worth a hundred clever solutions. We are obliged to face it. Perhaps the Politics of Aristotle, which he never wished to be separate from his Ethics, may give us a hint about the way of facing it. There, as I told you in my last lecture, he refers us to the Family as the underground of all National Institutions.

<small>No one without Education.</small>

But if that be so, is not Education presumed in these Institutions, presumed in the life of each one of us? The father *must* educate his child; so far as he has any authority over him that must be an Education. For what end he educates is a question of immeasurable importance: that there should be some end is inevitable. He may train his son to mere exercises of brute strength; he may train him to revenge and malice. But anyhow, we are saved from the necessity of considering the question what any child or man or boy would be if left to himself without education; because no one is. Each of us has had sufficient indications what he would have become if he had had his own way in any considerable degree; absolutely to have his own way is not given to child or boy or man.

Entire self-will impossible.

Authority then under some conditions or other —authority, as distinct from dominion—is implied in the existence of fathers; its correlative, *Obedience* as distinct from mere subjection is implied in the existence of sons. But I told those who listened to my lectures on the Conscience that Authority has been said to be another name for punishment; Obedience another name for the dread of punishment. I shall not repeat the objections which I made to that theory when I noticed it before. I wish you to reflect now that it is the best—the only—explanation which can be given of these two words and of all which they express, supposing the fact of the paternal and filial relation is overlooked, supposing it is not taken to lie at the root of human society. Then whatever difficulty there may be in settling who is to be the punisher; whatever difficulty in deciding the offences for which he shall punish, or how his punishment shall produce any effect except that of shewing how strong he is, and how weak the subject of his punishment is; I yet frankly admit that the

The theory which identifies Authority with Punishment inevitable if the filial relation is not confessed.

theory must be swallowed whole. The effort may be a difficult one, it may cause some disgust; but it must be made. On the other hand, if we assume the fatherly relation—the education which I have said is implied in it will include Punishment as one of its subordinate instruments. The punishment instead of being identical with authority will only have the slightest influence so far as the recognition of Authority precedes it. Obedience instead of being the dread of punishment may be destroyed by that dread ; will only be promoted by punishment so far as disobedience is felt to be an irregular disorderly condition which inevitably draws punishment after it. How to temper punishment so that it may be a witness for authority, and may never express mere dominion—so that it may foster obedience and not stimulate disobedience—is one of the hardest problems of practical education upon which we cannot too earnestly seek for light.

If it is a maxim of advanced Philosophy that Authority is identical with Punishment, one cannot wonder that it should be proclaimed, as it so often is, to be the foe of Reason. Suppose parental authority, as I have maintained, the very ground of Education, we must believe that through it all the faculties and energies which belong to a child are developed, that without it they would lie dormant. The obedience of a son is shewn in receiving those influences and impressions from a father's authority which most tend to quicken his own activity. No true father wishes his son to present an image of his opinions. He knows that the copy will be probably a caricature; that an echo conveys the sound not the sense of the original voice. On the other hand, the son whose opinions are most unlike his father's has often learnt most from him; in his latest years he probably discovers how much the father's authority has helped to mould the very convictions which appear to separate them. *produce identity of opinions.*

I have spoken specially of the father. In him most obviously dwells the authority which stamps itself on the life of a man. But the union of the mother's influence with the father's helps to distinguish authority from dominion; as well as to counteract any disposition which there might be in the male parent to demand of his son mere agreement with his conclusions. She never can regard a child as a possession; she never can appeal exclusively or mainly to his intellect. The authority is not weakened by her co-operation; it is divested of its inhumanity; it is made effectual for the whole of the child's existence, not for one section of it. I of course refer most to those cases in which there *is* co-operation—in which the two influences are not adverse. Even where they are so, we may clearly discern, by the disorder which the collision produces, what the true order of the household is. *The Mother.*

Effect of her influence.

I can never forget one sentence of Mr Buckle, which I confess I prize above all his statistics, and all his theories on civilisation. He said that *Mr Buckle's testimony.*

no mere arguments for Immortality had ever had much weight with him, but that when he remembered his mother he could not disbelieve in it. Such a testimony from a man who so greatly exalted the Intellect, who in words at least treated Morality as poor in comparison with it, seems to me of unspeakable worth. It contains, as I think, a most pregnant hint concerning the parental relation generally, specially concerning the maternal side of it. I have said that the mother purifies and expands the principle of authority, therefore gives to the principle of obedience a simpler and higher character. Still more does she impart the true form to that feeling of *Succession* which this relation brings to light; the feeling which leads the father to rejoice in the prospect of a race. In later times—in developed societies—nay, to a very considerable extent in all societies—this anticipation becomes connected with thoughts of what the father shall leave behind him, of what the son shall inherit. The joy of the poor man who has nothing to leave, in the sight or hope of those who shall bear his name in after days, seems to a luxurious age incomprehensible; so much do questions of property in such an age blend themselves with the domestic felicity which they mar. But, as Mr Buckle felt in his own case, there is something much more direct, more simply human in a mother's thought about the child that shall live after her; one wholly apart from any dream of possession, one that links itself directly with *personal* immortality. That thought communicates itself to the child; in the strictest sense he inherits it: not through a dogma which she has taught him but through his sense of a relation to her the thought becomes one of which he cannot divest himself.

But if this paternal relation, and this ἦθος of Authority and Obedience which responds to it are really what I have supposed, must there not be some signs of their effect upon the history of Mankind? Can it be only in particular families where the relation is exhibited amidst great varieties and contradictions that we are to realise the effect? You have a right to make this demand on me. If I cannot meet it satisfactorily, I shall admit that my method is a false one; that I am seeking to detect the rudiments of a Social Morality where they are not to be found.

Has the Paternal Authority left its mark upon History?

Mr Buckle draws a very striking distinction between the Nations which have succumbed to the powers of Nature and those which have risen above them and defied them. He distinguishes also between those which have been the victims of superstitious fancies about the unseen world, and those which have been able to grapple with hard material facts. Suppose I found amongst the races whom he has disparaged on either of these grounds, instances of a Society which had been shaped and moulded by the authority of the father—whose history and legislation through a number of ages were stamped and penetrated with it—I might be answered "That is just

Mr Buckle's division of Nations.

34   DOMESTIC MORALITY.

LECT. II. what we should have expected. Such a race was likely enough to have an inordinate appreciation of domestic bonds, especially to regard with great awe the paternal relation." But suppose the people to whom I referred for my example was the one which had most courageously confronted the powers of nature, and had overcome them, which had shewn the most capacity for dealing with material facts—with the prose of existence; suppose it deserved Mr Carlyle's praise of being an eminently 'thrifty people;' then it might perhaps afford a fair test of my doctrine. You will easily imagine that I am thinking of the Roman State, and of the influence which the *Patria Potestas* exercised over its institutions.

<small>The Romans fighters with the powers of nature.</small>

<small>Has our conception of the Patria Potestas been an exaggerated one?</small>

Certainly if we trusted to our schoolboy impressions that would seem a strong case in point. But those impressions may deceive us. Virgil has built Rome upon legends which modern criticism has exposed. Why should we attach any worth to his notion that piety to a father had more to do with the foundation or preservation of the city than its fancied Trojan ancestry? Why should the name of fathers given to senators, or of father to the Lord of the Capitol, be more than fictions? why should we endow these names with any significance?

<small>Maine's Ancient Law.</small>

I can answer these questions best by referring you to a book containing the ripest modern scholarship applied to the examination of Roman Institutions. Mr Maine has assuredly no prejudices in favour of the stories which were always suspected, and which our age generally discredits. He has not written on Social Morality, but expressly on Ancient Law. In his exceedingly able book he has discussed at considerable length the subject of the *Patria Potestas*. What he says about its influence on the latest Jurisprudence of Rome and of Modern Europe is highly important. What he says about the grounds of it, and the necessity of looking for it in a Society antecedent to all legal forms, concerns our present purpose still more.

The Roman Law about persons as well as property grounded on the authority of the Father.

One or two short passages will explain Mr Maine's view of the bearing of the Patria Potestas *on* Roman Law: "It may be shewn I think that the Family as held together by the Patria Potestas is the *nidus* out of which the entire law of *Persons* has germinated." Maine's *Ancient Law*, p. 152.

He expresses this opinion though he has taken pains to shew how much the power of the Father over the *person* of the Son, which existed at one period, was modified by later legislation or by the force of opinion. "But," he remarks, (p. 141), "though the power over the person may have been "latterly nominal, the whole tenor of the extant "Roman Jurisprudence testifies that the father's "rights over the son's *Property* were exercised to "the full extent to which they were sanctioned by "law." The law of *persons*, the law of *Property*, then, were both in the most marvellous way affected by this institution, and the habits of the people as much as either. He goes on :—

LECT. II.

The extent of the authority in legal times.

Its basis in an earlier time.

Its diffusion over the Roman world.

"There is nothing to astonish us in the lati-
"tude of these rights when they first show them-
"selves. The ancient law of Rome forbade the
"Children under Power to hold property apart
"from their parent, or (we should rather say)
"never contemplated the possibility of their claim-
"ing a second ownership. The father was entitled
"to take the whole of the son's acquisitions, and
"to enjoy the benefit of his contracts without
"being entangled in any compensating liability.
"So much as this we should expect from the con-
"stitution of the earliest Roman society, for we
"can hardly form a notion of the primitive family
"group unless we suppose that its members
"brought their earnings of all kinds into the com-
"mon stock while they were unable to bind it by
"improvident individual engagements. The true
"enigma of the Patria Potestas does not reside
"here, but in the slowness with which these pri-
"vileges of the parent were curtailed, and in the
"circumstance that, before they were seriously
"diminished, the whole civilised world was brought
"within their sphere." pp. 141, 142.

To what does this Institution point, fixed as it was in the heart of the strongest of all commonwealths, the one which has done so much to mould the Society of modern Europe? A longer extract is necessary that you may understand what Mr Maine teaches us upon the subject.

The unit of society.

"Archaic Law is full, in all its provinces, of the
"clearest indications that society in primitive times

PARENTS AND CHILDREN. 37

"was not what it assumed to be at present, a collec- Lect. II.
"tion of *individuals*. In fact, and in the view of
"the men who composed it, it was *an aggregation*
"*of families*. The contrast may be most forcibly Contrast between
"expressed by saying that the *unit* of an ancient earlier and later con-
"society was the Family, of a modern society the ceptions.
"Individual. We must be prepared to find in
"ancient law all the consequences of this differ-
"ence. It is so framed as to be adjusted to a
"system of small independent corporations. It
"is therefore scanty, because it is supplemented
"by the despotic commands of the heads of
"households. It is ceremonious, because the
"transactions to which it pays regard resemble
"international concerns much more than the
"quick play of intercourse between individuals.
"Above all it has a peculiarity of which the full
"importance cannot be shown at present. It
"takes a view of *life* wholly unlike any which
"appears in developed jurisprudence. Corpora- The per-
"tions *never die*, and accordingly primitive law of corpo-
"considers the entities with which it deals, *i.e.* rations derived from
"patriarchal or family groups, as perpetual and the family.
"inextinguishable. This view is closely allied to
"the peculiar aspect under which, in very ancient
"times, moral attributes present themselves. The
"moral elevation and moral debasement of the
"individual appear to be confounded with, or
"postponed to, the merits and offences of the
"group to which the individual belongs. If the
"community sins, its guilt is much more than

LECT. II.

Responsibility of the whole family for the offences of each of its members.

"the sum of the offences committed by its members; the crime is a corporate act, and extends in its consequences to many more persons than have shared in its actual perpetration. If, on the other hand, the individual is conspicuously guilty, it is his children, his kinsfolk, his tribesmen, or his fellow-citizens, who suffer with him, and sometimes for him. It thus happens that the ideas of moral responsibility and retribution often seem to be more clearly realised at very ancient than at more advanced periods, for, as the family group is immortal, and its liability to punishment indefinite, the primitive mind is not perplexed by the questions which become troublesome as soon as the individual is conceived as altogether separate from the group. One step in the transition from the ancient and simple view of the matter to the theological or metaphysical explanations of later days is marked by the early Greek notion of an inherited curse. The bequest received by his posterity from the original criminal was not a liability to punishment, but a liability to the commission of fresh offences which drew with them a condign retribution; and thus the responsibility of the family was reconciled with the newer phase of thought which limited the consequences of crime to the person of the actual delinquent. * * * * In most of the Greek states and in Rome there long remained the vestiges of an ascending series of groups out of which

The inherited curse.

"the State was at first constituted. The Family,
"House, and Tribe of the Romans may be taken
"as the type of them, and they are so described to
"us that we can scarcely help conceiving them as
"a system of concentric circles which have gra-
"dually expanded from the same point. The
"elementary group is the Family, connected by
"common subjection to the highest male ascend-
"ant. The aggregation of the Families forms the
"Gens or House. The aggregation of Houses
"makes the Tribe. The aggregation of Tribes
"constitutes the Commonwealth. Are we at
"liberty to follow these indications, and to lay
"down that the commonwealth is a collection of
"persons united by common descent from the pro-
"genitor of an original family? Of this we may
"at least be certain, that all ancient societies
"regarded themselves as having proceeded from
"one original stock, and even laboured under
"an incapacity for comprehending any reason
"except this for their holding together in political
"union. The history of political ideas begins, in
"fact, with the assumption that kinship in blood
"is the sole possible ground of community in poli-
"tical functions; nor is there any of those sub-
"versions of feeling, which we term emphatically
"revolutions, so startling and so complete as the
"change which is accomplished when some other
"principle—such as that, for instance, of *local*
"*contiguity*—establishes itself for the first time as
"the basis of common political action. It may

marginalia:
The ascending groups.
The family, the house, the tribe, the commonwealth.
Kinship assumed.
The great revolution.

"be affirmed then of early commonwealths that their citizens considered all the groups in which they claimed membership to be founded on common lineage. What was obviously true of the Family was believed to be true first of the House, next of the Tribe, lastly of the State." pp. 126—129.

Mr Maine goes on to explain, as Niebuhr had done, that the supposition of an ancestry was often a gratuitous one, "that men of alien descent were grafted into the original brotherhood," that legal fictions were invented to connect the old feelings of kinsmanship with the later principles of '*contiguity in place.*' To these remarks I must recur in the second part of these lectures, when I arrive at that period of social development in which Mr Maine is most interested, the strictly legal period. I must however give you the words in which he sums up his observations on the Family.

"The Family then is the type of an archaic society in all the modifications which it was capable of assuming; but the family here spoken of is not exactly the family as understood by a modern. In order to reach the ancient conception we must give to our modern ideas an important extension and an important limitation. We must look on the family as constantly enlarged by the absorption of strangers within its circle, and we must try to regard the fiction of adoption as so closely simulating the reality of

"kinship that neither law nor opinion makes the LECT. II.
"slightest difference between a real and an adop-
"tive connexion. On the other hand, the persons
"theoretically amalgamated into a family by their
"common descent are practically held together by
"common obedience to their highest living ascend-
"ant, the father, grandfather, great-grandfather.
"The patriarchal authority of a chieftain is as Authority continues
"necessary an ingredient in the notion of the as the bond of the com-
"family group as the fact (or assumed fact) of munity after its
"its having sprung from his loins; and hence we extension beyond the
"must understand that if there be any persons circle of blood re-
"who however truly included in the brotherhood lations.
"by virtue of their blood-relationship, have never-
"theless *de facto* withdrawn themselves from the
"empire of its ruler, they are always, in the begin-
"nings of law, considered as lost to the family.
"It is this patriarchal aggregate—the modern
"family thus cut down on one side and extended
"on the other—which meets us on the threshold
"of primitive jurisprudence. Older probably than
"the State, the Tribe, and the House, it left traces
"of itself on private law long after the House
"and the Tribe had been forgotten, and long after
"consanguinity had ceased to be associated with
"the composition of States. It will be found to Its effect on juris-
"have stamped itself on all the great departments prudence.
"of jurisprudence, and may be detected, I think, as
"the true source of many of their most important
"and most durable characteristics. At the outset,
"the peculiarities of law in its most ancient state
"lead us irresistibly to the conclusion that it took

"precisely the same view of the family group which is taken of individual men by the systems of rights and duties now prevalent throughout Europe. There are societies open to our observation at this very moment whose laws and usages can scarcely be explained unless they are supposed never to have emerged from this primitive condition; but in communities more fortunately circumstanced the fabric of jurisprudence fell gradually to pieces, and if we carefully observe the disintegration we shall perceive that it took place principally in those portions of each system which were most deeply affected by the primitive conception of the family. In one all-important instance, that of the Roman law, the change was effected so slowly, that from epoch to epoch we can observe the line and direction which it followed, and can even give some idea of the ultimate result to which it was tending. And, in pursuing this last inquiry, we need not suffer ourselves to be stopped by the imaginary barrier which separates the modern from the ancient world. For one effect of that mixture of refined Roman law with primitive barbaric usage, which is know to us by the deceptive name of feudalism, was to revive many features of archaic jurisprudence which had died out of the Roman world, so that the decomposition which had seemed to be over commenced again, and to some extent is still proceeding." pp. 133—135.

The more you reflect on these passages, the

more you will perceive that what I have assumed for obvious reasons to be the right chronology of our own lives is also the right chronology of human society. Mr Maine's opinion upon this subject is very distinctly expressed in an earlier passage which I passed over that I might not distract your thoughts from the evidence concerning Roman history, and that I might not take advantage of any apparent confirmation of my statements in the sacred records._ _{margin: The general and particular chronology not at variance.}_

"The effect of the evidence derived from com-
" parative jurisprudence is to establish that view
" of the primeval condition of the human race
" which is known as the Patriarchal Theory.
" There is no doubt, of course, that this theory
" was originally based on the Scriptural history of
" the Hebrew patriarchs in Lower Asia; but, as
" has been explained already, its connexion with
" Scripture rather militated than otherwise against
" its reception as a complete theory, since the
" majority of the inquirers who till recently ad-
" dressed themselves with most earnestness to
" the colligation of social phenomena, were either
" influenced by the strongest prejudice against
" Hebrew antiquities or by the strongest desire to
" construct their system without the assistance of
" religious records. Even now there is perhaps a
" disposition to undervalue these accounts, or
" rather to decline generalising from them, as
" forming part of the traditions of a Semitic peo-
" ple. It is to be noted, however, that the legal _{margin: The Patriarchal origin of society. Attempt to represent it as a merely Semitic doctrine.}_

DOMESTIC MORALITY.

<small>CT. II.
evi-
ce for
the
itu-
is of all
ls.</small>
"testimony comes nearly exclusively from the "institutions of societies belonging to the Indo- "European stock, the Romans, Hindoos, and "Sclavonians supplying the greater part of it; "and indeed the difficulty, at the present stage of "the inquiry, is to know where to stop, to say of "what races of men it is *not* allowable to lay "down that the society in which they are united "was originally organised on the patriarchal "model." pp. 122, 123.

<small>theory
rds
h obvi-
facts.</small>
Of this (so-called) patriarchal theory I have said nothing, because I wished to rest my case on the evidence of facts with which we are all familiar. Those facts, as I may try to shew you hereafter, help to explain some of the legal fictions of which Mr Maine speaks, for they tell us why of necessity the relations of the family must interpenetrate the later order of the Nation, and impress their own character upon it.

<small>gil's in-
ct con-
ed by
ntific
uiries.</small>
Leaving these more general remarks, much as they concern our subject, and recurring to the particular Roman Institution about which we first consulted Mr Maine, I think he has made it clear that the conclusions suggested by our ordinary reading will endure strict investigation. Virgil was not mistaken in his belief that the ground of his nation's stability lay in the reverence for fathers; that the authority of the Consul rested ultimately on his authority; the obedience of the soldier on the obedience of the child. The power of the Roman over material things must be traced

to the same source. It does not appear that any peculiarities in the atmosphere of Rome enabled those who dwelt in it to make roads and drain marshes. The habit of obedience, grounded upon a personal relation, made them victorious over material things, victorious over the men who wanting that obedience stooped to things. It is delightful to find a court poet still retaining his interest in the growth of vines and the assemblies of bees: it is more delightful to find him still hoping for the restoration of manners in Romans through the revived recollection of the sacredness which they once attached to the paternal name.

marginalia: Lect. II. The conquests over material obstacles must be referred to the same cause.

Mr Maine laments his inability to trace as accurately as he would wish the alterations in the *Patria Potestas* in its different periods; how it was modified by laws or circumstances or opinions. Such a historical survey, were it possible, would I believe throw a clear light upon that distinction on which I have insisted between Authority and Dominion. To the paternal *authority* Rome owed its strength and freedom. The claim of paternal Dominion resulted in Imperial Tyranny. In the third part of these lectures I shall have much to say respecting the influence of the paternal relations and the Authority which assumed it as its foundation upon the manners of the modern world. Here I will only observe that though the institutions of Rome especially testify to the Authority of the father or his Dominion, the influence of the mother is never forgotten in its most characteristic

marginalia: Parental authority the blessing; paternal dominion the curse of Rome.

legends, in its most trustworthy records. They shew how deeply the most masculine of all Societies was indebted to the female for the preservation, because for the softening and the humanizing of its strength; how much the degradation of the female was involved in its degradation.

While I speak of this combined influence on the most organic of all commonwealths I am reminded of a poem which relates to the history and destiny of the most inorganic of all tribes. You will guess that I allude to the *Spanish Gypsy* of George Eliot. That remarkable and beautiful drama has been represented by some of its critics as an extravagant testimony to the influence of Race in overcoming the effects of education, in breaking the chains of a passionate attachment. To me it reads much more as a testimony to the might of paternal authority. With what admirable truth the struggle of Fedalma against that might is told; how every feeling that is deepest as well as tenderest rebels against the inexorable command of the outcast and prisoner who claims her as his daughter; most of you well know. But the victory was complete. The lover is given up for Zarca; the heart-broken girl undertakes the task of which she despairs.

"Father, my soul is weak, the mist of tears
Still rises to my eyes and hides the goal
Which to your undimmed sight is clear and changeless.
But if I cannot plant resolve on hope,
It will stand firm on certainty of woe.
I choose the ill that is most like to end

> With my poor being. Hopes have precarious life.
> They are oft blighted, withered, snapped sheer off
> In vigorous growth and turned to rottenness.
> But faithfulness can feed on suffering
> And knows no disappointment. Trust in me!
> If it were needed, this poor trembling hand
> Should grasp the torch—strive not to let it fall,
> Though it were burning down close to my flesh,
> No beacon lighted yet; through the damp dark
> I should still hear the cry of gasping swimmers.
> Father, I will be true!"
>
> *Spanish Gypsy*, Book III. p. 253.

That is certainly the sublime of obedience, scarcely conceivable in a Roman son, possible perhaps for the daughter of a Gypsy. Beneath the profound melancholy of this passage and of the whole poem, I cannot but fancy I see a glimmering of promise. It may be that abject races, which cannot rise to a new life through the influence of Joint Stock Companies and competitive Examinations, may yet have seeds in them which a domestic culture might call forth. It may be that races perishing in a worn-out civilization may awake at the stern summons of a father's voice coming to them softened and deepened through notes of feminine devotion and self-sacrifice.

[marginal note: Hopes for fallen and falling races.]

(2) *HUSBANDS AND WIVES.*

<small>CT. III.</small> It would be commonly said that the filial relation is one of necessity, the conjugal relation one of choice. We find ourselves in one, we may enter or not into the other. That mode of speaking is inevitable if we begin the study of society from the units which compose it. I have given you my reasons for choosing another method.

<small>rences n the hod sued in last ure as he sub- of this.</small> A mass of separate human units never has existed; why should we imagine it to exist? It is all important for men to discover that they are distinct persons; therefore I would strive to ascertain when and how they make the discovery; I would not anticipate it. If I pursue the chronological method it seems right to put the fact of sonship before all others; that dating from the hour of birth. But the relation of a man to a woman is presumed in that fact; it might fairly dispute for the first place in our enquiry. I am bound to give it the second.

Do I then exclude the distinction to which I have alluded? Do I deny choice as an element in this union? Are all the affections which lead to it, which have formed a principal subject for the song as well as for the prose of Europe, to be lost in the dead fact of a material or of a legal fellowship? The more we contemplate marriage as a primary institution of society—the more we remind ourselves that without it society could not be—the greater will be our reverence for the affections which lead to it and are implied in it; the less we shall be inclined to resolve it into any brutal instincts, or into any artificial arrangements.

<small>Lect. III.</small>

<small>Marriage a primary institute of society.</small>

This relation is always in peril from the sentimentalist and from the legalist. The first dwells on the fact, the undoubted fact, that without attachment between the parties who enter into it there is no true marriage. He proceeds to the assumption that choice is the ground of it. Therefore all bonds are accounted hardships; that the union may be perfect, those who have formed it must be at liberty to dissolve it whenever they please. Such a doctrine the Lawgiver declares to be subversive of Society. The union of husband and wife exists, he affirms, by his permission. There is a Nature which he cannot fight against, which he may be obliged to tolerate. Marriage he claims as his; *he* pronounces what is to be called marriage, what is unworthy of the name. Such language sounds plausible; it provokes a vehement reaction. 'Can

<small>The sentimental and the legal conceptions of it.</small>

4

DOMESTIC MORALITY.

T. III. *protest ach inst the r.* you bind us in one by your decrees if there is nothing within to bind us?' Again Sentiment is in the ascendant. Compromises are very ineffectual. You cannot have a little law and a little sentiment. That experiment is as fatal to the true *conjugium* as either extreme.

rela- as- ied in v. For this relation, like the paternal relation, is not the creation of formal Law; but is implied in it, lies beneath it, must be recognised and adopted by it so soon as it comes into existence. It is a *Relation;* therefore neither is it the creation of the persons who enter into it. This phrase truly expresses the fact. They *enter into it.* All the inward feelings which attract them to it do not determine its nature; that is determined before. But without the attraction they cannot in any degree understand the relation; it is for them as though it were not. There must be in each the sense of incompleteness without the other; the belief of each in the other; the dependence of each upon the other; not of the weak upon the strong *nplies st.* more than of the strong upon the weak. So that Trust is engendered, which becomes as essential a part of the domestic ἦθος as the Authority and Obedience which are demanded by the relation of father and child, without which the Family can not subsist. The Choice and Affection of which the sentimentalist speaks are involved in this Trust. Unless there is choice and affection upon each side, it loses its name and becomes a nonentity. But the choice and affection are not, as in the creed of the sentimentalist, the gratification of a separate instinct; choice meaning a mere passive submission to an overpowering impulse; affection having very little respect to its object, being chiefly prized for its reflex operation upon the person who cherishes it. This Trust is not impatient of Law as a restraint. It welcomes Law as a check upon the vagrant inclinations which would undermine it.

<small>Lect. III.

The sentimental creed not one of Trust but of separate enjoyment.</small>

There is no Trust like that which is expressed and fostered by the conjugal relation. But it diffuses itself from that through all the household; the authority and obedience, though they have another root, cannot be separated from it—derive their chief strength from it. From the family it goes forth into the nation. It manifests itself in friendships between members of the same sex. It enters into all the intercourse of life; where it is wanting, society becomes an intolerable lie. Clever men try to build up polities on suspicion and distrust. If they can but make men sufficiently on the watch against each other, the highest ends of civilisation, they think, will be accomplished. But the Babels which are compacted with this mortar fall down. For the needs of trade—even for the needs of that most subtle complicated machinery which is brought to perfection on the Bourse or Stock Exchange of the most refined cities in the world —you ask for Credit. Credit is found to be a most sensitive plant, liable to expand and contract in different circumstances for the most myste-

<small>Credit and Trust.</small>

rious reasons. The importance of possessing it, the miseries which may ensue if it is weak, are no securities that it may not utterly wither. Practical men must learn to translate their refined word into the older monosyllable Trust. They must ask elsewhere than among moneyed men how Trust is to be kept alive. They may trace the earliest seeds of it, as well as the secret of their growth and decay, to the homes of nobles, of shopkeepers, of peasants.

I wish you to remember that I am speaking of no bygone period, but of our own England—of this 19th century. Civilisation does not throw off the family; the blessing or the curse of it penetrates every corner of the most artificial society. Look at the *Mariage à la Mode* of Hogarth. Meditate on that ghastly breakfast table which is the preparation for all the Tragedy that follows. The great painter of English Social Morality has told you there the history of commercial failures, of political distrust and baseness, as well as of domestic infelicity. But when we have thoroughly assured ourselves that none of these lessons are obsolete, none of them inapplicable to our own age, it is then useful to travel back that we may see whether this conjugal relation has *only* to do with Great Britain or with Christendom—whether if we overlook it or treat it as of secondary significance, we can understand any society, any literature.

We are wont to speak of Greek Society as

pre-eminently that in which individual force and energy made themselves felt, of Greek Literature and Art as containing the clearest and highest conception of sensuous beauty. Everything there, it might be concluded, was adverse to the kind of fellowship and restraint upon taste and appetite which is implied in any relation, especially in this relation. Let us see how the case stands.

Lect. III. The Greeks.

What light the Iliad throws upon the order and manners of a time preceding the strictly historical time, Bishop Thirlwall and Mr Grote have told us. We knew before how much it had connected itself in the minds of Greeks with the thought of an enduring conflict between their tribes and the monarchies of Asia, how Alexander felt that he was fulfilling the lessons with which the song of his childhood had inspired him. But the discoveries of scholars cannot make us indifferent to that which lies upon the surface of the story for every one who reads it. The later Greek, though he may have accepted Homer as a prophet of the destiny of his race, must have accepted him still more as a witness how his ancestors regarded the marriage vow—how they deemed the defence of it the sign and pledge of the fellowship of their tribes with each other, the reason and the bond of a common enterprise. Had the Rhapsodist preached to us on this subject his words would never have lasted to this day or have left an impression upon any day. He is no preacher; he simply presents

The witness of the Iliad respecting the sanctity of the marriage vow.

us with clear pictures of human life under various aspects—now favourable, now unfavourable to his heroes. They do evil deeds, and avow them. Agamemnon says openly that he likes the daughter of the priest as well as Clytemnestra. Nevertheless no poem in the world does so much homage to the hearth and the home and especially to wives as this poem. Amidst the clatter of spear and shields, in the Greek ships or the Trojan city, they are never forgotten. The reader is impressed before he is aware of it with the conviction that the Greek manners must have been mainly created by the conjugal relation, that the weakness and corruption of their manners may be merely traced to the violation of it.

That the other great narrative poem of this period, whether the author of it was the same or not, bears the same impress, no one can doubt for a moment who considers the plot of it, the heroine of it, the wanderings and the final reward of Odysseus. He may have become, as Mr Tennyson imagines, weary of Ithaca when he arrived there. He may have longed for the sight of other cities and other men. But home and the wife were, as far as the Greek poet knew, the ultimate goal of his thoughts and longings.

If these poems bear a true witness, the union of the husband and the wife was the ground of Greek Society; whatever was healthy, graceful, refined in the Greek people, might be traced back to it; that which was vain, gross and false in them was connected with outrages upon it. And we cannot but perceive the influence of this relation upon their institutions. The order of the Greek commonwealths was not like the order of that great city which we were considering in the last lecture. Authority is not what we first think of in them, though authority was there, though it made itself felt in manifold ways; the authority of descent, the authority of intellect. But the elements of taste and affection, those which are so prominent in the Marriage relation, and are always trying to become supreme in it, present themselves to us in the various forms of these societies, in the changes which they underwent. We feel that we are in a world where choice will always be asserting itself—where perhaps very hard chains of law will be forged to restrain it. If again we examine the qualities of the Greek Intellect or Imagination, we find ourselves in the presence of a faculty curiously combining the masculine and feminine qualities; aiming at that perfect balance between the passive or receptive, the active or creative temper, between the individual and the universal, which constitutes the complete artist; liable of course to great excesses on either side, especially to a predominance of the senses over the man who should rule them. We can see how these tendencies would work with and against those which we are wont to describe as moral or ethical; how the political institutions which combined both elements would affect them and be affected by them. When the æsthetic faculties had reached their highest point in the Ionian race and had given birth to the marvellous works for which Athens in the age of Pericles was glorious, the most earnest thinkers reverted to the marriage relation as the most radical and precious of all for the life of their people, as that which was most in peril from their new and higher civilisation. The Agamemnon of Æschylus is an entirely different man from the Agamemnon of Homer. The age of sombre reflection has succeeded to the age of sunny observation. Yet the bond of wedlock is the subject of the play as it was of the narrative poem. And it is not the progress of guilty love which a modern artist might have described that the Greek Dramatist sets before us. It is the tragedy of the broken relation, of the vengeance on the husband, of the vengeance on the adulterers, of the furies that tormented the matricide, which appealed to the Greek mind and conscience. Yet I do not mean that here more than in the earlier poetry there is a formal didactic morality. It is the morality of life, the morality of a man who read the legends of past days by the light which fell upon them from the experience of his own. He had not to translate the dialect of the heroic ages into that of the later age, because he understood that the same relations existed in both; that they were permanent; that the breaches of them were Tragedies for every period and every country.

HUSBANDS AND WIVES. 57

The moral effect of such compositions as these, so filled with the sense of an order which would assert itself, which no one could violate with impunity, must have been exceedingly salutary to a people so possessed as the Athenians were with thoughts of self-government, so open to the suggestion that there was no Law which they did not establish or might not alter. It is in this way that the force of those relationships which precede the Law of States made itself felt as the protector of Law; there was that which evidently was not formed by decrees or assemblies; it was that very bond which seemed so closely associated with preference and self-will. On the other hand, as the Greek came to look down upon the wife, to regard the marriage bond as merely a legal one, to seek elsewhere for the gratification of his tastes and appetites, there was a corresponding loss of the sense of political order, an ever increasing opinion that it stood in words and conventions which cleverer words, conventions established by a stronger force, could overthrow.

LECT. III.
The effect on the Greeks of an order which they did not create.

There is one important topic connected with the Greek idea of marriage which I have no right to pass over. M. Comte speaks of Monogamy as a blessing which we have derived from the Middle Ages. Mediæval Christendom was no doubt engaged in a great and enduring conflict with a faith which accepted and endorsed Polygamy, no doubt it associated the opposite institution with its own faith. But to confine Monogamy within the

Monogamy.

CT. III.
t a
diæval
even
'hristen-
n Insti-
ion.

Christian Age is to pervert History. Your classical books tell you of many moral corruptions; they do not exhibit, either in Greece or Italy, Societies under the influence of this Institution. I am desirous that you should notice that fact and meditate upon it—not the less desirous because it may suggest another to you. 'Our classical books, so called, do not give us indications of such a state; our sacred books do.' That is an observation which you must needs make and which may often puzzle you. I cannot discuss the relation of Husband and Wife properly if I leave it unexamined.

You will understand that I am not now concerned with the Mosaic law, how far it restrained or did not restrain Polygamy. All questions into which formal Law enters belong to a later part of this course. Still less is it my business to notice the times of David and Solomon, though they may present important points for our reflection, when I enquire into the influence of Law and personal government upon each other. What interests us here is that ante-legal or patriarchal condition of which Mr Maine finds the traces in Ancient Law, and for the leading characteristics of which he refers us to the Book of Genesis. He does not mention Polygamy among those characteristics. No one can say that it is necessarily involved in the patriarchal order; still we all feel that it is a conspicuous incident in the lives of Abraham and of Jacob. The discovery of that

:iarchal
ygamy.

fact did not much affect the commentators on the Scriptures before the Reformation; they could resolve all the events which they read of in the previous time into figures or types of what was to be in a more advanced time. The Protestant schools grew to be impatient of allegories, studious of the letter. To them these examples became perplexing. They explained them away as they could. Milton scandalised his Puritan contemporaries by the consistency with which he accepted them as warrants for Polygamy in the Christian Age. He was, as Mr Wordsworth has remarked, a Hebrew of the Hebrews; he breathed the spirit of the Old Testament; its domestic, if not its national, forms had a strange attraction for him. The elevation and purity of his character made his doctrine harmless for himself; they could not hinder him from doing a great injury to the book which was so precious in his eyes. A history which is strikingly progressive became stereotyped. A set of men whose great worth to us consists in their being the most ordinary specimens of the race were elevated into heroes; what is still worse, the very idea of a divine education of the race through these specimens of it was practically annulled. Milton has increased his manifold claims upon our gratitude by affording us the most illustrious example of a perverted method which one moment treats these records as exceptionally sacred, the next as affording models which all men may follow. We justify

Lect. III. How it was dealt with by commentators on Scripture before and since the Reformation.

Milton's defence of Polygamy.

the true meaning of both opinions and reconcile them, if we suppose that they are lesson books for mankind, teaching by experiment what is incompatible with the order of human existence, gradually discovering the principles which are at the root of it.

The practical use of these narratives.

Looked at in this way the patriarchal story may be (I conceive has been), more profitable than any other in making readers aware of the confusions which Polygamy must introduce into every family circle; nay, in shewing them how incompatible it is with the existence of a family. We find in these records the absence of any effort to make out a case for the patriarchs. There are in them no doubt pastoral pictures which artists of after times have delighted to dwell upon. There are, beside these, acts of brutal violence such as are most likely to occur in the lives of real shepherds; but which are altogether disagreeable to those who prefer Arcadian shepherds. The tenderness of Jacob for Rachel is exquisitely beautiful; along with it we have the quarrels of the sisters, his own partiality and the effects of it upon his children. That which I observed as a remarkable feature of the Homeric legends is even more conspicuous in the patriarchal histories. There is no talk about morality; no dogmas about that which ought not to be; but a narrative, revealing in acts what could be only imperfectly enunciated in words, even if the time had come for enunciating it. We may hail

Their sincerity.

with great delight the Hellenic freedom from the mischiefs of Polygamy. But Palestine, not Greece, has made us *feel* the mischiefs of it, has enabled us to perceive by what unseen processes, and under what living teacher, Greece must have attained to her exemption from its curses. Under what *living* teacher I say; for those who have supposed that Greece owed this or any other blessing to Hebrew traditions are obliged in the first place to interpolate history with fancies, and secondly to deny the testimony of Scripture that there is one Lord over all nations.

<small>Lect. III.

How any people have become Monogamic.</small>

M. Comte has assuredly, then, no right to credit the middle ages with the chief and most effectual testimony on behalf of Monogamy. What he means doubtless is that chivalry involved a reverence and worship of women, which cannot be paralleled, though there may be many foretastes of it, in the ancient world. That worship, as a counteraction of the Mahometan tendency to degrade women into servants or instruments of a tyrant's pleasure, was of inestimable worth. But the abuses of the Courts of Love to which M. Comte points as proofs that the mediæval Church—or as he calls it, Theology—was unable to vindicate the purity of the household, grew out of this worship; in this instance, as in every other, the idolater degraded the object of his idolatry. The superiority of the sex was asserted; its dignity was undermined. Why it must be so I think you may gather from

<small>The mediæval chivalry.</small>

the hints which I have brought together in this lecture. The relation of the man and woman which is expressed in marriage, the dependence of each upon the other, is lost in the attempt to exalt either at the expense of the other. Separate them that you may glorify the strength of the man or the tenderness of the woman,—the strength and the tenderness depart, either because the strength becomes brutal and the tenderness imbecility, or because the strength apes the tenderness and the tenderness the strength. Proclaim their union, not as the result of any system but as involved in the order of the Universe, as implicitly confessed by every society which has not been given over to brutality—and you may hope to see the meaning of the union better understood, the contradictions to it more thoroughly exposed by every fresh light that is thrown on past ages or on the present age. There are some who tremble when they hear of the attempts to found a new Polygamy in the West under the shadow of Christian civilisation. I apprehend such a spectacle may be of the greatest service to Christian civilisation if it is turned to right account. Let the Polygamy of the Mormons be presented to us in the most favourable light by the most impartial observers. Let it be declared as loudly as you please that those who are adopted as wives by any distinguished prophet are content with their position, even proud of it. Still there is no ques-

[Margin: Lect. III. The relation destroyed by the attempts to glorify either sex to the disparagement of the other.]

[Margin: The Mormon Polygamy.]

tion whatever that the position is one of servitude; that the women are used to perform certain works for their masters. If the civilised Christians have understood that to be the position of the one wife; if they have had no higher conception of the marriage relation—it is good for them to behold the full development of their own principle, to see how much more perfectly it may be realised if the form which they have deemed sacred is abandoned. It may be a startling discovery; it may shake all their surface morality. But it may drive them to ask for the ground on which their morality rests; to see whether it has been created by social conventions, or is itself at the very basis of society. Clearly the States by mere force have not been able to put down Mormonism. Most thankful we should be that they have not. By giving up Slavery, by overthrowing the horrors which it introduced into the marriage relation—horrors with which nothing in the worst records of Polygamy can be compared—they have borne the true witness against Mormonism. Reforming their own civilisation, they have taken the true course for protecting themselves against any attempt, organic or inorganic, to graft the Oriental civilisation upon it. Repenting of the blasphemy which led them to plead the divine authority for making women into far worse than chattels, they have done what they could to vindicate the true Scripture idea, that the man cannot be without the

LECT. III.

The lessons which it contains for American and other Christians.

woman nor the woman without the man if there is a Lord in whom they are one.

<small>The protest against the Subjection of women to Force.</small> Against every notion of the subjection of women to Force that doctrine has borne, and does bear, the most weighty testimony. Wherever Christians have adopted that theory of subjection, they may have quoted the Bible glibly in its defence, but they have known in their hearts that they were fighting against the Bible. All civilisation, so far as it has been Christian, has been at war with this theory; every return to it has been a relapse into barbarism. But the proclamation of the independence of women is not a counteraction of this theory—is, I believe, another road to it. That is an attempt to deny the physical order, under pretence of asserting a moral order; it ends in an invasion of one as much as the other. There will be perpetual alternations of slavery on both sides: slavish worship to the attractions of the weak, slavish worship to the <small>The Marriage union determines the relation of the sexes to each other.</small> force of the strong; until we look upon the relation of Marriage as that which expresses and embodies the principle of the union of the sexes, their necessary dependence upon each other. No statistics can in the least affect that position. In any given community there may be preponderance of males or females. Thousands of causes may make it the duty of numbers in either to prefer a single life to a married one. But there will be in the single man the habit of reverence, of chivalry, the desire to learn from women what

they can teach much better than men; there will be in the single woman the grace and dignity which belongs to the wife, most of the gifts and qualities which are seen in the highest form in the mother; always a willingness to receive from men what they better than women can impart. Every one has seen such approximations to this state of things, such proofs that it is what makes life useful, beautiful, human, that he may well join with M. Comte in exclaiming against boisterous self-assertion on either side as disorderly and injurious. He may join with the same writer likewise in his earnest protests against the licence of Divorce which some European countries have sanctioned, and which Milton—logically I think—connected with his defence of Polygamy. For these services we owe the French Philosopher great thanks, because he is maintaining with much positiveness a very ancient *principle* which, as he rightly says, the anarchy of our times has disturbed. When he seeks to build the worship of women on a positive foundation, he is maintaining a very ancient *practice*—one into which men in all ages and under various impulses have fallen; one which has been largely developed in our time; one which may be a needful protest against tendencies to brutalise instead of to deify the female sex; but which will vanish along with them to its great blessing whenever the true order of human life is fully recognised.

Single life a reflection of the married life.

The idolatry of women.

Any consideration of the legal status of women,

LECT. III. about which we have heard so much in recent controversies, would be manifestly out of place in such a lecture as this. I would however make this remark. The perfect Trust which I have maintained to be implied in the relation of husband and wife, would be wrongly appealed to by those who oppose any measures for protecting the distinct property of women unless they are willing to base all legislation upon this trust. It is Trust of each in the other; it cannot be demanded of one more than of the other. Where the true $\mathring{\eta}\theta o\varsigma$ prevails, any rules about property will be unnecessary; the cry for rules is an intimation that it does not prevail. The moralist, if he enters into the region of positive law, must take care that he maintains his own ground. He affirms the existence of a relation which the Lawgiver can neither establish nor ignore. He does not pronounce what regulations may be needful for the defence of Property where the relation has been forgotten. But if he is silent on this point, he is not indifferent to it. Property wants the help of the Relation, though the Relation can dispense with the Property. When Trust vanishes from the Family, commercial men may feel their need of it—may seek for it eagerly—but they will not find it*.

<small>Maxims respecting property and the laws which regulate it cannot be immediately deduced from the principles of Domestic Morality.</small>

* I would earnestly advise my reader to study a pamphlet "On the Education and Employment of Women," by Mrs George Butler. He will see how much I am indebted to it; how feebly I have repeated some of the sentiments which are beautifully and powerfully expressed in it.

LECTURE IV.

(3) BROTHERS AND SISTERS.

If I had thought that bright and beautiful pictures of domestic life would enable you best to enter into the subject of my last lecture, I might have found them in our English writers of poetry and prose. I deliberately left them for such a dark and terrible tragedy as that of the Agamemnon. For I would not have you think of relations as if they were—what some seem to consider them—the ornaments and embellishments of our existence; additions on the whole, though with many drawbacks, to the sum of its happiness. It is of relations as the core of human society that I speak, as implied not only in its well-being but in its very being. If we do not take account of those societies in which we must exist, we shall attach a very disproportionate value to those in which we *may* exist.

Lect. IV.

Danger of treating Relations as if they were not involved in our existence.

LECT. IV.

What the greatest number means when the Family is forgotten.

The Class and the Club will be superlatively precious and dear as the Family is lost out of sight. Men will recognise themselves more and more by their badges and colours when they cease to care about the ties of blood. So with all our talk about the greatest happiness of the greatest number, the number to which we attach any real importance will be after all a very small one. The greatest number for which we shall care will be that which uses our shibboleths, which favours our sect. If we can persuade the greatest number to identify their greatest happiness with those shibboleths and that sect we shall pay it honour; if the greatest number should have some other conception of happiness we shall regard it with as much contempt as the most exclusive haters of the common herd.

Houses cannot be disregarded by the historical critic.

My object is therefore to lead you away from what seems to me an utterly false method of estimating human beings; that which proceeds upon the principle of counting heads. I find men and women in families. I do not find that in practice we can overlook or ignore this fact. I do not see why we should try to overlook or ignore it in theory. History, I perceive, takes great note of it; more not less since it has become critical. Families and houses appear very considerable items in our most recent books; their effect for good or for evil upon the course of events in every land, is admitted with greater clearness just as our observations become more exact. The stock in trade of the sensation novelist consists in flagrant outrages that have been committed against them; these it is supposed will stimulate the jaded appetite of fashionable readers more than incidents of any other kind. The contrast between these stories and those of the early or the later Greek ages to which I adverted in my last lecture is sufficiently striking. There was clear, free, living description in the first; no fever, no violent excitement of any kind. There was deep reflection in the second; but the stories which were chosen by the dramatist were familiar to his audience, there were no starts and surprises in them; everything to solemnise the mind, not to agitate and distract it. Yet both had this likeness to the wonderment-maker of our times. Violations of domestic relationships supplied to both their most characteristic subjects. The legend of Ægisthus and Clytemnestra, of Orestes and his sister, was one that every Athenian knew. The poet sought for the meaning of it; traced the different steps in the story; saw how past acts had contributed to the crime; what after acts were the avengers of it; so left to all generations a witness how the relations which men and women trifle with are the ground of their existence; how social order is subverted when they are set at nought. Let it be admitted, nay let it be strongly proclaimed, that the poet was producing a work of art, not a sermon about the marriage bond. Because it was a sincere work of art, because he

Their place in the epic and the drama.

The legends not for the ear or the eye, but for the heart.

looked into the heart of facts and did not try to twist them for the sake of any conclusion, therefore this testimony to domestic morality, as something deeper than all maxims of moralists, as implied in the very constitution of the world, came out of his tragedy.

The story of Œdipus.

A precisely similar testimony with regard to another relation, that of which I proposed to speak this morning, is borne by that Greek Trilogy which concerns the destiny of Œdipus. That story too, even when treated by the greatest genius, could have had none of the effect of surprise on those who witnessed the representation of it. Every incident was familiar to them; they would have resented any wilful variation from the tradition of their childhood. But here the culminating point in the misery of the house is the fall of the two brothers. That rested in the Greek imagination as the result of the previous confusions; as the sign that the foundations of the Theban city were broken up and could only be restored by the death of both the rivals. Most exquisitely indeed is the horror relieved—most beautifully is the lesson of it deepened—by the devotion of the sister to that brother whose body the king's edict had condemned to lie unburied; by her belief in a primitive and everlasting ordinance which none imposed by a mortal could repeal. Art required both sides of the picture and Art was faithful to fact in presenting both. Through them, not contemplated separately but together,

Eteocles and Polynices.

we apprehend the ἦθος which the relation of bro- Lect. IV.
thers and sisters developes.

When I spoke of Authority and Obedience as that part of the domestic character which is involved in the relation of Father to Son, I took pains to shew you that what we learn from that relation, what ceases to have any meaning when the sense of that relation is lost, is nevertheless not confined to it. When I spoke of Trust as the characteristic quality of the conjugal relation, I did not the least question that without Trust there could be no real authority in the parent, no real obedience in the child. The parallel observation that there may be an obedience in the Wife, an authority in the Husband, I cared less to insist upon, lest I should be supposed to plead for the sort of subjection by which some earnest philosophers are scandalised. But having once maintained that obedience, instead of being another name for Slavery, is incompatible with it, is the one defence against it, I need have no hesitation in using the old language respecting the wife and in believing that it denotes a state of feeling which is elevating not degrading to her. So in passing to the relation of brother and sister, I may most fully admit that Trust belongs to the very essence of it, that without Trust it becomes a huge contradiction. I may admit also that Primogeniture often confers an authority of brother over brother; that the difference of Sex, and other differences, often lead sisters to acknowledge an authority in

The manner specially belonging to each relation is demanded by every other.

Trust indispensable to the brotherly relations.

brothers. I may hold that this authority, however liable to abuse and whatever false deductions may be made from it, is an important and healthy element in Social Morality. But yet I may still look for some quality which shall be *distinctive* of this relation as Authority is of the paternal, as Trust is of the conjugal, some quality which shall be its contribution to the domestic life, and through the domestic life to the life of the most expanded Societies. The story of Œdipus, with its beauty and its horrors, fixes the name which we may give to this brotherly and sisterly ἦθος. If I call it the ἦθος of *Consanguinity*, I may seem to choose a legal and technical name. But my object is now as in the former instances to shew what primitive and domestic principle is hidden under legal and technical names, determines their signification, expands as well as limits their application.

When I speak of Consanguinity I of course acknowledge a physical fact, I assume that fact as inseparable from any principle which may be involved in it. What I affirm is, that in human beings this physical fact is connected with a fixed relation, and that in this relation a certain habit or manner is implied. It is implied *in* the relation, not artifically attached to it by certain later conventions. Where it is lost the relation is denied; Society if it is more than a collection of brutes is subverted.

This sense of Consanguinity implies primarily the acknowledgment of a common origin; not necessarily the relation both to a father and mother, but undoubtedly to one. It is capable of very great extension; as Mr Maine has told us it may be imagined when it does not exist. Yet the developements of it through any degrees of cousinhood; the dreams of it in a remote age; the counterfeits of it by legal adoption; never really interfere with the first and pure form of it. In the most complicated Societies the brother and sister still retain their dignity and position. They are not lost in any tables of descent; families which can trace no descent feel this bond as firm, as imperishable, as those which are most conspicuous for their quarterings. The significance of the relation, its enormous influence, the monstrous rebellions against it, may be learnt better perhaps in the household of a peasant than of a prince. Yet it is more in the last than all possessions, all titles, all expectations. What homage is paid to it concerns nations more than all the circumstances of their outward destiny, than the wisdom or folly of any Legislature or any Administration.

Lect. IV.

The radical principle survives amidst all changes and developements.

I use that language begging you to meditate upon it. At first it may sound strange; then you may deem it the flattest of commonplaces. I would rather you rested in the latter opinion. It *is* a commonplace and may become a very flat one if we make it flat. It may also rise to an alarming height before each one of us, as he thinks within himself—'In this relation I am or

The grandeur of the brotherly relation.

'I have been. What has been its importance to 'me; how have I fulfilled it?' No one who seriously asks himself these questions every day will doubt that this Consanguinity has been a mighty power for him; whether he has turned it to a good or a bad account, it has been more to him than all the controversies in all the schools of philosophy, in all the diets of kingdoms or consistories of churchmen.

In every English household of our day we may study this relation; we may trace its effects upon our national society. But you may study it also in the Hindoo village of the present and of former ages. You will be presented with the most startling phenomena concerning it as you read the history of the Ottoman Empire; the brothers' murders which were necessary to consolidate it and to preserve the succession. There is no monarchy of Christendom which does not teem with illustrations of it. Aristocracy in all its aspects brings us back to the primacy of brothers as well as their conflicts with each other. You have signs wherever you look that what concerns you more than the outward economy of the world, equally concerns all people in all parts of the world. The lessons of the Dramatist are graven on the records of mankind. The frightfulness of Incest, the temptation of brothers, for the sake of dominion, to lift themselves up against each other with a ferocity to which there is no parallel in the quarrels of mere neighbours, the way in which, amidst all these outrages upon it, the common blood asserts itself, the triumph of the human relation over the savage instincts which set it at nought—the triumph won by feminine weakness and devotion—these truths could only be illustrated by fiction because Sophocles had realised the force of them in the actual history of his land.

<small>Lect. IV.</small>

<small>Literature a witness to facts.</small>

No land indeed afforded such a witness of them as that one in which democratic institutions had established themselves, in which the claim of wit and talent to rule was most intensely felt. Why should one man have possessions rather than another; exercise authority more than another? Not in virtue of brute strength, that was a barbarian's notion of power; the man could subdue creatures that were vastly bigger than himself, provided with beaks or talons that he had not. For he had an inward art, a craft that was not theirs. By that same art or craft he could prevail over the stupider, if they were the more bulky, parts of mankind; he could overcome the apparent force of the Persians, in whose land he was settled; he could bring his own countrymen to bow before him, to confess his supremacy. It was a mighty persuasion; how many encouragements there were in the experience of the past, in what he saw around him, to make it good! What a restless desire for dominion and conquest it created! How sure it was to find its way into the heart of families, to make the clever

<small>Greek democracy.</small>

or cunning brother feel that he might overreach one older and less vivacious, might perhaps displace him in his inheritance or his father's affection! Why should there be anything in a family but this strife of intellect, this struggle for predominance? There it encountered the troublesome antagonist, the sense of consanguinity. The feeling of rivalry, the passion for dominion, did not dwell alone in these members of the household, who seemed to stand all on the same level, whom so many circumstances seemed to point out as equals. They might be equals but they were kinsmen. Which recollection was to be the stronger? The struggle was often deadly between them; often the passion for independence triumphed; often all thoughts of kin were cast to the winds. What were they? Why should clever men be bound by them? They were gossamer threads; a child's knife might cut them in twain. But then again what strength there was in these invisible threads! How they wound themselves about the hearts of those who were most impatient of them! How when they went forth on their cruise of independence, in the search for worlds where they might have their own way and not be checked by old associations, the old associations came back. Neither seas and mountains, nor the sight of new men, nor the hearing of new tongues, succeeded in dissolving the old spell. The family, the tribe, reappeared in the untrodden soil; the names, the customs that had belonged to the hearth and household, drove out those which they found, or, blending with them, transformed them. It was the glory of the Greek in his native home to assert his independence and superiority. Is it not his glory in the new land to assert his Doric or Ionic derivation; to shew what it is to be one of a race?

Lect. IV.

How it works in the foundation of new societies.

See how Consanguinity works in those who give the greatest signs that they were determined to have a way of their own, that they were born to be founders of Societies! Their zeal to be independent becomes the instrument of asserting relationship. So soon as they begin to found Societies they acknowledge a Society which was founded for them.

Amidst all the whirl of events in the Greek cities, amidst all social strifes and schemes of legislation, speeches of rhetoricians, theories of philosophers, we cannot then forget the brother and sister. Turn to a history which is free from these interests; one in which law and policy have not yet appeared. Consider that book of Genesis to which I referred last week for its illustration of the marriage relation, as well as of the effects of polygamy in confusing it. There you have another and much simpler exhibition of the brotherly relation. Simpler but not the least more flattering. Free from the impediments of law, from the social complexities of later days, you have the family life, especially in these aspects of it, clearly set before you. I leave critics to discourse about documents,

The Hebrew records.

what their value is, or whence they come. I merely take what I find. I know not what omissions or alterations could convert it into a more instructive commentary on ancient life or on modern life; on the smallest commonwealth of classical Greece, or on the greatest democratical community of the western world.

Isaac and Ishmael.

In the house of Abraham we have an indication—little more than an indication—of the strifes which might arise between brothers like Isaac and Ishmael, with a common father, with hostile mothers, one a concubine. After the separation and the establishment of one as the head of an Arab tribe or horde, the sense of a common blood brings them together at their father's grave; amidst all the conflicts of after ages the old tie of Ishmaelite to Israelite is never forgotten.

Esau and Jacob.

Far more distinct and vivid is the picture of the relations between Esau and Jacob. The plain man with his tendency to craft and cowardice, the genial hunter full of outspoken affection and hatred, have reappeared in every age, have been claimed as representative figures in every region of the earth. Amidst the strifes of characters so opposite, each desirous of dominion, each connecting it with a father's blessing, there is still the mightiest sense of consanguinity. They plot against each other, and they embrace; the name of the father about whose favour they dispute, and his grave, are still meeting points for the Edomite chieftain and the heir of the Covenant.

Then follows the story which has had such power over the minds of children and adults, a story full of fierce passions and wild deeds, but exhibiting the sense of a common blood, in those who are taking a crafty and brutal revenge for the seduction of their sister, even in those who are punishing their father's partiality by casting their brother into a pit. The sense of relationship is conspicuous in the oppressors as well as in the victim. It goes with him into the prison and into Pharaoh's palace; it is awakened in them by a punishment which appears to have no connexion with the crime. Of course I accept the story like that of the patriarchal polygamy as the genuine record of a divine Education. But since it is the education of men with the coarsest natures, as little disposed as any could be to fraternal sympathies, it illustrates the ordinary history and experience of mankind more completely than any other can. In this case as in the one I considered the last week, if I accept the Scripture narrative at all, I must accept it as teaching how Greeks or any human beings were enabled to rise above their own selfish tendencies and prepossessions and to become capable of any Social Morality. I may shew you in a subsequent lecture that their own apprehensions upon the subject, if very different from those of the Hebrews, were not different in this respect; both traced human relationships to a divine origin.

I have dwelt much on the word Consanguinity

Lect. IV.

Joseph and his brethren.

An illustration of ordinary domestic antipathies and sympathies.

LECT. IV. in this lecture in connexion with the brotherly relation. We shall hear in due time of trade brotherhoods, of religious brotherhoods and sisterhoods, of a universal brotherhood. We shall have to enquire into the force of language which has been so widely diffused throughout Christendom. But we must not antedate these enquiries. We may weaken our belief in the reality of the domestic bond, if we introduce more general thoughts prematurely. I have purposely taken my illustrations from two countries which we are wont to consider specially exclusive; from the family of Abraham, with its Covenant and its special rite; from the Hellenic race, the very name of which marks it as antagonist to the Barbarian. Whatever principles might be hereafter developed in the history of either or both of these peoples it is important to remember that consanguinity bore for each of them its most direct and obvious signification. There might be a temptation sometimes to extend it, sometimes to contract it. But the thought of an actual brotherhood was assumed in the existence of the Jewish tribes, and was never obliterated. We know from a familiar story that the Greek disputed the right of a Macedonian monarch to attend the Olympic festival, because the purity of his blood was suspected.

Wider notions of brotherhood not to be considered here.

Strictness of the Greek and Jewish conception.

I do not wish you to forget the connexion between brotherhood in its most limited and in its most comprehensive sense. I wish you to preserve the feeling of that connexion. I shall have to shew you what modern Europe has lost by turning a word into a metaphor which should have represented the greatest reality. That is my reason for deferring the consideration of this use of the word till we can find some substantial ground for it. But there is one remark which I must make in this place. Fraternity has in later days been closely associated with Equality. We have seen from the history of the Greek republics, as well as from the simple patriarchal narrative, how naturally the thought of Equality springs out of this household relation, and what was in the earliest times the restraint upon it. There is a sense of equality in brothers which there never can be between fathers and sons; which only starts up artificially, when the feeling of the relation has been enfeebled, between husbands and wives. Brothers are to be the founders of new households, perhaps of new cities and commonwealths. Among them appear all distinctions of temper, taste, intellect. One has this claim, one that, to superiority. The common English household explains the working of these influences; Greek factions were the result of them. Equality is asserted in them—Equality is disturbed by them. Fraternity comes in partly to soften the cry for equality, partly to make the fulfilment of it possible. The competition of interests is checked as the sense of the relationship is strengthened; with the sense of the relationship comes also the feeling of distinct powers which each may put forth for the help not the overthrow

Lect. IV.

Equality and Fraternity.

The conflict between the two ideas.

of the other, of distinct vocations to which each may devote himself, and so may make the destiny of the whole family more complete.

<small>Lect. IV.</small>
<small>The fellowship of brothers.</small>

That is a very simple statement of what you all have in some degree experienced—the statement of a principle, as I think, of the profoundest importance and the most unlimited extent. I dare not tell you how much I feel that competition which some deem the great sign of social advancement, the great help to modern learning, is threatening the existence of Society, is undermining knowledge. Yet I have no dream of checking it by artificial expedients. I shall endeavour to shew you hereafter how it becomes associated with that consciousness of a distinct life, which I believe cannot be too vigorous in a man, without which nations must perish. It is the brotherly relation in which I find the true antidote to the destructive tendency of competition, the true vindication of all in it that is sound and healthful. History bears that witness to us; may each of us realise it for himself!

<small>Competition.</small>

That we may do this, I have given you in the patriarchal records evidence enough that the contentions of brothers are not produced by the circumstances of civilization; that to wish those circumstances away for the sake of obtaining a more affectionate brotherly intercourse, is in the last degree idle and ungrateful. In the household stripped bare of all arts, luxuries, refinements, there are rivalries, hatreds—the impulses that lead

<small>Civilization not the cause of disorders between brothers.</small>

to fratricide. But learn the other part of the lesson also. These rivalries, hatreds, impulses to fratricide, are all rebellions against an established order, are all violations of a relation in which we actually exist. You may call them natural if you please; as I have said again and again I do not complain of that word. But if so submission to Nature means ceasing to be men; the choice of an inhuman state.

And whilst I am most anxious not to charge any improvements or progressive developements of Social Life with evils which become apparent in its earliest stages, I must also repeat the maxim that every step onwards is a blessing or a curse, according as the first steps are securely taken. The craving for ownership, for dominion, is that which distracts the household. Whether that is turned into a healthy craving, or becomes the seed of all mischief to him who cherishes it, and to all with whom he is brought into contact, depends upon the question whether it is harmonized with the feeling of relationship, or whether it tramples that down. If the desire of possession and rule is stronger in any man than the sense of brotherhood, he may be a tyrant or a slave; or both in one. He in whom the sense of brotherhood is uppermost may be a sufferer and a victim, but he will help to preserve Society from destruction.

Lect. IV.

But what civilization shall be is determined by the degree in which these disorders prevail in the family or the order conquers them.

LECTURE V.

(4) *MASTERS AND SERVANTS.*

<small>Lect. V.</small>

<small>The Domestic Institution.</small>

A PHRASE was heard very frequently in the Southern States of America when Slavery prevailed there. It was called a Domestic Institution. No arguments of those who aimed at the abolition of Slavery were so powerful as this language of its defenders in causing it to be regarded with disgust and loathing. For those who listened to it knew —those who uttered it could not be ignorant— what kind of domestic Morality was associated with the legal dogma that the negro was the chattel of his Master, and ought to be dealt with as other chattels were. All relations of father and child, of husband and wife, of brother and sister, were thrown into the wildest confusion by the practice which that tenet sanctioned. It was no question of colour or race. The white was more degraded by the presence of this anomaly in his household

than the black. For the honour of his skin, for LECT. V.
the dignity of his parentage, he had need to demand at any price a deliverance from it.

But now that that deliverance has been effected—now that we have no excuse for speaking harshly of any southern planter or of his apologists—it may be right for our own sakes to consider what this plea meant. An expression does not gain such currency as this gained, if there is not some foundation for it. We were often reminded by slaveholders that there are servants in most English households. We were asked whether the only difference between these servants and slaves is that they receive certain wages, and that they may at their pleasure change one master for another. We were urged to consider that "this "privilege has its attendant disadvantages; that "the affection of the hireling is often far less than "that of the Slave who has grown up, who has "perhaps been born on his Master's Estate, who "has never known himself in any other character "than as attached to him. There is no doubt," it was said, "some difference in the independence "of a man who lets himself out for a time, and "one who is transferred altogether to an owner. "But it is a question of degree not of kind. "Money settles in what position either the "Slave or the so-called Servant shall stand to his "Master. Money is more clearly and distinctly "required as the bond of union in the latter case "than in the former." Reference was also made

Wherein does the servant differ from the slave?

Arguments for the second.

LECT. V.

The Greek, the Roman, the Jew, all slaveholders.

The Greeks.

Aristotle.

to history. "The Greek Republics which were "most democratical, in which the sense of Equality "was most predominant, recognised Slavery. It "was no offspring of Monarchy. It was intimately "associated with the sense of Freedom and "Citizenship. The Greek felt what he was, what "he ought to be, when he contemplated the dif- "ference between his race and the races that were "merely animal. Was not the slave like the Son, "a part of the Roman Family? Finally, what "can be said of that Society which Christians "believe to have been divinely set apart, divinely "organised?"

No questions are more pertinent to our present subject than these; I should conceive I was treating the subject of Domestic Morality most carelessly if I passed them over or only offered loose and general answers to them. I will try to examine them in the light of history. I hope I shall not shrink from applying the lessons of the past with all strictness to our own practices. I will take the Greeks first, since the most careful and systematic of their writers on Social Morality has handled this topic and has given us a kind of help in the investigation of it which we shall scarcely find any where else.

Aristotle, as I have observed already, begins his Politics from the Family Relations. Amongst these he includes that of Master and Servant. He accepts in the fullest sense the Greek faith about Slavery; he sustains it by his own arguments; he shews how thoroughly his mind was penetrated by it. There was a supremacy due to Intellect, *i.e.* to the man over the animal. The Greek clearly possesses this supremacy. However it came to him, it is his; he must assert it. He can rule. He must shew that he can. The position has often been maintained since; it has been applied to other races than the Hellenic; it has never been more vigorously asserted or in more various modes of speech than in our own day. But I am not aware that Aristotle's reasonings have ever been improved, that anything has been added to them, except a little violence of temper into which he was seldom betrayed. He had a thorough mastery of himself and of his doctrine. It was not with him a rebellion against some other; it was a calm deliberate assertion of what he perceived to be a fact, and of an inference from that fact which appeared to him inevitable.

<small>Lect. V.</small>

<small>The dominion of the intellect over the animal.</small>

According to this doctrine certain men should be instruments, organs, through which certain other men effect their purposes. There should be no genuine difference, as I observed in my lecture on the paternal Relation, between the plough and him who drives the plough, between the apparatus for cooking and the cook. But *is* there no difference between them in Aristotle's estimation? Assuredly the widest. For the servant is part of the Family, if ever so subordinate a part. There is a relation between the Master and the Servant; a relation which is afterwards to be unfolded in the

<small>What such a doctrine *should* involve.</small>

88 DOMESTIC MORALITY.

LECT. V.

Why it does not involve this.

Aristotle's theory overcome by his reverence for fact.

The battle of relations and property.

civic order. Because this relation becomes associated with those of which we have spoken already, the slave rises unawares from a possession, an instrument, into a man. His position may be justified by his animal tendencies. He may be marked for servitude. He may be deemed incapable of rule. But however incredible it may be, he is *related* to the ruler; that bond between them must not be denied.

'*Must not be;*' you will say perhaps, 'in the theory of a Philosopher.' By no means; the philosopher's theory would permit that it should be denied. It is the philosopher's faithful study of facts which surmounts his theory, which compels him to confess what his theory would contradict. But no philosopher and no plain man could force any Master to admit the slave as one of his relations; could hinder him from saying 'He is my property. I have won him with my sword. I have purchased him with my money.' That assuredly would be said; it was the ordinary tendency of every man to say it. All the circumstances of his position, all the lessons of his wisest counsellors, seemed to point it out as the most reasonable language. What proved it unreasonable? Simply that fact of the most ancient, of the most modern, experience that the language which is applied to one part of the family will gradually be applied to the whole of it. The belief in Property will become the absorbing belief in the mind of the Father; it will convert his authority over his Son into mere Dominion. It will be a question between the husband and the wife which shall have dominion over the other; notions of Property will regulate *their* union. Brothers will view their relation in the same aspect; it will be a struggle which shall possess most of that which the father leaves. Here is the test of the two principles. They will be always fighting in every man to whatever Society he belongs; democratical, aristocratical, monarchical. If he admits the principle of Property in any case to be the ground of his connexion with one of his own race, that principle becomes predominant in his whole life; if the domestic feeling is stronger in him than the feeling of possession, that will work itself out in him till it leavens his thoughts of every one with whom he is brought into contact.

<small>Property must be supreme over all relations if over any.</small>

I take Aristotle then as expounding to us the conditions and the contradictions of Greek Society, and as foretelling what would be the conditions and contradictions of Society in all lands. The American who said that the acknowledgment of Equality did not overcome—could not overcome —in him the contempt of an inferior race, that the fact of inferiority was stronger than any theory, had a precedent for his statement in the experiences of the Hellenic races, and in the most enlightened commentaries upon those experiences. The American who spoke of Slavery as a Domestic Institution might also turn with much profit and hope of confirmation for his doctrine to the same

<small>How far the Greek precedent availed for the modern slaveholder.</small>

source. Only then he would encounter the discovery—of which he could also supply abundant illustrations from his own age and land—that Domestic life must either subdue Slavery or be subdued by it.

The Roman slave.

The Roman Family may teach us more on this subject than the Greek, not through philosophers, but through the acknowledged facts of the history. The Son, as you know, was in the family as a Servant; he had need of emancipation before he could rise to his proper rights as a Citizen. The Slave was in the Family, and might also be emancipated, might become a Citizen. Here was in a strict sense a domestic Institution. What was the effect of it? That question cannot be answered by an appeal to one set of facts. There are two opposite sets of facts each resting on clear evidence. In one of the debates on West Indian Slavery in the House of Commons, when Sir Thomas Fowell Buxton had proposed a resolution declaring it to be incompatible with Christianity, Mr Canning appealed to the Sixth Satire of Juvenal as shewing what the Slavery of the Roman Empire was when Christianity appeared in the midst of it. He quoted that speech of the Roman Matron which ends with the well-known line,

Mr Canning's appeal to Juvenal.

> Sic volo, sic jubeo; stet pro ratione voluntas.

What it proves.

Well! that speech points to one class of facts quite indisputable; there might be the most reckless tyranny exercised over the person of the slave. If Mr Canning's respect for his audience and for the public opinion of England had permitted him to adduce other passages from the same Satire, he might have shewn what an utter decay and overthrow of domestic life generally was co-existent with this violence. He might have proved that the saying 'omnia Romæ venalia' was illustrated by the son plotting for his father's death, the wife for the husband's, the brother for the brother's. But when we have wearied ourselves with looking into those dreadful records, it is some refreshment to recollect that the body of Roman freedmen, not to speak of those special instances of the class which we have been wont to connect with very graceful portions of Latin literature, bear witness to an influence of the other kind — to an elevation of the servant, not a degradation of the son. I am not considering how far Legislation contributed to either result. I am maintaining that the Roman state could not have existed, that Law would have perished altogether, if family Relations had not counteracted the mere money power; asserting for the slaves a place among Romans and men.

Lect. V.

This Satire does not refer only or chiefly to slaves.

The other class of facts.

But undoubtedly the Society of Palestine was a more favourite argument with the supporters of Slavery in the Southern States of America, than that of Greece or of Rome. Had it not a sacred even more than a classical sanction? What I said on the subject of Polygamy in a former

The Hebrew slave.

Lecture makes any formal answer to this question unnecessary. But I am glad to speak of it in connexion with the phrase 'Domestic Institution.' We have seen how thoroughly the order of the Jewish Commonwealth was laid in Domestic Institutions, or, to use a less ambitious phrase, in the Family. All its after Legislation is only intelligible when this ground is assumed for it. The highest promise to the Family of Abraham was that through it all the families of the earth should be blessed. However slight a meaning might be attached to that promise by those who accepted it and spoke of it as the Israelite privilege, this at least was an inevitable deduction from it. All captives in war, all slaves purchased with money, came into the circle of the children of the Covenant; their condition might be comparatively ignominious; they could not be treated as mere animals. They were in a very practical as well as formal sense members of the Family. The legislators and prophets of Israel in general encouraged the slaughter of enemies in war, discouraged the taking of them as prizes to enrich the Conqueror. They dreaded, no doubt, the multiplication of Slaves; they saw the peril in which it would involve the native Society. But all bondsmen, however they might be claimed and dealt with as the property of particular householders, came—in that very character—under the cognisance of the whole Commonwealth; could not be excluded from its protection. The Master and Slave stood of necessity in a relation to each other; Property in this as in all cases did homage to the Relation; not the Relation to the Property. I do not mean that the lust of Property rebelled against this Relation less among the Jews than among the other peoples of the earth. That Rebellion is most conspicuous through their whole history. Every age exhibited some fresh instance of it. Every Prophet lifted up his voice against it, saw in the prevalence of it the ruin of the land. In the final days of the Commonwealth the maxims of Property subdued all others; the religion became mainly a calculation of Profits and Losses; Mammon was worshipped in the Temple and in the corners of streets as the true Lord of Heaven and Earth. It did not signify much then whether the servant was bought or hired; whether he was or was not esteemed a part of the Family. For what is the Family in a Society of that kind? What man feels that he is related to any other?

The principle of Jewish society.
Its overthrow.

If these observations are true, the supporters of modern Slavery had an unquestionable right to claim for it a Latin, an Hellenic, or a Hebrew ancestry. They had a right to say that it was in Greece, in Rome, in Judea a Domestic Institution. The resemblance might have been pushed further. It might have been shewn that the disorder of the Modern Nations, like the disorder of the ancient, was inseparably connected with the disposition to treat men as property; that the order of the

Inferences from those statements.

LECT. V.

Modern slavery not inherited from the old world or the middle ages.

Modern Nations, like the order of the Ancient Nations, has always manifested itself in its struggle against this disposition, in a victory over it. These historical parallels may be of great profit to us. But if we try to prove that we have inherited Slavery either from the old world or from the middle ages, the most notorious facts confute us. The Slavery in our West India Islands, and in what were our colonies on the American Continent, had not the faintest connexion with the ancient Serfdom of Europe. It cannot be traced, as we like to trace our abuses, to feudal or papal traditions. It is of Protestant birth; it belongs to the Trade age. Men of high intelligence may plagiarize from the Greeks and apply their doctrine of the dominion of intellect over brute force to the case of the white and the negro. But they know that the white stooped to the brutality of the negro in the act of capturing him; increased his brutality in the process of holding him; found his interest in warring against intellect in those whom he possessed; therefore gradually lost all feeling of the difference between Intellect and mere force in himself. Let us make all possible excuses for those

It is strictly the creature of trade.

who purchased slaves or received them by inheritance; but the arguments from reason and religion must be regarded as altogether *ex post facto*. The spirit of Trade, the desire for Property, must be credited with the origin of the traffic, with the maintenance of it, with the resistance to every proposal for abolishing or even mitigating it. I wish you to remember this, not because I am anxious to escape the force of those arguments of the Slaveholders to which I have referred, but because I feel how strong they are still. They have survived the extinction of the laws and customs which they were first invoked to defend. The statement that the hireling servant, whether in the household, the farm, or the factory, may be as little regarded as any one who is bought and sold, is one which we cannot afford to disregard. It is strictly true. It points to a tendency which is in all of us—a tendency very little affected by theories concerning Government—not touched by any of the contrivances or comforts of modern civilization—strengthened rather than weakened by the mercantile dogmas which have supplanted the old feudal dogmas. The habit of regarding separate possession as the basis of Society, as the end which all Society exists to secure, leads directly to the expressions which we hear so often: "I have paid the fellow for his services; what more can he ask of me?" That is, in other words, "Between me and him there is no relation; the only bond between us is that which money has created." That is the feeling on the master's side. And the servant's of necessity corresponds to it. "I owe him nothing: he has had my work out of me. What more have I to do with him?"

Force of the old arguments for slavery against ourselves.

Wages do not affect the relation between master and servant.

There are men, generous and noble men, who listen indignantly and impatiently to this kind of discourse; who think it is increasing, whom it fills

96   DOMESTIC MORALITY.

LECT. V. with apprehensions of that which must be coming upon a Society where it prevails. To them the obvious, the only, remedy for it seems a proclamation that the terms Master and Servant are grounded upon a false and unrighteous assumption; that they ought to be banished from the vocabulary of true citizens and well-constituted societies. I respect their feeling; I share their terrors; I utterly dissent from their conclusion. It seems to me that what we want is not a repudiation of service as inhuman, but a much profounder reverence for it; not an assertion that all have a right to rule, but far rather a conviction that every one is bound to serve, and may claim service as his highest privilege.

The two modes of curing this social evil.

I am uttering no paradox. I am merely affirming that our ordinary speech is not treacherous and hypocritical speech. We talk of military Service as honourable. The rulers of the land are those whom we call the Queen's Ministers. Of course we may mean nothing by these words. We may mean nothing by any of our words. They may all be merely counters which we pass off upon one another without attaching the least value to them. But suppose for an instant that we are not doing this—that all our commonest expressions are not impostures—in that case it would not be at all necessary or desirable to get rid of these names; no one would be elevated, every one would suffer, by the loss of them. Indeed, what good do we ever obtain by unmaking facts, or by determin-

Service assumed in our common speech to be noble.

ing that we will not recognise them? Men will direct others in the doing of certain works, will teach others certain lessons. Men will ask to be directed both in their works and their thoughts. The only result of saying "It ought not to be so; there should be no master and servant," is that some will exercise dominion because they can do it, that others will be submissive because they cannot help it. That is to say, the condition of owner and slave will be substituted for the relation of Master and Servant. *Lect. V. Consequence of rejecting the notion of Service.*

When we come to speak of the Legal or National State we shall find an explanation of Equality very different from this, much more satisfactory. At present we are in the domestic region, that region in which Manners are formed, from which we learn what Manners are. The ground of these cannot be Self-Assertion; that tends to brutalise Manners; that is always threatening Social Intercourse. Deference, courtesy, observation of the feelings of those with whom we live, these habits are cultivated by the interdependency of the members of a household, by what I have described as the inevitable duplicity of every relation. But this manner—this essential part of the domestic ἦθος—attains its highest developement when there is a reciprocal reverence between the Master and the Servant; it is shattered to pieces when that reverence is destroyed. *How Manners depend upon it.*

Do not suppose that I have any *arrière pensée* about a condition of Clanship, or that I wish

Anglo-Saxons to become Celts. My principle is good for nothing if it depends upon social accidents, if it is not as valid for those who pay wages as for those who claim the fealty of vassals. Family Relations last on through all changes; I claim the Relation of Master and Servant as one of these, as overshadowed and interpreted by the relationships of blood and in turn protecting them from the perils to which they are at every moment exposed. I rejoice in all those facts which prove that the Servant has a legal status; that he has as much claim against his Master in the courts as his Master has against him. But I am sure that neither his position nor his Master's is made a pleasant or even a tolerable one by these arrangements. I am sure that unless they learn that reverence for each other which neither feudal bonds nor legal securities can create, they will become more and more enemies to each other, and the enmity will spread from that relation to all others till the entire Household is infected with it. A full discovery of the reasons which make Service venerable, which render the ambition to rule only moral, only human, when it means ambition to serve—must be reserved for a subsequent part of these Lectures. But if I have given you a hint how much that doctrine, strange as it sounds, has been recognised in our language and in every modern language—I must follow up that hint by reminding you that every one of you will be called to some position in which he will be both Servant and Master, in which he will be under authority, in which he will have some under his authority. What your lives shall be, what good or mischief you will do to your country —will depend mainly upon the question how you understand this position, what you suppose to be the nature of this authority. Just so far as you forget that the position involves a relation—just so far as you confound the Authority with Dominion your manners will become brutalised, just so far you will help to brutalise all with whom in any capacity you are associated. I will not go through a host of instances. I will take one which will illustrate the whole subject and its bearing upon the most modern practice. Some of you may become civil or military servants in British India. You will have native servants under you. You will be tempted as others have been before you, to think of those servants as members of an inferior race. You will not of course call them 'Niggers' as some have done. You will not disgrace our Education here so much as to exhibit that stupid ignorance. But without resorting to any of the epithets which stamp vulgarity upon all who condescend to them, you may be tempted to say, "We have a right to treat "these people as brutes, for in many ways they "shew themselves to be so." Understand that they have a brutal nature in them as you have a brutal nature in you. If you speak to the brutal nature in them—if you assume that there is nothing else

Lect. V.

Importance of recollecting that fact.

Native servants in India.

The plea for brutality towards them.

in them but that—you will cultivate it in yourselves. The distance between them and you of which you boast will diminish at every moment. You will sink to their level. It is only to the force which your country wields that you will appeal for the preservation of your superiority. And that force you will be weakening. Your treatment of the natives will be doing more to shake it than a hundred blunders in legislation. For the manners of men affect men more than the acts of Councils or the decrees of Judges. If England reigns by Force, her reign must come to a speedy end. If she reigns by Justice and Gentleness you her sons must shew forth those qualities in your acts. No one will believe in them because we talk about them, because our Newspapers say that the world ought to admire us for them. By our fruits we shall be known and judged. By our conduct to Servants it will be shewn whether we are fit to be Masters, or whether we must sink into Servants of Servants.

LECTURE VI.

FAMILY WORSHIP.

We have now considered the different Relations of the Family, including among them, for the reasons which I stated in my last Lecture, that of Master and Servant. What shall we call these Relations? If I said they were *artificial* you would denounce my language as monstrous. Supposing it were possible to treat Service as a mere arrangement—supposing it were not an outrage upon our deepest convictions to describe Marriage by that name—it becomes merely ridiculous when it is applied to Fatherhood or Brotherhood. No wonder then that men have been wont to speak of the relations and the affections which correspond to them as *Natural.* But we have found great difficulties in the use of this epithet. Rousseau's confusions—those against which his successors have most protested—arose from his belief that Domestic reformation meant a return to Nature.

Lect. VI.

Objections to the name.

Every exercise of the parental authority involves a restraint upon certain natural inclinations of the son; every exercise of obedience by him implies a restraint upon inclinations of his own nature. The plea for the dissolution of the conjugal bond, on some other ground than infidelity to it, is that the husband or the wife finds it an inconvenient check upon the impulses of nature. It is a natural impulse which leads every brother to tear asunder the tie of Consanguinity. It is natural for the Master to beat his servant, for the servant to run away from his Master. These are not verbal puzzles; they cannot be removed by an explanation of terms. They belong to the practice of Life. They have presented themselves to each new age. Each age has been obliged to consider what they mean.

Theological explanations of facts.

M. Comte tells us that in the infancy of the world men sought for theological explanations of facts which they could not understand. How long that infancy continued, when it terminated, or whether the majority of us are still in it, are questions of considerable interest upon which many of M. Comte's readers complain that he has not

Are they chiefly physical facts of which these explanations are offered?

given them sufficient light. Perhaps we should gain some if we considered more seriously what were the facts which came most home to men in this infantine stage, and of which they had most need to demand an interpretation. No doubt those who were liable to tempests at sea, to earthquakes, to inundations of rivers, to alternations of rain and sunshine, would be glad to know whence the blessings or the calamities which they experienced from any of these accidents proceeded. No doubt we may gather up their guesses and conclusions in the general formula, that they referred natural events to a supernatural origin. So we may account for the varieties of worship in different regions; the phenomena being different we may assume that the agents to whom they were ascribed would be different.

But why ascribe these phenomena to living agents at all? Why look at all beyond the tempest or the earthquake, the sunshine or the rain? If men bow down to powers above themselves these are the powers. And such would assuredly be the tendency of men, such *is* their tendency now as much as ever it was. What counteracts this tendency? There are other facts more precious, more important than these, of which they *must* get at the meaning if they can. They are sons, brothers, husbands; these relations are more serious to them than the tempests and the earthquakes; affect them more than the sun and the rain. They are with them at all times, at all times there is a disposition to cast them off. To be rid of this order is impossible; yet every father, son, husband, wife, brother, sister, master, servant can produce an effect upon it which he can not produce upon the fall of the rain or the heat of the sun. It was not then an impulse of mere curiosity which led men to ask what these relations signified, how they were upheld. The demand becomes inevitable for any people who have perceived their worth, who have become aware of the perils to which they are exposed.

<small>The existence of fatherhood explains better than 'a Law of Nature' why men enter upon these enquiries.</small>

Moreover these relations explain in the most simple and direct way how this enquiry is suggested to men. You may say with Virgil that the man is happy who has been able to know the causes of things; you may say with Hume that the man is a fool who thinks he can know anything about causes. But Virgil's felicity implies the existence of Civilization and Philosophy, Hume's denunciation is supposed to imply a special maturity in Civilization and Philosophy. When you say that men in the infantine stage enquired into the causes of things, you have to beg a law of Nature to account for their doing it; then afterwards to shew that the law of Nature was either high Art, or that it deceived those who yielded to it. On the other hand if we go so far as to admit that a child or a man has a father, we may, without attributing to him any wise or vain desire to understand the cause of volcanoes or of rain, confess that he must own a cause of himself, or if the word Cause is disagreeable, an Author, or if you would rather not say Author, then Parent; the word with which we started is just as good for my purpose as any we can substitute for it.

My position is that instead of conjuring with 'a law of Nature' which is itself either a theological or metaphysical phrase—and a very treacherous one whichever it is—we may understand from an obvious condition of our existence how we are led to look beyond ourselves that we may account for what we are. We cannot help it if we try. We have fathers, we have ancestors. And since it is also notorious that we make guesses when we have no means of arriving at certainty about the origin of phenomena in the outward world, the next question would be 'Which kind of guess prompts the other?' 'Which kind of guess has been on the whole most interesting to human beings?' 'Which is most nearly associated with their manners and their social progress?'

The human interest in natural objects.

For the answers to those questions I would point you to some facts which are not less important subjects of reflection because every schoolboy is acquainted with them. What strikes you as the characteristic of Homer's Mythology? How was it connected with the life of Greece? You hear of Zeus the Cloud Compeller; you hear of Poseidon the Lord of the Sea. You hear of Phœbus who sends his invisible arrows into the midst of the hosts, striking sheep and mules and at last men. You hear of Hephaistos the great Mechanician. Have you arrived at the secret of the worship yet? Let us try by a comparison.

Homer's Mythology.

Is it derived from Nature?

There have appeared lately some exceedingly interesting translations of Vedic hymns by an eminent Oriental scholar. They are, he thinks,

The Vedic Hymns.

some of the most ancient compositions in the world. Through his version we can discover that they have much poetic merit; we may assume on his testimony that there is much more in them which our ignorance makes us incompetent to appreciate. These Hymns are addressed chiefly to the Winds, or to some of the great Powers and Energies of the outward world. Hereafter Mr Max Müller foretells they will be carefully studied by Scholars. Since the Language in which they are written is older than the Greek— since we are assured that the knowledge of it would contribute more than any thing else to throw light upon the Greek forms and inflections —our children or our children's children instead of neglecting these may add to them an acquaintance with Sanscrit. Should that event occur, do you imagine that any ordinary human being will care for these hymns as hundreds of thousands in all ages and countries have cared for the Homeric Poems? I believe no Sanscrit scholar, however devoted to his work, however inclined to exalt the genius of these Vedic Songs, would for a moment cherish such a dream. And why not? Is this Mythology more grotesque, more alien from our habits of thinking than the Homeric mythology? The Winds are about us as they were about the writers of these Hymns. Where are Zeus and Phœbus and Hephaistos?

The grand difference is this. The Homeric

Why they are less interesting to us than the Greek Songs.

Poems are poems concerning the relations of men with each other. And being such, they are Poems concerning the relations of men with the Gods and their relations with each other. The Father and the Child, the Husband and the Wife, the Brother and Sister, the Master and the Servant are there, the names belong to those who inhabit this earth, to those who dwell on Olympus. One of these may gather the clouds together, another may raise the tempest, another may send the pestilence, another may forge armour for heroes. But they are persons, they take account of human interests; they form a Society; they have Manners and Habits, as those have who form human Societies.

You have learnt perhaps to call these 'personifications.' Do not let a word cheat you of a broad simple fact. Personifications belong to a later period; when that theological infancy of which we are told had long passed away. Pope personified with great skill and effect in the *Rape of the Lock;* but he introduced sad confusion when he tried the same process in his translation of Homer. His original did not personify at all. He described living persons, whether in this world or any other; not shadows, not abstractions. Therefore it is that his voice has been heard in generations far removed from his own, in countries utterly unlike any which he ever saw, among people possessed by Hebrew and Christian convictions. The effect of his mythology on the literature of such

Lect. VI.

Relations on earth and above.

Personifications and persons.

peoples can never be forgotten. No more serious poets surely are to be found in the world than Dante and Milton; the one a Catholic theologian of the middle ages, the other a stern Puritan. Yet the legends of Greece have coloured the *Inferno*, the *Hymn on the Nativity*, *Comus*, *Paradise Lost*, even the purely Hebrew drama of *Samson Agonistes*. In the last century the talk about Apollo and the Muses became a foolish affectation. But Goethe and Wordsworth, in their *Iphigenia* and *Laodamia*, shewed how living the thoughts connected with the Greek mythology still are; how closely associated with human affections and relations.

I accept most thankfully any helps which learned men can afford us respecting the localities and circumstances which have given shape and colour to these legends, respecting the use or abuse of words which may explain the names of particular divinities. Still I am convinced that the simplest way of considering them is also the deepest. The Hero is the son or descendant of a God. He attributes himself to a divine Ancestor. His House has become one, for a God has called it forth. The founder of a race, the builder of a City has a divine progenitor. Is the founder Poseidon? That you will say is because the chief came across the sea, because he introduced some arts or customs from a foreign land. Very possibly. But a man cannot think of his ancestor as derived from the unfruitful ocean. He must speak of Poseidon; of one more like him than the waves through which his oars and sails make a path-way. Let the horse be brought over the seas; a man brings it, a man tames it. The man has been taught to bring it, and to tame it; how?—By some other horse? or by some one more highly endowed than he is with the art and wisdom which is emphatically man's? Let it be the olive which is introduced. But it is the culture of the olive that we want; it is the knowledge of the way to use the fruit when the fruit is gathered. The man who has that has a skill which the olives did not impart. Who did? The Lyre is a wonderful instrument. To ask who made the instrument is something. But to ask who brought those sounds out of it which speak to the human ear, who brought the harmony out of it, which speaks to the human heart, that is a deeper question. There may be a wild kind of music in the Æolian harp; it may impart a certain pleasure to those who can associate with it the music that has been poured out from human lips, that has been drawn forth by human fingers. But those lips, those fingers suggest a Teacher. The artist cannot have learnt from the winds though it may be that his instructor also plays upon the winds, uses them as his instruments. You have here not the fruits of an infantine conception; far rather the roots out of which those fruits are produced. The hero feels in himself an insight and a foresight; a capacity for overcoming that which encounters him

<small>Lect. VI.

The Horse, the Olive, the Lyre.

Arts coarse and fine.

Courage and wisdom.</small>

LECT. VI. in the shape of brute force; a courage to endure and to defy. He is sure that these were not derived to him from the things which he observes, from the animals which he bends to his purposes. They must have been derived to him from some one who is a sharer in these faculties, in this courage. He only holds his heroism on the acknowledgment of the source from which it flows. He is inclined to appropriate it; to say 'I have it,' as if it were his own; to play with it or do violence with it. Then there come to him all those rebukes of which Greek poetry is so full; those warnings that if he has a master, he is also a servant; that if he is related to a God he must not presume on the relation. Lessons of this kind come forth in legend after legend; but they all presume that the relation exists; the outrage is only possible because there is that which can be outraged.

Warnings against the confidence of heroes in their gifts or in their birth.

M. Comte would of course have been able to explain, some of his successors may inform us, when and how this early stage of thought ceased; when in the proper order of developement men learnt that their arts and wisdom were their own or were caught from the things with which they held converse. I have no doubt that such a time did come to the Greeks, that it has come to most people on the earth. Whether it has been a time of progress or of declension, a time of discovery or of hard System which stifles discovery, we may consider hereafter. But if

The loss of this worship.

you would read Homer with a real living interest, if you would find out what he felt and thought and believed, you must observe that it is not chiefly the vicissitudes in the outward world, keen and clear as was his eye for them, which he refers to the Gods. It is the courage of Diomed, the wisdom of Odysseus, the authority over the host in Agamemnon, which they impart. These are the heroical qualities, and they are ascribed to some in whom they dwell more perfectly, whom they must more thoroughly characterise. *(Moral qualities the specially divine qualities.)*

Again, as I observed before, the relations of the Heroes to their wives and children correspond to relations between those from whom they are said to descend. There is a family in the superior world as well as in the lower. Here we at once find ourselves among the perplexities of the mythology; here begin the particulars in the legends which offend us. The Relation of Marriage is that on which the Greek dwelt most; the invasions of its sanctity were those to which he was most tempted. The acknowledgments of its dignity along with the violations of it reappear in the celestial region. They blend with observations on nature; the disturbances in earth or sky where the Gods are supposed to rule recal to men the disturbances in households, the confusion of plans and purposes in them. Fables rise out of both; each contributes an element, the human being always the predominant. The visible object would never suggest thoughts, if there *(Mixture of human anomalies with the divine order.)* *(Mixture of physical phenomena with the same order.)*

were not the nearer commentary upon it. As that becomes more muddled by the discords in families, by the craving for independence, the outward world presents the likenesses of these; then those who preside over it are either contemplated as avengers of these discords, or as affording examples to justify them. I avoid as far as possible all reference to those points of the mythology which assume the existence of laws or national Institutions, and seek to account for *them*. It is with the domestic aspect of the fables that I am concerned. That aspect of it called forth the indignant animadversions of Plato in the *Republic*. The Gods he said were treated by Homer, not as patterns of what men should be, but as the images of what they are. A hint of deep and far spreading significance, touching the very heart of the subject. But Homer has his truth as well as Plato, one which his critic could not appreciate. He felt that domestic relations were in *some sense* divine relations. If the divine could become practically what Plato felt it must be in principle, the archetype of the human, would these relations be extinguished in communism? Might not the Homeric anticipations be fulfilled? Might it not be shewn in *what* sense they are divine?

<small>Lect. VI.
Conceptions of the Gods as as images of mortal life.

The Platonic Protest.

Rome.</small>

When I was speaking of Roman life in connexion with the *Patria Potestas*, I could not avoid an allusion to the household gods or to the Jupiter of the Capitol; so curiously do they illustrate the union of the domestic with the civil order of the

Commonwealth, so strikingly do they mark the characteristic distinction between the Greek and Latin habits of thought. That subject properly belongs to the present Lecture. As no worship became more strictly *political* than the Roman in the best and the worst sense of that word—as it will be necessary hereafter to point out with some care what I mean by this best and worst sense—I am anxious to remind you that the foundations of it were, what Virgil has proclaimed them to be, domestic. There is no pretence in this case for speaking about Powers in Nature or over Nature. Jupiter became the air to the Roman when he had ceased to acknowledge any force in the name, when it had nearly lost all significance for him. *Nearly* lost, for it remained to him a terror still. There might be loud noises in the air; there might be explosions of pent up air. They might have something to do with acts done on earth—done in the households of the city. Dire superstition, an intense craving for magical powers and Babylonian numbers, was, so Gibbon confesses, characteristic of the period when scepticism about the gods had become general. But till that time came, Jupiter was assuredly the father of the city; the authority of particular fathers had its support in his authority. That was not enough. Each household must have its own Penates. There must be a divine superintendence over each hearth. Since we only know Rome in its national period, it is impossible to separate this religion from that which was of a

Margin notes: Lect. VI. Jupiter not a power in the air. What happened when he was reduced to that. The Household gods.

LECT. VI. formal and legal character. In the earliest legends of the city, Numa appears as the establisher of sacerdotal institutions, of a prescribed worship. But the outlines of a domestic worship are traceable in the priestly system when it was most developed—just as Mr Maine has traced the outlines of a domestic order in the Jurisprudence. The paternal relation to the Latin, like the conjugal to the Greek, was felt always to have its ground in one which was more radical, more universal; which was Divine yet essentially human. But it is impossible not to perceive that the word 'Divine' being connected in the Roman mind with that relation which speaks of Authority, acquired a grandeur and awfulness which it could scarcely vindicate among the Greeks. With them it was, at all events, continually in danger from familiarity and grossness. How likely, on the other hand, the reverence for Authority was to be exchanged for the dread of Dominion in the celestial as in the terrestrial region, we may easily conjecture. But that subject cannot be fully illustrated till we arrive at the third part of this course.

The formal Priesthood does not obliterate the original Family Worship.

General Inference.

If we consider either the Latin or the Greek worship, then, we are forced to the conclusion that their apprehensions of the divine arose from no study of the external world—its blessings or its curses, its fixed forms or its incessant changes—but from the human relationships in which the inhabitants of each country found themselves. That relation of which they most realised the worth was that which linked itself most directly to the belief of a divine relation which corresponded to it, of some divine person who had appointed it and could uphold it. When the sense of the domestic fellowship became weak—when it gave way,—then indeed the weight of the external world became overwhelming; then, whether its powers were contemplated in themselves, or were associated with names and persons, it might become a field for the exercise of demoniacal caprice, which men might try to divert by skill or by sacrifices, but which must ultimately prevail: Death being obviously the great Dæmon of all, that to which all the rest did homage. And since he could not be for any long time kept off by arts or propitiated by offerings, the aspect of the universe was hideous enough; the temptation to forget as long as forgetfulness was possible nearly irresistible. With relationships is associated Memory and Anticipation; with them the thought of immortality is intertwined. The Death Power cannot have called them into being.

The Demons no longer domestic, but Ministers of Death.

But there is, you must observe, a perpetual tendency in both these Nations to identify the Ancestor with the God. The Hero must trace his lineage back till it is lost somewhere; not in a cloud surely, but in a Person, whether he dwells in a cloud or not. And that Person must in some way have been in a relation to a human creature; else the Hero cannot connect himself with the world below as well as with that above.

The Hebrew History.

LECT. VI.

The Patriarch simply a mortal,

The House must have had a founder; how he came to found it must be explained; the explanation is here too a union with some mortal. We say at once "these are legends; they involve all the dangers which Plato pointed out. The Gods do acts which for man are unlawful." When we pass to the patriarchal history of the Israelites we are conscious at once of an amazing difference. Abram is no hero. He is an ordinary shepherd. He claims no divine birth. His parentage on both sides is carefully recorded. Nor has he any distant ancestor who boasts to be different from other men. Is he then unlike those we have spoken of in that the Family is to be of less worth to him? Is his worship to be connected with the Sun or the Stars, not with that? He is led to observe, we

but the root of a family.

are told, the number of the stars. But it is that he may be encouraged to hope for a progeny as numerous. Every thought that is awakened in him has to do with a Family. He lives in a Family; is never safe beyond the limits of it. But there is an Awakener of his thoughts. There is One who leads him to dwell on the mystery of birth; to feel and understand how he is related to those who are about him, how he will be

In what sense the family has a Divine origin.

related to those who shall come after him. According to the book of Genesis the God of all the families of the earth, the God who has made not heroes but man in His own image, calls out this particular man to know Him as his Ruler and

Guide, the Ruler and Guide of those who shall come after him, the God of Abraham and Isaac and Jacob.

That I hold to be the difference between Theology and Mythology as they present themselves to us in this first stage of our enquiries. Accepting the belief that the God of all families does reveal Himself to men through the relations of the family I can appreciate the mythology which recognises that belief, I can value every conception which men have formed about a union between the human and divine. I can see why those conceptions must become false when they assume the human as the ground of the divine. It might drive one into madness to fancy that generations of men in the countries which have left most mark of themselves in History have been living upon a lie; have been thinking their best thoughts and doing their best acts on the strength of a lie. It is worse than madness to fall in love with lies; to say they are so pretty that we cannot part with them, to suppose that we have no means of testing the gold and the alloy. We *have* no means of determining in any man's case how much he has in him of gold or of alloy; it is assuming the throne of the supreme judge to attempt *that* discrimination. But we may exercise very clear and satisfactory discrimination for our own guidance if we will remember that we are members of families as much as Greeks or Latins or Hebrews were; that the domestic relations signify as much to us as they did to any men of former generations; that what our manners shall be—savage or human—depends primarily on the use which we make of them, on the life which we lead in them. I do not know when the theological age—according to the Comtist definition of theology—terminated: if my definition of it is the right one, I believe it will terminate whenever men set at naught the authority of fathers and the obedience of sons, the trust of husbands and wives, the respect of brothers and sisters for each other, the honour of the master for the servant of the servant for the master. In desponding moods one may dream that a worship based upon our own conceptions and likings—a worship which because we invent it for ourselves will represent our lowest thoughts and confirm and deepen those in us—may conquer all that has struggled with it, all that has borne witness to us of a Life which is higher than our own. But when we are in our right minds we know that this cannot be. The more steadfastly and earnestly we labour, as the Comtists bid us do for the progress of Humanity—the more we agree with them that all interests are subordinate to moral interests—the more we recognise an order in the Universe before which all discords must at last disappear—the more will the Worship to which domestic Relations have led the way—the Worship which seeks for a ground of Humanity beneath itself—expel the superstitions into which vulgar men and philosophers equally are betrayed when they make gods of their own and bow down before them.

I have not spoken in this lecture of any forms or modes of worship. The diversities of these belong to a later period than that with which we are occupied. But it is impossible not to connect Sacrifice with the domestic age, as well as with those which are to follow. One of the darkest of domestic tragedies blends, as I had before occasion to remark, with the Greek conception of Sacrifice. No offering but that of a daughter could propitiate the power that kept the fleet at Aulis. Though that legend manifestly belongs to a time of Kings and Laws, still it suggests the thought that the Gods reckoned a child a more precious offering than any animal could be. Under that most frightful of all perversions was hidden a conviction which would ultimately become the profoundest for social life and morality. The story of Abraham's offering indicates the right desire and the wrong mode of expressing it which were working together in the patriarch's mind, as well as the process by which they were separated. So considered it is a commentary on the records of other nations; it enables us to understand by what practical methods the belief that a living Sacrifice is of more worth than a dead one, may have been imparted to them.

NATIONAL MORALITY.

LECTURE VII.

THY NEIGHBOUR AND THYSELF.

I ENTER to-day on the second Division of my Course. You will not, I hope, misunderstand the subject of it. I am not leaving the plain highway of Morality that I may discourse of the special Morality which belongs to Kings and Tetrarchs, to Ministers of State, or to members of Parliaments. You and I are members of certain families. So are we also members of a certain nation. One is just as much a fact of our lives as the other. We are Englishmen as we are sons and brothers. What it means to be an Englishman, what Manners are demanded of us because we bear that name, we are to enquire.

There is, you all know, an English manner which some affect. Foreigners call it the John Bull manner. It consists—first, in boasts of our doings, our courage, our power of ruling, our justice; secondly, in contempt for the customs, habits, traditions of other peoples in denunciations of their cowardice, or feebleness, or injustice. The more obtrusive and vulgar forms of this insolence are so ridiculous that every cultivated Englishman is ashamed when he meets with them. But though he may not display it, he may be conscious that he has it within him; he may detect himself in acts of intolerance and unfairness to those who have grown up in practices different from his own; he may find that he is secretly giving himself credit for virtues which perhaps are not visible in his conduct, excusing himself for faults which are far too visible. In revenge, he not unfrequently makes a violent effort to divest himself of his native qualities. Whatever is British becomes offensive to him. French manners, German manners, how much better they are than those of his stupid countrymen! He imitates what he admires; every one observes how awkwardly the new drapery sits on him; to what artifices he is driven that he may adjust the folds of it to his figure. And after all he does not rid himself of that which he inherited from his fathers, of that which was planted in him by his education. It cleaves fast to him. It betrays itself in his efforts to hide it or to throw it off.

Where is the escape from these two opposite dangers which yet lie so near to one another, which are likely to attack the very same person at different stages of his life? I believe it lies in an increased reverence for our position as members of a nation, in a more earnest purpose to understand that position and fully to realise it. If I count it an unspeakable blessing for myself to be the citizen of a nation, I must count it an unspeakable blessing for every man. If I, being an Englishman, desire to be thoroughly an Englishman, I must respect every Frenchman who strives to be thoroughly a Frenchman, every German who strives to be thoroughly a German. I must learn more of the worth and grandeur of his position, the more I estimate the worth and grandeur of my own. I cannot shift my colours to please him. I shall honour him for not shifting his colours to please me. If I retain my distinctive characteristics, he may learn something from me. If he retains his, I may learn from him. Parting with them, we become useless to each other, we run in each other's way; neither brings in his quota to the common treasure of humanity.

LECT. VII.
The National Manner.

When I insist upon this fact as an all important one in my existence that I am not merely the member of a certain family, that I am also the member of a nation, I am no doubt taking up an exclusive position. That position has been given me. I cannot deny that my country has boundaries; that my speech is not the speech of Spaniards or Frenchmen or Italians; that my laws are in many respects different from theirs;

How far an exclusive one.

that I am under a Queen who is not their Queen. But this very exclusiveness forbids the desire that their national features should be the same as ours. I abdicate all right to determine what is best for those who have their own battles to fight, their own ground to maintain.

An authoritative definition.

When we use this language about Nations or the distinction of Nations, we are often encountered by a question and answer both delivered in that lofty oracular tone which is so alarming to quiet men. "And pray, Sir, what *is* a Nation? *I* take it to be a mere collection of Individuals. You of course have some mystical conception about its nature and essence." It is a great satisfaction to me that I can entirely accept this definition. I want no addition to it, mystical or other. I only want to know what a collection of Individuals is. In a former course of Lectures

The value of it.

I spoke of the word '*I*' as one which specially concerned a student in my department. It encountered the student in every department; but none seemed disposed to investigate it. Important as this word was, I could not pretend that its force is at once recognised by those who use it most frequently. There is a time in a life in which it is not used. A child speaks of itself in the third person. Slowly, as Mr Tennyson reminded us in some very striking lines, the self-consciousness is awakened. The complete awaken-

A boy finding out himself,

ing is reserved for a later period. There begins to be a restlessness in the son, in the brother, of a family. He does not like to admit that he is only a son or a brother. The wisdom of the parent is shewn in his treatment of these indications. If he merely indulges them the family life is destroyed. If he crushes them the child is dwarfed; it is not in the way to become more than a child. As long as the boy abides under the parental roof the discipline continues in the same hands. It is very hard indeed to combine the old habit with the new craving for independence. Yet it is not merely a craving for independence. With that is mixed the craving for a wider Society than that of brothers and sisters. There are perhaps cousins not far off. They form a distinct household, their ways are not exactly the same as those in which he has grown up. There is the hint of another fellowship. That is not enough. Why should not the boy or girl find friends among those who are called *neighbours*? Evidently these two feelings —that of personal distinctness, of self-assertion, and that of desire for wider intercourse, seemingly hostile are closely allied. One cannot be gratified without the other. In the School they are in some way adjusted. In the School each boy or girl must be treated not as the member of a certain household, but as the member of a new community in which all are equals, or if not equals are arranged according to no maxims of kinsmanship. Each one brings certain recollections, traditions, instincts, which others do not share in, which are perhaps discovered, perhaps carefully concealed, but

and also craving for neighbours.

The School.

which are felt to be incongruous elements in the new atmosphere. Mr Trench introduces his amusing *Realities of Irish Life* with an account of his own school experiences at Armagh. They illustrate curiously the transition from one stage of life to the other. He is solemnly warned by an experienced adviser when he first enters the school never to answer any one of his comrades who questions him about the names of his sisters; he is to intimate significantly that he is too wise to make any such announcements. He follows this advice and is thrashed by a bigger boy for his reticence. He is soon involved in all the new school interests, learns to regard the Master as a common enemy, takes part in a barring out, and so forth. This narrative Mr Trench rightly considers an artistical prologue to the drama that follows; that being intended to exhibit the combination and conflict of clannish sympathies in a clannish people with the sense of a Law that does or should deal with all persons impartially; which may be claimed as a protector or repulsed as an enemy.

The Lectures of last term will have shewn you how the particular household and the particular school illustrate the relation between domestic and national life generally. Mr Maine tells us that Ancient Law implies a State previous to its establishment—the unit of Society in that State being not the Individual but the Family. There comes a time, he says, when the new principle intrudes itself. Law as Law assumes *Contiguity of place* not Kinsmanship, as the ground of Social existence. Law as Law treats each man as a distinct person, not one as responsible for another. The change from the first of these conditions to the second is so amazing, so mysterious, that Mr Maine can only speak of it as one of the greatest of Revolutions. How it takes place he does not attempt to explain; that it has taken place before any Community can be described as legal or National he is sure. He is equally sure, and the observation puzzles him still more, that when there is the fullest acknowledgment of the new unit, the old unit cannot be forgotten. They wind themselves curiously into one web; legal fictions are needful to make them *appear* compatible; yet somehow they *are* compatible; you cannot take either away without causing the Society to crumble. It is seldom that a legal antiquary so frankly, so modestly, exposes his difficulties; when they are exposed, how they help us to understand our own difficulties, those which meet us in every day's experience! We belong to households, we belong to a nation. How to reconcile the positions is often a perplexity. We may try fictions to make them harmonise, as the lawyers do. But there must be a harmony between them which is not fictitious, since it is suicide to part with either. The formation of a manner which shall not be utterly unsocial, utterly destructive of Society, depends upon their fellowship.

Lect. VII.

The old and the new trying to combine.

Fiction and Fact.

To form that manner, to establish that fellowship, we must distinctly admit that two-fold principle of a National or Legal Society which Mr Maine has set forth. No description of it can be better than his. The two elements, *Contiguity in place, individual distinctness,* constitute it. Or to translate that language into Saxon, "my neighbour and myself;" these are the factors which I must take account of, if I want to know what I mean when I claim to be the member of a City or State. Supposing I forget either, I forget the other. I cease to recognise the distinctness or worth of my neighbour, if I do not recognise my own; I cease to recognise my own distinctness and worth, if I do not recognise his.

You see how admirable that account of a Nation is which our lofty critic gave us; how foolish I should have been if I had demurred to it. England, France, Germany, Spain, is a Collection of Individuals. That is just what makes it so hard to maintain an England or a France, a Germany or a Spain. How came this Collection into this menagerie or this Jardin des Plantes? Who brought it together? These creatures have great powers of injuring each other—claws, talons, hoofs of a very alarming kind. Who are their keepers? What arts of taming do they practise? These are questions which History has to answer; which press very heavily upon the Social Moralist. He is often disposed to cut them short with an answer of this kind: "There can be no Society until this

"Individuality is extinguished. It is the unsocial "principle; the immoral principle. Men cannot "behave to each other as they ought while each is "striving to assert himself." There is great plausibility in that statement. I shall have to shew you in these Lectures—still more in those of my next division—how many have adopted it, and what schemes they have devised for giving effect to it. But I adhere to the definition which has been forced on me. I maintain that a Nation is a Collection of Individuals; that there can be no Nation, if those who compose it are not Individuals. Conversely, I affirm that there will be no Individuals in the full sense of that word, where there is not a Nation in the full sense of that word.

I approached this subject from the other side in my lectures on Casuistry. I was then speaking of an eminent philosopher belonging to the end of the last century and the early part of this—Johann Gottlieb Fichte. I described him, *par excellence*, as the egotistical philosopher; the philosopher of individuality. I said that he was also the philosopher who had most practically, most vehemently, maintained the freedom of Germany—its right to a national existence. It seemed to me that the one part of his belief explained the other; that he could not have been the assertor of Individuality, if he had not been the defender of his nation. If he had not striven to raise his countrymen out of the condition in which he found them plunged,

Marginalia: LECT. VII. The Nation demands the Individual, the Individual the Nation. Reference to the German Egotist.

he could not have asserted that which he had accepted as the only maxim for his own life. I explained to you why I said this. Fichte had found that he might read many books, study many sciences, but that unless he was a living person the books would be dead letters to him, the sciences would become sciolism. To be a man, to know that he was a man, was the first condition of understanding what he learnt about men, even what he learnt about things. Therefore when he heard the cry of Frenchmen to be owned as men at the Revolution, he felt it as an electric shock through his whole being. That was what he wanted, that was what every German wanted. If each of them made that demand, the student would become an actual student, the soldier would become an actual soldier. He could listen, therefore, to the French message about the rights of *man;* whencesoever it came, it was true; it belonged to him and his people. But then followed a fearful interpretation of it. Germans were not to be Germans; they were to be a portion of a French Empire. To be men, they must part with their own distinctness; their own memories; their own hopes. This was the universal right; to be individuals no longer! Why that was just what he had complained of before! He had said, "We are members of certain faculties; we are "doctors, we are lawyers, we are soldiers; we are "not individuals." And now the preachers of freedom appear under a leader, who has converted

them into a set of wonderful machines—still instinct however with a living force, because they
have the sense of being Frenchmen—to force
this doctrine upon us. Thus was the truth brought
home to him, "We are not yet a collection
" of Individuals, we are only a collection of Atoms.
" If we could become a collection of Individuals,
" we might cast off this accursed yoke. And why
" may we not become so? If we once discover
" that we are Germans—if a German heart can
" be put into us—we shall indeed become a col-
" lection, not of dead creatures determined by
" some force from without, but of individuals
" quickened by a fire within; therefore able to
" move together, to move irresistibly."

Shall they extinguish us?

That these were not only the thoughts of a recluse in a solitary chamber; that they penetrated
into the halls of science, into the hovel, into the
palace; that they called a people again into existence; that a new army arose out of the corpse of
the old, uttering in acts the mind of a people;
that the French Goliath fell beneath the sling and
the stone of the peasant warrior—this I had occasion to tell you before; the lesson I had then to
teach compelled me to speak of these facts if it
were only in passing. I must repeat them now,
for I fear they are almost forgotten by this generation. I fear that amidst the revived worship of
organisation, which has its meaning and worth—
when it is *not* worshipped—they are scarcely believed. Some of us can remember the kindling

The revival of the present.

LECT. VII.

The revival of the past.

eye, the trembling voice of old men who partook in the inspiration of those days; how they testified that then the past and the future were linked together; that they knew what their country had been; that amidst the greatest disappointments they could still contemplate what it was to be.

For that is a point on which I would insist, since it greatly concerns our subject, and relieves the statement which I have adopted from Mr Maine of some apparent difficulties. With the revival of individual life all the traditional beliefs of Germans revived also. The sense of the present did not obliterate the past, but called it out of the tomb. Those who talk about progress in our day measure their steps by the forgetfulness of all which they leave behind. These Germans realised their progress by their lively memory of their ancestors. They were one people with those who listened to Luther at Wittenberg, with those who overthrew the host of Varus. It was no sentimental admiration of other days; it was the sense of communion with them; the conviction that a people lives on through generations; that it is not Progress but Slavery which severs one generation

The Family rising with the Nation.

from any which has preceded it. Here is that immortality which Mr Maine connects with the Family making itself felt in the period which he affirms to stand on the other principles of neighbourhood and individual distinctness.

Nevertheless nothing is truer than that these principles made themselves manifest in the awakening of Germany, make themselves manifest in the awakening of every people to national consciousness. Each man in such a crisis feels himself to be a man, therefore feels his neighbour to be a man. He cannot help reverencing himself because he has learnt to reverence his neighbour. He cannot help reverencing his neighbour because he has learnt to reverence himself. The 'I' and the 'Thou' stand out confronting each other, making each other intelligible. There can be no account given of those wonderful moments of revival which is so true, so satisfactory, as this. The songs of patriots express it, the deeds of patriots express it. For an instant—it may be only for an instant—jealousies, discontent, murmurings about precedence are suspended. They may—they will—all appear again; but that instant wherein the leader exercises authority and the soldier pays willing obedience, where there is a trust of man and man, wherein Neighbourhood assumes the likeness of Consanguinity, wherein all are glad to serve, and yet the Master establishes his right to rule—that instant is felt to be the one which determines what a Nation is intended to be, what it may become. *The Crisis of a people's renovation explains its history.*

There is a sad counterpart to this German story in the records of another Nation. I must refer to it because that Nation was even more than Germany linked with the thoughts and hopes of England at the same time, and because the history of its fortunes and misfortunes has done *Spain.*

LECT. VII. more than anything to excite in us a distrust of individual energy, a confidence in mere organi-

The hope of what it might do for itself.

sation. Before the dry bones in Germany began to move, before they rose up a great army, Spain had proclaimed itself independent of the same oppressor, had invoked the co-operation of England. The heart of our people responded to the call; the stirs of life in a Southern race kindled our Northern blood. Wordsworth sung

> The power of Armies is a visible thing,
> Formal and circumscribed in time and space,
> But who the limits of that power can trace
> Which a brave people into light can bring,
> Or hide at will—for freedom combating
> By just revenge inflamed?

Inference drawn from the progress and issue of the Peninsular War.

Ah! reply the dispatches of the Duke of Wellington, the history of Sir William Napier, the limits of that power can be all too easily defined: the revenge, savage enough, was indeed there; the combat for freedom was weak, capricious, interrupted by the vulgarest disputes, the meanest suspicions. And the "formal and circumscribed" power of armies, on the other hand, proved that it could effect the liberation which the so-called patriots only attempted. Can we resist that argument, if we exalt facts above theory? I do not wish to underrate the worth of discipline. I look upon it as a divine gift to Nations, without which no other gift will be of much worth. But I entirely deny that the errors of the Spaniards at that time were any evidence that Individual Life is not a more precious, a more essential endowment of a Nation, even than that. Indeed, I know of no history which establishes this position so triumphantly. Individuality had been most laboriously extinguished in the Spanish people by those rulers, civil and ecclesiastical, to whom they had bowed before Joseph Buonaparte ever visited their land. They had been taught that Individual Death was the very highest perfection of the Saint; they had felt it to be the chief comfort of the sinner. For such a people to become a Collection of Individuals was the hardest thing conceivable. The throes of birth were terrible; the result might be at the time a miserable abortion. Yet that struggle may have been a preparation for better days; the Spaniards may remember the times of old, instead of merely trying to make all things new. They may learn that the best manner of chivalry may be revived in the 19th century, without any of the fantasies which Cervantes shewed to be the caricature and debasement of it. Not arrogant self-assertion, but that self-assertion which is sustained by a man's respect for his Neighbour, may come forth to make laws living, not mere letters on paper. Years of degradation and despotism may yet teach lessons to a noble race which they could not learn from any foreign allies, however well organized and successful.

The inference not justified but confuted by facts.

I have used these words "thy neighbour and thyself" because they express better and more simply than any that I know the meaning of a Na-

Title of the Lecture explained.

tion's existence; the ἦθος which must keep it alive. You know whence the language comes. Its connection with other lessons, borrowed from the same source, I shall not consider in this lecture. But I would observe to you that the Revolution which Mr Maine supposes must precede the passage from the Family condition to the legal or National is described in the Scriptures with a precision and minuteness which one cannot find anywhere else. The Patriarchal Horde does not emerge into a Nation till it has passed through a period of oppression and slavery. Deliverance is inscribed upon its Law, is made the very foundation of it. The recollection of ancestors and relations enters into every part of it. We hear the suspicious murmurings of a people unused to individual freedom. But there is a moment in which they awaken, like the Germans of later days, to life and liberty and song.

Passage of the Jew out of patriarchal to national existence.

LECTURE VIII.

LAW.

I SPOKE in the last Lecture of the School as the passage out of domestic life into the life of neighbourhood, which is also the individual or personal life. A line from George Herbert, which I quoted in a former course, defines this transition, "Then Schoolmasters deliver us to *Laws.*" The school is the preparation for National Life. When we contemplate men in a Nation, we contemplate them as under a Law. The expressions are interchangeable.

Under a Law, you observe; that is the marvel we have to consider. There may be a great many theories about the making or unmaking or remaking of Laws; who are to be the agents in making or unmaking or remaking; what principals employ the agents. But apart from all these disputes, there is for each of you and for me this fact. We find a Law; it claims us as its subjects; we learn by degrees that we *are* subject to it.

marginalia: LECT. VIII. — A Nation implies a Law. — The Law given to us.

The acknow-ledgment of it.

That is a very great discovery. We are slow in arriving at it; very slow in confessing the full force of it. Just so far as it is brought home to me I know that I am a distinct person; that I must answer for myself; that you cannot answer for me. I perceive also that each of you is a distinct person; that each of you must answer for himself.

That is the effect of Law; that effect warrants me in connecting it with Social Morality. If you recollect the principles which I laid down in my first Lecture, and which appeared to be recognised by writers of the most opposite opinions, you may suppose that I have nothing to do with Law; that Law and Morality stand wholly apart from each other. For I said that the Moralist is primarily occupied with a certain State or Character; only with acts as they exhibit a character. And I think, as most people think, that Law is chiefly concerned with Acts, that it cannot undertake the task of forming the character from which acts proceed. It forbids murder and robbery; if it tries to produce good temper or charity it will try in vain. I will go a step further. If it tries to make us just it will try in vain. Justice, as we shall find, is nearer of kin to Law than Charity is. But Justice, like Charity, is a Disposition or Habit; and of Dispositions and Habits the Law cannot take cognisance. The Lawgiver may find good habits to be very necessary. He may enquire earnestly how they can be formed. He will cer-

Wherein Law and Morality are opposed to each other.

tainly be compelled to own that he cannot form them.

I find myself under a Law. A Law, what is that? I have been used to hear commands from a Parent. I have learnt to recognise his authority over me, to distinguish it from Force. When he tried to compel me by force I could resist. His authority was a subtler thing. I did not know exactly with what weapon to strive against that. But here is no parent. It is a command which has issued from I know not where. He who repeats it to me, he who enforces it upon me, does not pretend that he has invented it. He assures me that he has not; that he is as much bound by it as I am. He has the same facilities —probably much greater facilities for breaking it than I have. He says he *must* not break it. What is this *must* not?

On what compulsion must I? tell me that.

When Bellario, the jurist of Padua, sent the most charming of messengers to represent him at Venice in the great cause of Shylock against Antonio, she said, having heard of the bond,

Then must the Jew be merciful.

A harsh voice answered,

On what compulsion *must* I? tell me that.

Portia and Shylock.

And Portia, after making her splendid speech on the quality of mercy, admitted in her legal character that Antonio must pay the penalty, that the State of Venice would not be safe if Covenants were not observed to the letter. Here is

140   NATIONAL MORALITY.

Lect.
VIII.

The bond cannot be evaded.

the true faith of a legal, commercial Community, such as Venice was. There is an Obligation upon each individual of the State; there is an Obligation upon the State itself. Nothing can break or set aside either. Against the most popular and beloved citizen it must be maintained, in favour of the most detested. The position is all the stronger, because it comes forth in a poetical legend, not in a legal treatise. Shakspere adopted it; for it was the only maxim upon which English Society, in the days of Elizabeth, could stand.

Very mysterious assuredly this sense of Law is. It breaks through such prejudices as those which surrounded the person of the Jew in the middle ages. It sets at nought the dignity of birth, the advantages of position. It mocks even the ecclesiastical indulgences which appealed to a power above Law. I cannot explain it away by any philosophical phrases. I can merely bid you take notice of the facts. They are, you see, vulgar facts.

The Law above Christian and Jew.

I have purposely dwelt upon the commercial character of Venice, that you may connect this authority of Law with the incidents of property. It springs out of no dreams of sentiment; rather, it scatters all such dreams. A bond! a contract! what a commonplace thing that is. Very commonplace, referring, in this case, to a loan by one merchant to another; enforced by the penalty of a pound of flesh. But the loan did not create the reverence for the Law which protects it; the penalty did not create it. The loan could not have been, the penalty would have been nothing, but for the sense in the mind of Christian and Jew that there was a Law, that it was mightier than both.

<small>LECT. VIII.</small>

Now no sort of moral sympathy was produced either in Christian or Jew by this Law. The Christian did not spit on the Jew less for it, did not call him less foul names for it. The Jew did not hate the Christian less for it, did not the less desire to ruin either his faith or him. But the Law nevertheless spoke to both; threatened both; protected both. Each had an interest in twisting it; the Christians being in the ascendant had the power to twist it. Still they bowed to it. The Jew feeling himself a proscribed man could yet invoke the Law of the very people which proscribed him. They might interpret it falsely, they might exalt force against it; but if they did they were overthrowing their State; that State stood by Law, meant the triumph of Law over force.

<small>The condition of a State to exalt Law above its own pleasure.</small>

Therefore though this mighty and mysterious Law is incapable of moulding the mind or character of any individual, it has *this* faculty. It makes him feel that he is tied and bound, that, whether he likes it or not, there is a yoke over him to which his neck must adjust itself. There is an *obligation* upon him; no other word but that expresses his position; he can substitute no other for it. 'Why am I obliged? Why may I not have my own way? Who obliges me?' All these questions I may ask. And I may find answers

<small>Individual obligation.</small>

<small>Ground of it.</small>

to them, such as these: 'It is the will of a Majority of those among whom I am dwelling.' Yes! and supposing the Majority should agree to dispense with all Law; should say, 'We will have nothing to do with it,' what then? There would be an Anarchy. Just so. And if in the midst of that Anarchy some two or three should proclaim the dignity of Law, and should say, 'We at least will obey it,' those one or two would constitute a State, and till the Majority joined with them, the Majority would be no State at all. You may say again, 'The penalty of violating the Law leads me to observe it.' Possibly; but who attached the penalty to the Law? who keeps it attached? If the majority do not choose to enforce the penalty, as in the case I have supposed, what will the penalty avail for any individual? We may go round and round in this circle; we shall find that at last we take for granted the Law, and an obligation in us to keep the law; that neither the Will of the Majority nor any terrors for transgression mean anything unless I assume something which governs the Will of Majority, something which it as well as every individual can transgress.

Looking at Law simply as Law its action upon the members of a Nation is this: It makes each of them aware of an obligation; it makes each of them aware that there is a line which he has an inclination to pass over, and which he is not to pass over; it awakens in him the feeling of a wrong which he may do to another, of a wrong which another may do to him. Taken by itself Law awakens me to these convictions; that is its office. But Law cannot be taken by itself. It finds me one of a family. It is unable to dissolve any of the relations in which I exist before I became aware of its claims. All of us to whom the Law speaks are Sons. It does not add anything to the affection of the Son for the Father, or the Father for the Son. It cannot call forth an affection which does not exist. But it stamps an obligation upon the Relation. There is something which every son owes to his father and mother because they are his father and mother. So again, it stamps an obligation on Marriage. It does not form the union; it cannot beget any trust in those who are united. But it guards every Marriage-bed. It denounces Adultery. The movement onwards into the age of Law—revolution as it is—yet gives all that preceded it a sanction. The Law takes under its care not only me and my neighbour, but all the conditions under which it finds me and my neighbour.

Why it cannot be considered alone.

Its effect on relations.

The change even in this respect is very great, the progress very remarkable, though it seems to be only the ratification of that which was already established. It is one thing for a man to feel a tie to his parent or his wife; it is quite another to contemplate that tie as one for his neighbour. The relation is not only for his household; it is for a multitude of households. And yet how clearly

The new sense of separate and common obligation.

the individuality of Law makes itself manifest. Each man is taken apart from every other. Each one is met with a 'Thou.' The Law is over families, but it is addressed to every one who hears it separately, without reference to his ancestors or his descendants. The corporate feeling descends upon the Law, as Mr Maine has shewn so admirably, from the House; the Law accepts the legacy with some awkwardness; but its own formula excludes all participation in responsibilities, recognises each one as the doer of his own acts and the sufferer from them.

The corporate feeling does not overshadow the individual.

Does the Law then only confirm that which was already to some extent characteristic of the Family?

Effect of Law on the reverence for human life.

1. With respect to human Life it introduces what must be called an altogether new conception, though one which does not really clash with older conceptions, but unfolds and deepens them. The life of the child, of the sister, of the wife, is bound up with the life of the father, of the brother, of the husband; the kinsman has a difficulty in contemplating it except as the life of a kinsman. The life of his ox, or his sheep, is also precious in his eyes; he may claim the power of taking it away for the food of his own household; but it is surely more precious than that of an invader from any other household. He has not yet learnt to distinguish the life of a man as such from the life of another animal. Both are contemplated domestically, if I may so speak. It is difficult to

express oneself with perfect accuracy; as it is difficult to distinguish the streaks of dawn from the light of the risen sun. But there is a clear difference between the sense of the sacredness of a man's life, in a legal and in a merely patriarchal community. The difference arises from the growth of a consciousness that a man is not accidentally but essentially different from a beast; that men form a Society of which beasts are not a part. There may on this account be often less of humanity to animals in the more developed than in the more primitive Society; the Arab's care for his horse may be an example to those who have a sense of legal bonds to which he is a stranger. Apparent—nay real—retrogressions may accompany a veritable progress; they should not hinder us from recognising the distinction of the human life from the animal life as one of the greatest of all the blessings which Law confers on us.

The distinction of the man from the animal.

2. As each man is brought forth into distinct prominence by the Law it becomes evident that he needs protection for something besides his bodily life. He has a reputation which may be injured; words can inflict a wound upon him as well as swords. That is a subject which we shall have to consider more particularly in the next lecture. I advert to it here because it denotes very remarkably what kind of advancement it is which I am describing. Each man acquires an importance in himself. Each man is obliged

Character.

to recognise the importance of his neighbour to himself. An injury to character falls into the circle of positive acts of which the Law takes cognisance. Its function is not the least to mould a man's character but it can decree that his neighbour shall not interfere with this more than with his visible possessions.

3. The last sentence reminds me that I have not yet spoken of that which is in some respects the most important topic connected with the legal or national state as distinguished from the domestic.

Property. How can I dare to speak of *Property* in these terms when I have already treated of *Life*,—emphatically of human life? I use this language precisely because I wish you to be aware of the transcendent superiority of Life to Property and because there is the greatest fear that you may lose this feeling altogether if I am not careful in pointing to you how Law and Property are related to each other and what position Property assumes in the crisis of Society which I am now examining.

Two observations have presented themselves to us in the lectures on Domestic Morality: one is that Property in its strict sense does not exist *The Family Stock.* in the Family, that there is a common stock, which is vested in the father and is only dispersed among the children when the family is broken up; the other is that a craving for separate possession may be always traced among the members of a family and is the chief interruption of their fellowship. Now the Law by its primary condition of treating each man as separately responsible, though it cannot destroy the family relations, though it cannot more than to a certain point disturb the custom of succession or inheritance which it finds, yet does unquestionably give an altogether new weight to Property, does ratify the disposition of each man to say 'this is mine.' A Law attempting to create Communism or assuming Communism as its basis is a contradiction in terms. It must recognise separate ownership; it must forbid each man to interfere with that which his neighbour owns.

This truth has impressed itself deeply upon the Citizens of Nations and the Rulers of Nations. With it has been combined the observation—brought home to them by accumulated evidence—that questions of Property are those which disturb, more than most others, the peace and order of a Community, tend specially to provoke assaults upon the life or reputation of its members. The inference seemed natural, 'The main function of Law must be to grapple with these questions; to devise means for preventing the holders of Property and the seekers of Property from coming into collision with each other; to settle their disputes when they arise.' And when Legislators have found themselves defeated in their experiments for these purposes, even in those which seemed best contrived—suggested by the experience of practical men as well as the wisdom of

Marginal notes: LECT. VIII. Law must admit separate ownership. The owner tormenting the Law-giver.

LECT. VIII.

Will the interest in Property cause laws to be obeyed?

Philosophers—they have begun to think, 'Law after all wants some support besides its own authority; whence must the support come?' The most popular answer has been, 'It must come from a sense in the holders of Property and the seekers of Property, of that which is for their own interest. If they perceive *that* they will devise reasonable laws; they will know where it is best to dispense with Law.' All this sounds very plausible. I do not say that it is only plausible. But you observe that it changes our position altogether. We thought Law was to guard Property; to protect men from invading each other's Property. Now it appears that Property is to guard Law. The feelings, or if you will the intellectual perceptions, of men about what it is good for them to have and good for their neighbours to have are to prescribe what the Law shall be. I venture to think that those very facts which would be appealed to in favour of this doctrine directly confute it. The latest experience that I know of is that of the gold-diggers in California. The story is told at considerable length on the authority of an eye-witness in a chapter of Sir C. Dilke's *Greater Britain*. I wish you would read that chapter and consider it carefully. It shews unquestionably that a set of reckless vagabonds who had come from every country to seek for property, and who committed the most ferocious acts against each other in order to obtain it, were at first restrained by an extemporised Lynch Law, and at last became

Sir C. W. Dilke's Greater Britain, Vol. I. Chapter on Lynch Law.

an orderly Society. Can we infer from these facts that the lust of gold suggests the policy of confining the lust within certain bounds? or may we rather conclude with Sir C. Dilke that a few people having the sense of Law derived from the traditions of a 'law-governed' Community were able at last to awe a multitude of ruffians much stronger than themselves,—were able to call forth in the very people who were to be restrained— and whom mere force could not overcome,—the sense of an order which they must not transgress? Looked at in the last aspect I know of no recent record which is so cheering, none which throws a more brilliant light upon the testimonies and the beliefs of other days.

<small>LECT. VIII.</small>

<small>Law conquering the craving for Possession.</small>

Turn back, for instance, from these recent facts to that splendid fiction of which I spoke before, a fiction embodying the principle that is hidden in a great many facts. The faith of Shylock in law— even a law which was to be administered by the Courts of Venice—strikes me as magnificent; it proves him to be the member of a race which, more than any other, has borne witness of Law, has diffused the reverence for Law through the Nations of the West. He is sure that Law must somehow prevail; he recognises in a Christian who expounds it honestly " a Daniel come to judgment." If that had been all, his character would be not ignominious but sublime. What makes it ignominious? He regards Law only as an instrument for securing his property. He is not without family affection,

<small>The Jew's grandeur.</small>

but he cannot separate his ducats from his daughter. There is the reverse of the medal; there is the mean Mammon worshipper. The two tempers may dwell in the same man; because there is a deadly war within him; because hostile principles are struggling for the mastery of him. But the craving for Property will never beget reverence for Law. And the Law, instead of fostering his covetousness, will make the man conscious of it, will make him know how much it interferes with his submission to that which in his heart he honours most.

4. That is another of those great functions which Law performs for morality—functions all the more valuable because they prove how utterly unable it is to make us moral. The Law, taking each of us apart, treating each man as an individual, brings him to perceive what there is in that very individuality which leads him to struggle with it, to be at war with Society. He wants something for himself; he wants something which is his neighbour's. The Law which forbids him to meddle with another's property shews him that he has a *wish* to meddle with it, leads him to doubt if that wish can be separated from himself. That makes Law so terrible—not its punishment for any specific transgression which he need not incur, which he could easily endure; but the detection in him of that which appears to be hopelessly at variance with the condition under which he does exist and must exist. The sense of obligation to his neighbour

ends in the discovery of an intense dislike to the obligation, of a passionate longing to be free from it; while at the same time he eagerly insists that his neighbour is obliged to him; he must have the forfeit of *his* bond.

<small>LECT. VIII.</small>

Were this the only effect of Law, or were there nothing to qualify it, we might shrink from the national State as from one that only lays upon us a heavy burden of which in the earlier stages of life we had no experience. No doubt each step as we advance does make us more aware of that which we have to lift; *this* stage teaches us that the heaviest weight which a man has to bear is himself. That is surely a hard lesson if there comes with it no promise of a way in which he may throw off himself. He has had hints upon that subject in his previous experience. Each family relation has said to him something about the possibility of losing himself in another; has taught him that he only realises a blessing when he confers it. This remembrance is not enough for his present growth; his personal distinctness has been discovered to him; he cannot merely fall back upon domestic sympathies. But they may remain to illuminate the new road which he has entered; there may still be a way, by which he can lose himself and so find himself.

<small>The terrors of Law and its blessing.</small>

In the mean time the Law does not only bring to him the conviction that there is something wrong in him; something very close to him, a part of himself, if not his very self, from which he needs to be

<small>Wrong and Right.</small>

152 NATIONAL MORALITY.

LECT. VIII.

emancipated. There can be no Wrong if there is not a Right; he cannot be unjust to his neighbour or his neighbour to him, if there is not some justice which is over them both. The sense of being under a Law forces that belief upon us. We may explain it away afterwards. Philosophers may shew us that we have been misled in the use of the word 'justice,' or that it can be resolved into elements altogether unlike those of which we have supposed it to consist. For this we must be prepared. But though the explanation may remove the impression which Law has made upon us, that is the impression. That is what it has made upon all nations. When they have been submissive to this Law it has been because they took it to be what they called just, when they have protested against it they have named it unjust. Wise men may expose the folly of this vulgar speech; but that it is of this kind wherever nations exist, there is no question. That fact is all I am concerned with at present. I am considering the operation of Law upon us; if its operation is to deceive us, still I am bound to notice the deception. Many acts may be deemed wrong in one place which are not deemed wrong in another; many acts may be praised here which are blamed there. But the epithets are given, the praise and blame are bestowed. "Ah, but perhaps wrongly." Perhaps so; but you are resorting to the very word which you wish to banish from our discourse.

The Law though it only prohibits wrong acts, makes me conscious of a Right which is over myself.

Justice has unquestionably a relation to Law

which mercy or charity has not. But as I said at the beginning of this Lecture, that Law could as little produce habits of Justice as habits of Mercy, so I say at the end of it that there is a sense in which the formula of Law may be applied to Mercy. 'Then *must* the Jew be merciful' was Portia's language. She spoke as a woman, doubtless, but the phraseology of her adopted character suited well with her own. She felt that there is an obligation to shew mercy. I do not imagine we shall ever shew much if we think otherwise. Sentiment is but a weak support for one part of morality or another. It must rest at last on a Command. Whence that Command issues, why it must enjoin Mercy, is a question for a future Lecture.

<small>Lect. VIII.</small>

<small>Obligation above Sentiment.</small>

LECTURE IX.

LANGUAGE.

<small>Lect. IX.</small> You have heard doubtless many jokes about the name which we give to the Council of our Nation. It is a place for talk. Mr Carlyle calls it the great National Palaver.

<small>Parliament, is it a contemptible title?</small> It may be well for those who are members of this assembly to reflect on such remarks. They *may* make Parliament a place for talking, not for doing. We who are not members of it, though greatly interested in its proceedings, shall be wiser perhaps if we remember that Speech need not degenerate into Talk; that it may express individual convictions and beliefs, that it ought to be the bond of intercourse and communion between citizens. If the obvious derivation of Parliament is the right one, I can think of no fitter word to denote a body which ought to collect the thought of a people and to make it effectual. I gladly avail myself of that Etymology to intro-

duce the subject of which I propose to speak this morning. The first characteristic of a Nation is that it has a Law. The second is that it has a Language. What the Law has to do with the Morality of a Nation I enquired last week. What its Language has to do with its Morality I propose to consider now. *Speech the sign of a Nation.*

The subject belongs strictly to this branch of my subject. The distinction of Nations is represented by the distinction of Languages. All attempts to overthrow the distinction of Nations have been accompanied by attempts to introduce some common language which shall efface the national language. The use of Latin in the Middle ages, the diffusion of French in the age of Louis XIV. indicates the weakening of nations. Both subjects will come before us again in this Lecture.

I am not inviting you to enter upon any philological questions. Experiments to ascertain what is the primitive language of the earth may be as clumsy as that which Herodotus attributes to Psammetichus, as much grounded upon fallacious preconceptions as those which M. Max Müller has exposed, as promising as any which he or any one endowed with the like learning has inaugurated. But there is for all of us one undoubted primitive language; that which our lips first utter, that which we first understand when it comes from the lips of others. Whatever may be believed about former ages it is this which bears witness to hidden springs in ourselves, to hidden *The primitive speech.*

156 NATIONAL MORALITY.

LECT. IX.

The beginnings of articulation.

The strange discovery.

springs in our *neighbours*. I recur to that word on which I have dwelt so much in the last two Lectures, for it is through Language that we begin to apprehend the force of it. We have been gradually finding words to denote our kinsmen; words for things which we have or which we want; words to denote that in any person or any thing which attracts us or repels us; words for acts that we do or for impressions that we receive; words that declare whence we are coming or whither we are going; words that link other words together. These, succeeding the cries, the mere ἄσημα κνυζήματα, as Herodotus calls them, of pure infancy, may shape themselves into sentences without waiting for any syntax to decide how they shall succeed each other. The syntax is extemporised, it is determined by imitation of what is heard without or by some inward impulse before the rules of it are acquired by rote or are fixed in us by custom. All this might be merely a peculiar family jargon, certain signs of intelligence between the brother or sister, the mother and child. But others not of the family appear. They utter this same kind of speech, they give a sense to that which they hear from us. Somehow or other all who dwell within that circle, larger or smaller, which we call a neighbourhood speak—not in the same tones and inflections of voice, not always in the same order,—yet on the whole the same words; we know what they mean or at least a little of what they mean; they know what we mean more or less. It is the same with those who come from any city, London, Liverpool or Exeter, not strictly in our neighbourhood. It is so with women as well as men; with children as well as with the full grown. We are not the least surprised that it is so. We are surprised when we meet with a child or man who is dumb. We are surprised when the sound of some foreign tongue reaches our ears for the first time. But that we should be able to make ourselves intelligible to any about us, that they should be able to make themselves intelligible to us; this does not astonish us at all; we are angry if we cannot exercise either of those rights which seem so natural to us, so inherent in us. It appears a hardship, almost an injury, if people address us in our own tongue without making their intention evident to us; we are inclined to call them naturally or wilfully stupid if we cannot make our intention evident to them.

The power of understanding and making ourselves understood claimed as natural.

So it was when we were young. I am not at all sure that we cease to claim the same right to understand and to be understood when we grow old. But we have probably passed through some experiences which make us far less hopeful as to our power of establishing these rights. We have not understood those who have spoken to us in very clear beautiful English. We have not been able to make very intelligent persons understand us. Both experiences may have been strange and irritating to us at the time; they may have given

How we learn to regard it as a marvel.

rise to painful reflections afterwards on the defects in thought or expression, or in something deeper than both, which interfered both with our apprehension of what our fellow citizens meant, and with our faculty of discovering our meaning to them. But there should be another result besides that, one quite as salutary and more consolatory. The power of communicating thoughts instead of being regarded any longer as an ordinary treasure should be accepted as an amazing gift. A man who has never suffered from a bad digestion scarcely knows that there is a digestion. Those who have never been asthmatic scarcely believe in respiration. Dyspepsia and short breathing bring a man to confess that the organs which receive food and inhale air do not exist merely in books of physiology or pathology; that they are real.

He who has mistaken others, through preoccupation with his own conceits, will feel with especial keenness the delight of receiving a flash of light from some book which he had passed by, some man whom he had regarded with indifference. He who has been mistaken by others will accept the slightest recognition from them with grateful astonishment. And when he strips off the rags of vanity which may cleave to his thankfulness he will regard the possession of a common speech much as one just escaped from a sick chamber regards the common air. He does not despise it because it is breathed by weary day labourers and jaded artizans. That is its charm. Like Faust passing from his pedant-haunted demon-haunted study to the assembly of peasants on the Easter Morning, he cries "I am a man, I dare to be one."

You must not suppose that I am demanding this discipline of you, any more than our Medical Professors would wish you to learn by bodily weakness or derangement the truth of their teaching. I hope much that you may learn to appreciate the worth of your national language at a far less cost; though those who have incurred this may consider the compensation an ample one. The Morality which I associate with the speaking of a language is very ordinary Morality indeed. It may be fitly called dame-school Morality. Only the dame is England, and we all, young and old, men, women, Ministers of State, Lawyers, Merchants, Divines, Professors, Students, are sitting on the same forms, repeating the same lessons, threatened by the same rod, encouraged by the same smile.

An illustrious man, John Locke, laid it down in his *Essay on Government*, that there was, at some time or other, in some place or other, a compact between Rulers and those whom they were to rule, which determined on what conditions they should rule, under what circumstances they should cease to rule. Practical people have enquired anxiously in what time or at what place the Compact was made, whether any ancient MS contains any record or trace of it. Charters, they

LECT. IX.

Is not language itself such a Contract?

say, there are of great interest and validity, written on durable parchment, declaring certain acts to be violations of the obligation which rulers owe to their subjects. But these are all subsequent to the birth of Society; they are written in known words; they presume the existence of rulers. The earlier compact which called them into existence, where is that? These questions have been felt to be very puzzling. Mr Maine pronounces Locke's conception to be utterly 'unhistorical.' So I am afraid it is. Yet one is unwilling to believe that a writer so averse from fictions as Locke was, composed a fiction upon so serious a subject with no basis of fact. He was a truth loving, a truth speaking man. Had he not the sense of a compact which binds men to speak the truth to each other, not to practise frauds upon each other? Such a compact I hold there is—not limited by the technical terms 'rulers and ruled,' but extending to all the inhabitants of a land; the ground of all other compacts that can be made between them. In the ancient transfers of land there might be a visible sign, that A gave a certain possession to B and to his heirs, for some consideration which he received. But these signs were accompanied by words. If the words had one meaning for the vendor, another for the purchaser, the compact was a fraudulent one; it was no compact at all. The sincerity of words, the strict significance of words, therefore is implied in all such transactions. A covenant not to lie is implied in the language of every people under heaven.

"You have indeed brought us to our ABC" some one will exclaim. "A very grand philosophy which bids us abstain from telling lies!" Very grand I think, the foundation of a Moral Science and also the climax of it. Holding that opinion strongly I wish to know how the lesson may be made effectual. A good parent of course desires above all things that his child should not utter a falsehood; there is no offence which he treats with so much solemnity. But the mere general precept, the mere punishment for the special act, will avail very little; if he trusts to precepts or punishments,—if the first are merely formal or the last vindictive,—he may make cowards who will be continually lying. Only a resolute sincerity in his own acts, a punctual observance of his own promises even in trivial points to his children, can cause them to appreciate veracity. They have a reverence for *his* words, but they will not learn at once to reverence words as such. Children are great actors and romancers. They are apt to twist their words like their other playthings into irregular shapes, to dress them in grotesque costumes, sometimes in haste or violence or from mere wantonness to break them as they do their dolls. To cultivate respect for them should be a primary object, but the cultivation will proceed slowly amidst many obstacles. In societies which are merely patriarchal lying is only felt to be an

The domestic discipline for the prevention and cure of falsehood most important but only preparatory.

offence against the members of the Clan. Dean Ramsay relates a story of a devoted Highlander in 1745 who perjured himself enormously to save his Chieftain's life, and who, being asked how he could venture on such a crime, answered at once that 'he had rather trust his ain soul to the Almighty than his Master's body to those scoundrels.' Such a curious compound of faith and falsehood could certainly find no parallel in the most authentic record of patriarchal life which we possess. But that honest story tells us that both Abram and his son, faithful in their tents, lied through fear of personal danger when they went down into Egypt and so exposed their wives to the greatest peril. Jacob again was perpetually trifling with truth. If we accept these as records of a Divine Education, nothing can be more instructive to a parent than the hint that all who are in the infantine stage, not yet brought within the bonds of law, must be led to the discernment of the wrong by the misery which follows it. But there is no anticipation of the time when lying will be presented to him who utters it as *the* evil which undermines his own life and makes social life impossible.

So soon as members of different households have transactions with each other, even if they are kinsmen, words will begin to assert their power and sacredness. The words in these transactions appear to derive their worth from the objects to which they refer. 'These cattle belong to my herd, those to yours,' 'you shall not interfere with mine, I will not interfere with yours.' Such promises acquire a still higher sanctity, especially in an Eastern country, when they are about springs of water which may be common to two households and which either may close. They reach the highest point of all when they concern the marriages of daughters, or places of burial. But a time comes when words are felt to be more sacred than things. I do not say more sacred than *persons*,—but sacred because they express bonds between persons which there cannot be between things or between persons and things. That is the great sign that men are beginning to look upon themselves as members of a Nation. A Nation— I am not speaking too strongly—is held together by words. A certain portion of land larger or smaller is included within its domain. But this land may be increased or diminished. If the whole of it is supposed to be vested in the Ruler or Chief of the land, yet it will be divided into various properties which this and that man will claim as his. These possessions then cannot be the ground or witness of the fellowship between the inhabitants of the land. They separate one from another, they may be the occasion of numerous disputes. Words must be the media of all intercourse between the disputants. And thus that those words should represent—not things but— the purpose of him who speaks them, that his neighbours should be able through them to judge of his purpose, becomes the great demand of the citizen.

<small>LECT. IX.</small>

<small>Words acquire a new force when personal responsibility begins.</small>

<small>Words represent not things but purposes.</small>

LECT. IX.

Greek sense of a falsehood as an act of incivisme.

We often speak of the Greeks as specially cunning, of the crafty Odysseus as the typical specimen of a Greek. But the Greeks had in their earliest ages of which we have any record the keenest sense of civic life, and Achilles gave full expression to that sense when he declared that he hated as the gates of Hell the man who spoke one thing with his lips, and hid another in his heart. Even in days when we suppose that the standard of veracity had become anything but exalted among the Athenians, Euripides could not put into the mouth of Hippolytus the sentence, 'The tongue has sworn but the mind is unsworn,' without subjecting himself to the bitterest taunts of his comic foe, taunts which he was sure that his countrymen whatever their own practice might be would endorse.

Mental Reservation, who were its defenders?

The language ascribed to Hippolytus is the ancient form of that doctrine of mental reservation which has had so wide a diffusion in Modern Europe, and which is often accepted under another name by those who repudiate it when they associate it with a certain religious system. I allude to it because I wish you to observe that this doctrine sprung up and flourished and was sanctioned by skilful casuists, among those who despised national life, who treated it as a low, almost as an accursed thing;—to be endured and turned to account like all other evils—but which ought to be trampled upon by the priesthood unless it could be reduced into their servant. All who form this conception of a Nation, whatever creed they may profess, will also be bound by a higher logical necessity than they are themselves aware of to treat veracity—that is to say, the conformity of language to the purpose of him who uses it—as a cheap and secondary virtue which it will be often a merit for higher ends to part with. Nor, if I read history aright, has there ever been in any country a revival of horror and disgust for falsehood which has not been accompanied by a revival of belief in the sanctity of the Nation's life and the language which is the expression of it. I do not say for a moment that any creed commands a man to lie, or encourages him to lie. And I am convinced that a man who is penetrated with the feeling of his obligations as the citizen of a Nation, will find in his creed, let it bear what name it will, the strongest warnings against lying. But I hold also that if under any temptation we part with the feeling of those obligations, we shall turn our creed, whatever it be, into an excuse for lying. It will be removed from the catalogue of deadly into the catalogue of venial sins. I know not what priest or congregation of priests received authority to draw up either of those catalogues, but I do know that a lie brings death into the conscience and heart of every English citizen, and that he must continue in that death unless there is some one higher than any priest or congregation of priests who will raise him out of it.

We are thus better able to perceive what we owe

Lying always deemed pardonable and tolerable by those who are careless about national life.

LECT. IX.

Dante the restorer of his people's language.

to some great men of different lands whose names are familiar to us. The Italian may delight to speak of Dante as a politician, as a theologian, as a lover; may feel that not from one of those characters separately, but from all united, his poetry derives its power; that he could not have been a poet if he had not first and chiefly been a struggling, suffering man. All this he may see and testify; still I think the greatest debt he owes to the Florentine is that which we can least appreciate—the unfolding of the hidden powers of that speech which belonged not to the School or the Church, but to the Italian as an Italian. The stern, even savage, hatred of insincerity and untruth which worked in the heart of the singer, which led him to believe that the deepest doom was for those who had been in the highest places on earth, exercising an authority to which he paid willing homage—this hatred was linked inseparably not only with his patriotism, but with his reverence for the native words, with his awe of perverting them to any base or treacherous signification.

Wycliffe.

If we pass from him to a man who, not much after his time, did a work for our land, of a not less wonderful kind, though demanding far less genius, we shall see the same truth in another aspect. John Wycliffe was a great Schoolman, honoured in Oxford, honoured in foreign cities, in Prague especially, for his subtlety in disputation, and for his defence of Realism, which was identified in his mind with a belief that what we speak of and think of is not shadow but substance. He might have argued for ever on that thesis, and might have left us to this day in doubt whether he was not bringing us among shadows, whether some of his opponents were not at least as good witnesses for what is substantial as he was. But the great Logician was led to care for the English soil on which he was born; to see among those who met him when he came out of his rooms in Balliol, not quiddities or entities but living human beings; to discover that of the same blood with them was the Prince who for a while patronized him in London, were the peasants to whom he preached at Lutterworth. He perceived that the English tongue which all these spoke to each other was as sacred a tongue as the Latin. It was not framed merely for the purpose of buying and selling any more than that was, though it might serve such purposes as the Latin had done when Cicero and Cæsar conversed in it. Accordingly he believed that the language of the English people was not less fit than the language of the Latin *people*, was more fit than the language of the Latin *schools*—for expressing the deepest truths that could be uttered. A translation such as his, however imperfect it was and he may have felt it to be, yet was the greatest work for English citizens that had yet been accomplished; the surest foundation of an English Literature. It was a consecration of the words which peasants

First a Schoolman then an Englishman.

His Translation.

were continually speaking—a witness to them that those words had a truth in them which they had no business to twist to any temporary convenience. That witness was so much the more powerful because Wycliffe had been for years in battle with the Friars, especially on these two grounds, that they exalted their obedience to a foreign prince above their duty to the English king and law, and that they trifled with words or substituted for words mere pictures and images addressed to the senses. He was, in the strictest sense, the asserter of a national Morality in connection with a national language.

Its connection with his hostility to the emissaries from Italy.

I have not used any of the customary phrases about Wycliffe,—such as that he was the Morning Star of the Reformation,—not only because they do not concern my purpose, but because I believe they mislead us respecting the real point of his resemblance to the great German Reformer. Between him and Luther lay a most important century, which made a huge chasm between refined and cultivated men of the different nations and those clowns with whom Wycliffe claimed fellowship. The day of the Schoolman had gone down, the day of the scholar had risen. Latin had shaken off, to a great extent, its mediæval dress, and had striven easily or awkwardly to walk about in such robes as it wore in the reign of Augustus; Greek had fled from Constantinople, now become Ottoman, into the West. To study the speech, the literature, the art of Greece became

The relation of Wycliffe to Luther not a sectarian one.

the passion of Italians. Medicean Princes—sometimes eminent Popes—seemed as if they would inaugurate a Commonwealth of letters in connexion with, or as a substitute for, the Catholic Church. Germans caught the infection. Earnest students of the new lore, as well as of Hebrew, appeared to the great scandal and terror of many of the monks, but often supported by the smiles of the higher Ecclesiastics. Only in Bohemia, where Wycliffe's words had been heard, and Huss had left disciples to wreak their wrath upon his murderers, was there a vehement national movement against ecclesiastic domination mixed with vehement contempt for the new, or as it was deemed by the Hussites, the old Pagan, learning. It was amongst such circumstances, utterly unlike those which had surrounded our countryman, that the Saxon monk appeared. He found himself in a Germany divided into a number of electorates, secular and spiritual, feebly combined under an Emperor who could not resist the brigands in his own land and yet was expected to prove himself the centre of European politics. Luther, occupied with Aristotle and Aquinas in his lecture-room,—occupied with intense agonies of conscience in his own chamber—seemed as far removed as a man could well be from any of those general interests which affected the throne of the Cæsars, or the seat of the successors of St Peter. But as he more than any one was to prove that a man who would be truly an individual must be intensely

The fifteenth century a reaction against native languages.

The Monk and the College Teacher.

LECT. IX. national, who would be truly national must be vehemently individual, so he was also to prove that the ancient learning which threatened to extinguish the dialects of the particular nations could be effectively used only by one who loved one of these dialects better than the Latin, which had become a half native—never a mother—tongue to him, better even than the Greek and Hebrew which he welcomed as containing divine treasures that the Latin had debased. Germans therefore exalt Luther as the preserver and restorer of their proper speech. And with the preservation of this speech was associated an intense horror of the notion that words might be turned into falsehoods at the pleasure of men. Words, Luther said, were not dead things, they had hands and feet. It is the notion of them as dead things which makes us fancy we may use them as we like. When they confront us as living powers, we dare not trifle with them.

Emphatically the German.

It may seem to you that this very phrase "words" is an ambiguous and deceitful one. Do I mean by reverence for words, reverence for letters, reverence for print? I will answer you by referring to the instances which I have given you already.

Are words chiefly in books?

There were no writings, except the sacred writings, which Dante honoured so much as Virgil's. None, he said, had done so much for the cultivation of his mind; he delighted to think that his own Italian, if it were ever so unlike the Latin which

Virgil and Dante.

he read and respected in the schools, was the off- *Lect. IX.*
spring of that in which the Mantuan had con-
versed. Yes, *had conversed;* for it was impossible
to shut up Virgil in the *Georgics* or the *Æneid.*
He was a man. He had spoken to Dante. There *They speak*
had been a real hearty intercourse between them. *together as Friends.*
So by no idle fiction, but because the old poet had
been in truth the guide of the younger one through
dark ways till he had the glimpse of a higher
light, Virgil becomes lovingly and personally associated with a poem which embodies the highest
conceptions about the world visible and invisible,
that the Catholic Church had cherished.

Do you say that this was owing to the imagi- *The*
nation of a great poet? Wycliffe was no poet; *Jewish preachers*
was emphatically prosaic. But he inwardly be- *in England*
lieved that he was bringing before the priests, the
nobles, the farmers, the mechanics of Great Britain not a version of certain Hebrew letters which
Isaiah or Jeremiah had written down, but that
these old prophets were speaking to his countrymen just as directly as they spoke to the priests,
the nobles, and the farmers, the mechanics of
Palestine, on subjects in which both were equally
interested.

With Luther this was even more remarkably *And in*
the case. Apostles and Prophets were for him *Germany.*
never men of another age; they belonged to his
own; they denounced the princes at Worms, the
cardinals in Rome. The word which they spoke
was to him an everlasting word; one which, when

it came forth applied to the circumstances of every period. It was his vocation to speak that word, not merely to preserve it in letters whether Greek or German.

So men felt at the time of the Reformation when they were inspired with the conviction that they were Germans or Englishmen. So I think they must feel again if they are to care for that which is contained in English or German books. What treasures some cry may we not open to our boys and girls in the highest classes and the lowest! what information respecting Science and Art; respecting Morals and Politics and Religion, and all the other topics on which Newspapers deliver their oracles! By all means make these treasures accessible to them. Call human spirits out of the vasty deep of ignorance and brutality. But will they come when you do call? Not at the bidding of any letters. Only if a living voice is heard speaking from the letters. Only if it is felt to be the voice of a spirit mightier than their own. Nor will that Morality, which I believe is cultivated by a common Language be at all apparent amongst us merely through the charms of print. Reading and writing may come as Dogberry thought they did by Nature or as we suppose by blackboards and spelling-books; in neither case will they of themselves teach us not to lie.

The Educational Reformers who say, "Give us in your schools things not words," will fully assent to this proposition. They desire to bring their pupils face to face with facts; not to let mere descriptions be a veil between them. It is an honest desire; but I do not see how the neglect of words which express what we mean, what we are, can make us truthful. I believe we need to teach words much more, much better, than we have done; to make our countrymen feel how they touch the core of our nation's existence and of our own. *You* have the privilege of studying other languages besides your own. Prize it greatly for the sake of your own. Prize it that you may enter more thoroughly into the speech which you share with every English peasant. The old languages are national languages. They express the strength and life of great nations. They enable us to think more of the mystery of words than we are apt to do when we are merely using them for the occasions of every-day life. Still we are all as I said in a Dame's school. We are all learning to speak English. The hardest blows we receive are for the solecisms and false concords which we have each our special temptation to commit. Heavy punishments descend upon us when we use words not to express thoughts but to disguise them; when we change the mother tongue for the cant of a particular circle. I do not mean that each profession must not have its own nomenclature. There are forms of speech used in each of the Lecture-rooms of this University which are out of place in any other. Still our work in a University is to subordinate all peculiar forms of culture to a common

[margin: LECT. IX.]
[margin: Other languages precious for the sake of our own.]
[margin: Technical phraseology.]

end, to find some centre towards which all lines of thought converge. That is what we mean when we speak of Universities as Institutions for the Nation. In like manner the greatest lesson which we want in the business of life is to be according to the good old expression, "men of our word." He who is that as Merchant, Lawyer, Divine, fulfils his function; he may often prize silence much more than speech; but his speech will be worth listening to, his country will be the better for it.

A man of his word.

Let us not think that we can ever make our English more dainty by mixing with it foreign phrases or slang phrases. They do not merely separate us from the great writers of other days, from Swift and Addison, from Taylor and Milton, from Hooker and Shakespeare. They also introduce an element of untruth into the feelings and habits of our own time. Language is vital and growing, capable of continually sending out new shoots; but the grafting from other stocks is always perilous; we shall generally adopt what least deserves to be adopted; we shall derive our borrowed phrases from the worst sources. The vulgar tongue is never vulgar in the bad sense. The peculiar tongue which coxcombs exchange for it is essentially vulgar if by that adjective we mean coarse, ill conditioned, incoherent.

Duty of Englishmen to their language.

You will not suppose from anything I have said that I am exalting English speech above other speech; or am dreaming that it is ever to become a universal speech. It makes me tremble

"English speaking lands."

when any one speaks of that possibility. When I come to the last division of my subject I may shew you that there was a justification of the attempt to make Latin a universal Language, greatly as I rejoice that the different dialects of modern Europe rose up to confound it. The diffusion of French through all the courts and countries of Europe led I think to the death of the continental nations; the revival of a native Literature among Germans was the beginning of renovation: still I dare not say that French does not possess some qualities for general use which none of our northern tongues can claim. Instead of wishing that English should contest the honour with it I can think of no fate that would be worse for her. The lust of imperialism is far too strong in us already. Nothing will counteract it more than the recollection that our Language is a national possession; that only as such does it bind us to the past, that only as such does it help to maintain the veracity of which we boast, and of which our boasting is too likely to deprive us. We have indications in the presence of Celtic tongues close to us, in Wales, in Scotland, in Ireland, that whatever powers the English speech may be endued with, its power of exterminating the rivals of which it is most suspicious is limited by laws which we cannot alter. What the limits are we cannot know. Those sentimental persons who wish that the Welsh should talk Welsh because it is a beautiful old language when they are minded to talk Eng-

Latin and French both more fit to be universal languages than ours.

The Saxon and the Celtic tongues.

LECT. IX. lish, are doing it seems to me a very vain thing.
It may be, as experienced people tell us, that the coexistence of the two forms of speech leads to prevarication and falsehood; that witnesses in a Court of Justice have time to consider and invent evidence while the interpreter is translating. If so, to make the language stand on its feet when it is falling

A language cannot be kept alive by artificial props.

Est propter vitam vivendi perdere causas;

the final and highest aim of language being truth, you are losing that end that you may gratify your fancy of preserving one. If it can live it will live; if not a greater than you has sentenced it.

In India we have had lessons quite as remarkable which may either minister to our vanity or check it as we receive them. English has undoubtedly made mighty way through our arms, our administration and our schools. But Englishmen have been taught that they are face to face with languages of which their own has been a younger sister if not the offspring. A literature has been discovered to them which had existed for generations among the darker races when their fathers knew scarcely the use of the commonest tools. These are surely reasons for something better than self-exaltation; reasons for hoping that we have been permitted to educate nations which are to have a great future of their own, a future far better than their past but which will not be unmindful of that. May we prize that high calling and

The oriental tongues.

despise all miserable ambition for the spread of our speech or our power which stands in its way. And we have a calling at home, that which I must once and again tell you is the most difficult of all, the call to speak the truth, the whole truth, nothing but the truth. We have been made trustees of a glorious Language because we are citizens of a glorious Nation. That I may end where I began, a Parliament may easily become a mere place for talking, if we whom it represents are merely talkers. If the speech of each of us is sincere and manly the collective speech will not be frivolous and false.

<small>LECT. IX.

Speech may be silver if not gold.</small>

LECTURE X.

GOVERNMENT.

<small>Lect. X.

Law and Responsibility twin conceptions.</small>

A Law, I have said, appeals to the individual man, makes him aware that he *is* an individual. It is only another way of expressing the same fact to say that Law makes each man aware of his responsibility. To feel myself an individual—a distinct living person—is to feel myself responsible for my acts. They are mine; I can shift them on no one else.

But to whom am I responsible? Since the sense of having neighbours is awakened at the same time with the sense of being an individual, I might say generally I am responsible to my neighbours; to each of them, to all of them. The particular neighbour whom I injure may make me understand that he holds me responsible to him. Then he is said to take the *law* into his own hands. Or my neighbours may meet together and call me to account before them. Then they are said to pronounce or execute the *law* upon me. So that I am driven back upon this word Law.

Unless I assume a Law I cannot recognize a meaning either in the personal vengeance or the general sentence. Law lies beneath each. It is to a belief of the authority of Law in me that both appeal.

<small>LECT. X.</small>

We must keep this thought steadily in our minds. It will be often slipping away from us. We say to ourselves 'Law, what is Law? Why do you talk to me of its might? It only means this.' 'It only means that.' When we examine what it only means we find the answer is 'Law.' The three letters may be exchanged for a ponderous polysyllable, or a troop of polysyllables. But we cheat ourselves in the process. We show that we are very learned, that we cannot speak the common language. But the power of Law, the terror of Law remains for us; just as if we were not wiser than other men, and were not armed with any polysyllables.

<small>Law mocks those who mock it.</small>

Is Law then a mere dark Abstraction? Surely not. If it makes me feel my own personality, if it reminds me that my neighbours are persons, I cannot be content with abstractions. I ask who administers or executes the Law? I ask whom does the Law command me to obey? Here begins that manner or habit which the name of Loyalty so happily describes. That denotes the sentiment which I cherish—which a nation cherishes—for certain persons whom it associates with Law, who represent the Law to it. They save it from becoming a hard letter.

<small>Loyalty.</small>

12—2

LECT. X.

The Law demands administration.

Forms of Government.

Is Loyalty merely personal?

They connect it with living acts. It must be connected with these if it is to have any living force, although the connection is always a perilous one, is always threatening to make Law the servant of those whom it should rule.

I propose to consider this question in reference to the different forms of Government which we are wont to describe by the names Monarchy, Aristocracy, Democracy, as well as to that blending of these forms which is implied in the Order of many countries, but which we suppose to be peculiarly characteristic of our own. In a society where each of these forms prevails I believe Loyalty in its strictest sense may exist; in each of them it is exposed to certain special dangers.

The sense of Loyalty is often supposed to attach itself almost exclusively to a Monarch. We speak of the loyalty of our Cavaliers to Charles I., of the loyalty of the Scotch Highlanders to Charles Edward. The Roundheads and the Whigs we say have other claims to a reverence but it is not this. I think the Cavaliers and the Highlanders *were* loyal to these Stuart princes; and that their loyalty is entitled to our sincere respect. If I examine the feeling of either I find it to be no doubt in great part personal; that is to say they always asked for a man to whom they should pay homage, they never could contemplate law as law. But in both cases there was a sense of reverence for law underlying the personal attachment. If the Cavalier had not looked upon Charles I. as embodying and representing a law which had lasted for generations, his fidelity would often have been shaken by what he heard and experienced of the monarch's untruthfulness. He could forget that,—he could clothe his master with all splendid and beautiful qualities of soul and body— because he associated him with a certain right which was not absorbed in him, which belonged to the past and the future. In such men as Hyde and Falkland this law became the conscious and paramount object of reverence. Charles was to them little more than the expression of it. But in the military Cavalier who had none of their learning, to whom they would have seemed mere formalists, the same feeling was unconsciously at work. Take away the Law and what was implied in it and Charles would have shrivelled into nothing. With the Clansman of Scotland this was not equally the case. He had never risen to the apprehension of Law. He was still in the patriarchal stage of existence. Yet his devotion is entitled to the name of Loyalty because it was a prophecy of Law; the particular person belonged to a line with which the Highlander associated a certain right to govern. He resented the intrusion of a Stranger into the throne as he would the intrusion of a robber into his homestead.

In all cases Loyalty implies the union of a Person with an order or a Right.

The Roundhead and the Whig resisted the Monarch for the sake of the Law. For a long time during the civil war the Parliamentary forces fought in the name of the King against the King. They could not give him up because they beheld the Majesty of the Law in him. Cromwell and his soldiers proclaimed such language to be a fiction. A fiction no doubt it had become. But the endurance of it by men of particularly stern and vigorous minds showed that it expressed a very deep truth to them. When it had lost its power, when the Monarch and the Law had been absolutely divorced from each other it was scarcely possible that any result should follow but that which did follow. Men trained to the reverence for Law said 'there must be a Law—which can pass sentence upon every man.' Milton with his stern conception of the awfulness of Law, of its celestial origin, could rejoice in a death which seemed to him the vindication of it; his intense belief in the government of a King of Kings hindered him from perceiving what a shock Law itself suffered in that experiment to assert it.

This instance, contemplated on all sides, may show better than any other how Loyalty links itself to the person of a man, and yet how suicidal it becomes whenever it tries to exalt the man above the Law. Loyalty may be exercised most simply and directly towards one man or one woman. Nearly all of us drop naturally into language which indicates that conviction. But it is just as true that Loyalty so exercised is always liable to lose its meaning, to be false to its etymology. And whenever that result is reached there will be some crisis which restores the word to its proper significance or which ends in the anarchy of a land.

Some of the greatest assertions of the dignity and ascendancy of Law have been made by the nobles of our land. The most familiar of all examples, the winning of Magna Charta, is for us at least the most instructive. It was an act of apparent rebellion; it was in the strictest sense an act of Loyalty. John had been disloyal. He had undermined the foundations of his own authority; he had behaved as if choice and self-will were the ground of it. Those who represented the old families of the Nation,—those who kept alive the tradition of its permanence—said that that could not be. It was a subversion of Royalty to rend it asunder from Law. *[Defence of Law by an Aristocracy.]*

Think again of the complaints which have been made so often and so truly against Aristocracies; those for instance first deep, then loud, which were heard in France before the Revolution. On what did they turn? On the claim of the nobles to be a "privileged order," that is to be exempted from the conditions and restraints of the Law which bound other men. Those who raised the cry might sometimes covet the same exemptions. Nevertheless it was and must always be a righteous one. It must always ascend from the inner heart of a people. Privilege has no sort of connection with Government. It is the foe of Government. If a Government is in the hands of an Aristocracy it is *[Violation of Law by an Aristocracy.]*

LECT. X.

Government and Privilege not synonymous but hostile words.

an act of Loyalty to that Government to insist that those who administer it shall have no exemption from the burdens of other citizens, no indulgences for their transgressions. These pretences to exemption and indulgence destroyed the Nobility of France and at last France itself

If this force is given to the word Loyalty there can be no reason why a democratic Society should not be a strictly loyal Society. The members of such a society may confess the supremacy of Law over them one and all; they may be loyal to the Judges who declare what the law is; to the particular Magistrates who enforce it in any district; to the general Magistrate whatever be his name, who is the acknowledged head of the Commonwealth. Such Loyalty may be diffused through a Society. It may be a perpetual curb upon the lust of dominion and the lust of gain; a security that the interests of the present shall not cause the past or the future to be forgotten; a guarantee of history and of letters.

Democratic Loyalty.

Perils to Loyalty in a Democracy.

But on the other hand a Democracy has its own special motives to be disloyal. Does not the Law proceed from its mouth? Does not the Law bow at last to its will? If the multitude breaks through the cobwebs which bind it, where are the spiders that can preserve or refit those cobwebs? Have not we been proclaimed sovereigns? Are not Judges, Magistrates, Presidents, merely our ministers to be disposed of as we list? Such language sounds strictly democratical. Those who utter it would say if they were accused of disloyalty, "To what do we owe loyalty but to the people's voice? Are not they—that is to say, are not we—masters?" I apprehend that there is an answer to this language; that first Anarchy, then Despotism has been always the answer to it.

Do I present these facts to you that I may deduce Pope's moral from them:

> "For forms of Government let fools contest,
> That which is best administered is best"?

Pope's dictum requires careful examination.

No! That couplet like many others in the *Essay on Man* contains, it seems to me, a mixture of the poet's admirable common sense with the philosophical strut and political ambition of Bolingbroke who inspired his song. Pope I doubt not, had been tormented as well by noisy talkers about divine rights, as by classical pedants who vaunted republican heroes. The discourses of both seemed to him weary, flat, and unprofitable. His friend who had a scheme for combining opposite parties against the administration of Sir Robert Walpole had a different reason for denouncing the special theories which held them apart. When such opposite feelings enter into the composition of a maxim there will almost necessarily be something in it by which we may profit, something of which we must beware. It is true that there are very foolish contests about forms of government. It is not true that we can settle all questions between them by saying that any one of them will answer if it is well administered. That may be either an arid platitude or a falsehood. It is a platitude to say that if a Monarchy, an Aristocracy, or a Democracy is well administered it is the best form of Government. That is merely to affirm that whatever country is well governed is well governed. It is a falsehood to affirm that a Monarchy, an Aristocracy, or Democracy is equally adapted to every country; that any country under any one of these forms would be equally well administered. The principle which I think Pope would have expressed in some clear exquisite sentence if he had not been perverted by a passion for epigram and by the affectations of his friend is that those who dispute about forms of Government are not aware that the forms are determined for them; that the forms affect their arguments and are not the least affected by them. Their minds have been moulded by the order under which they have grown up; they may be deformers or reformers, but they must confess a form which they wish to break or renew before they are either. They may labour that that form shall be well, and not ill administered. To argue about the advantage of some other is child's play not men's work. That doctrine I deem very important to National Morality; I will endeavour to illustrate it.

Most citizens of the United States who have the means of travelling visit the different cities of Europe. They must hear in them many arguments in favour of Monarchy and Aristocracy. They may sometimes possibly be struck with points in which the administration of States on the Continent—even of our island—have a superiority to their own. Suppose an inhabitant of Boston or New York returning with the impression of these arguments or of these observations strong upon him—suppose some particular weakness, either in his institutions or in those who administer them, to be brought strongly home to him on his arrival—he may reflect, I think with great advantage, on Pope's first line. He may say to himself: "Well! whether I see or not at this "moment the force of the arguments for a republic "which I learnt by heart in my childhood—whether "or not they have been shaken by what I have "heard elsewhere—this land is my land, these insti- "tutions are the institutions which I have received "from my fathers. 'For forms of government let "fools contest,' I will not be troubled by wise saws "or modern instances. My life, my education has "been moulded into this form. Whatever it may be "for others it is good for me." If the second line should occur to him, if he should be tempted to say: "Yes, but I see many faults in the adminis- "tration of my country. Is it not a safe rule that "'that which is best administered is best'?" he will be bound to answer himself again: "On that point "too I can decide nothing. I have not the faculty "of comparing administrations. But certainly, this "land of mine will not be rightly administered "upon some other principle than its own. There "must be some compass to steer the vessel by.

[margin: Lect. X. A citizen of the United States returning from his travels. His doubts and his determination.]

LECT. X.

The genuine loyalty implied in it.

The abolition of Slavery a grand act of Loyalty.

"If we lose the compass I may talk about the "management of it as I please. It will drift "away, I know not whither." As the result of which consideration he would, I hope, resolve to labour that he might understand the form of his government better than he had ever done; that he might struggle for it more steadfastly; that so he might correct whatever he saw was faulty and inconsistent in the administration of it. Such a man I should deem a loyal man; loyal to something better than the conclusions of his intellect, which are always liable to fluctuations; loyal to what he perceived to be the principles of his Nation's existence and therefore those with which the life and thoughts of an American citizen ought to be in harmony.

What I am saying is no imagination. It is on this principle that the most admirable citizens of the United States have been recently acting. They found an institution among them which did not exist among us their progenitors, or in the other States of Europe. We taunted them with it. We made it an excuse for denouncing their form of Government. They listened, sometimes with displeasure, sometimes in silence. But they did not abandon their form because they found a practical anomaly among them from which other countries might be exempt. They declared that it *was* an anomaly; that loyalty to their land, to its form of Government, demanded the removal of it. Amidst all difficulties, against all oppositions of interests in one part of the land and another, they maintained their doctrine. The will of the multitude gave way before the convictions of a few; the worship of the dollar before the willingness of men and women, of young and old to sacrifice their money and their lives and lives which were dearer than their own, to purify their land from an abomination. They did purify it, and a great Republic has held forth a spectacle for us to wonder at, an example to make us ashamed.

I dwell with more interest and satisfaction upon this instance of true loyalty to the form of Government established in a land because the youth of the American States might be so easily pleaded, has been so often pleaded, as a reason why they need not be faithful to the lessons of their fathers, to the order which they have inherited, why they may consider all questions about Governments as open questions to be settled by the balance of reasoning or authority in favour of one or the other. I hold it a high honour to Americans that they had not been misled by these plausible suggestions. Some of them may, no doubt, be convinced that Democracy, as such, has proved itself to be the only tolerable form of Government for the Universe. But I hope and believe that those who hold this intellectual persuasion most strongly do not rely wholly or chiefly upon it. If they do I fear they will after all be poor citizens, not ready, like those who shed their blood in the war, to give themselves up for their

marginalia: LECT. X.

A young State should be as tenacious of its Institutions as an old one.

Poverty of mere intellectual conclusions.

LECT. X.
Loyalty for a people not for a select class.

country. Loyalty I am persuaded is deeper in them, as it should be in all of us, than any judgments of the understanding which are liable to continual shocks and vicissitudes. Loyalty may bring them into fellowship with the commonest dwellers on their soil. Suppose these had the information or the faculty for applying it which would enable them honestly to accept the proofs and conclusions of learned men, would that do them as much good—would it as much elevate their hearts as the thought, 'Here we were born; here are the graves of those who went before us; they won this order for us; we will not let it perish or be corrupted'?

The English Constitution according to Blackstone.

That distinction I would apply with rigour to our own case. Sir William Blackstone, the accomplished and popular Jurist of the last century, told first his pupils at Oxford—then the people of England generally—that we possess a machine called a Constitution; the various parts of which fit so curiously and marvellously into each other, as to make one wonder how it should ever be out of order. 'There are great merits but also con-'siderable defects in a Monarchy. But we have a 'monarchy the defects of which are remedied, the 'merits of which are developed by an Aristocracy. 'An Aristocracy has also great excellencies and 'some weak points. But we have a House of 'Commons as well as a House of Lords. That 'House exhibits the most perfect kind of Democracy 'supplementing what is not found in Monarchy and

'Aristocracy, preventing them each from being too 'strong for the other.' Recommended by the legal knowledge and graceful style of Justice Blackstone how could such a theory as this fail to charm the people whom it pronounces so much more fortunate than all others upon the earth? How could they help extolling the wisdom of the ancestors who had contrived such a machine, or feeling some considerable self-congratulation that it was still at work among themselves, that they perhaps were in their own way contributing to move or at any rate grease its wheels? A young man appeared in the University in which Blackstone was lecturing, who instead of echoing his admiration of this exquisite piece of machinery, gave his reasons for thinking that it could accomplish nothing; that the action of one part of it must always be interfering with the action of every other; that altogether a clumsier invention had never been produced in the world. That was the doctrine of Mr Jeremy Bentham's *Fragment on Government*, the first of a long series of works which were to illustrate the same position; though in later times Mr Bentham was quite as busy in constructing what should be an efficient scheme of government and legislation as in demonstrating the feebleness and incoherencies of that which he had been commanded to admire.

The same Constitution according to Bentham.

Many of us can remember when these conflicting theories were first presented to us; how very clever and exact the arrangements of the Constitution seemed to us when they were described by

Effect of the two doctrines.

the Judge, how they crumbled to pieces before our eyes—how absurd we deemed them—when they were dissected by the critic. And then as we got a slight glimpse into the records of the past, how they evidently appeared to make in favour of the censor, to prove the dogmas of the eulogist untenable! We could not find those wise ancestors who had composed this finely balanced Constitution. We heard of a number of opposing influences which had produced laws and repealed them, of men who had aimed at usurpations and had resisted them. We could sympathise with one or other of these influences, we could complain of this or that man; but where was any elaborate scheme for adjusting one part of a government to another? In what workshop was that perfect fabric devised which had been handed down to us and which we were to cherish? Mr Bentham certainly was a Vulcan; we could see his forges at work; we could examine the engine which was produced in them. Had he not excuse for telling us that all who preceded him were mere bunglers, mainly occupied in gratifying some interest of their own or of their masters?

I certainly should for myself have acquiesced in this conclusion if I had been forced to choose between the opinions of Judge Blackstone and Mr Bentham. But it struck some of us, that perhaps we were not driven to this alternative. We began to think that if our Constitution in Sovereign, Lords and Commons was worthy of the honour that was demanded for it, to treat it as a clever machine was scarcely the right way of paying it honour. That was to glorify the ingenuity of a particular expounder. We need not rob him of any praise that he has earned by his cleverness. But as I have had occasion to observe before, a man does not find the Constitution of his own body in a medical treatise; he learns what it is, either by the enjoyment of regular health or by fits of gout and diseases of the lungs. He has a certain state of body different from that of his neighbours in some points as well as one in its essentials resembling theirs. But to be contemplating it as if it were outside of him, instead of doing what he can to preserve its order and cure its disorders is scarcely judicious. If we applied this analogy, it seemed to us that we might accept all the facts of history which had shaken our faith in Judge Blackstone's perfect scheme,—we might even admit all that Mr Bentham told us about its practical failures,—and yet might retain our loyalty to it as the Constitution that had been from generation to generation proving itself to be ours. We should have no occasion then to credit our ancestors with any grand architectural genius. We should credit them with just what we found they had done; with their efforts successful or unsuccessful to remove confusions which they discovered; with the errors or insincerities by which they made the confusions greater. We should learn from their wisdom, and therefore should not be enslaved by their opinions; we should profit by their righteous acts, and not copy them in circumstances to which they did not apply.

I have spoken of Blackstone's and Bentham's contests about the form of our Government. In the present day our propensity is rather to accept Pope's second line—to resolve Government into Administration. For instance, it has been maintained by a very ingenious writer that 'the Cabinet' which constitutes the centre of what is popularly called 'The Administration' really absorbs the Monarchy of England; that the person whom we call Monarch is merely an ornamental appendage to this Cabinet; not useless, because the imagination of common people asks for pictures and gewgaws, cannot altogether dispense with them, but useful in that way only. Such an opinion is not only plausible; to those who contemplate Government merely as an instrument for securing certain external advantages to the inhabitants of a country, in any given period, as having no relation to the past or the future, it must be irresistible. That it is possible for a man—quite an ordinary man—*not* to contemplate it in this way, I can perhaps shew you best if I give you the experience of a person whom I once knew, nearly in the words in which he reported it to me : "I was a boy," he said, "in "the time of the Regency. I was told about the "fopperies of the Prince and his profligacy. I "was taught to despise the one and hate the other. "I was bred to admire Milton for his republicanism

Monarchy treated as a merely ornamental appendage to Government.

"as well as his poetry; to connect them together.
" I learnt that Washington was one of the worthi-
"est because the simplest of heroes. Whatever
"cultivation was given to my imagination was of
"this sort. That is to say, the capacity for taking
" an interest in any kind of shows was not developed
"in me. I never have been able to cultivate it in
"myself, though I have sometimes longed for it.
"My dislike of George IV. and his court has deep-
"ened with fresh knowledge; my reverence for
"Milton and Washington. I have seen nothing of
"courts, I have lived chiefly with those who detest
"them. And yet I am convinced that not the
"outside of my mind—not my fancy, which is as
"dry as the remainder biscuit after a voyage—
"but my inmost convictions, my way of considering
"all those subjects which affect and interest me
"most, would be utterly different if I had not been
"brought up under a Monarchy. I have watched—
"from a distance—the changes of Cabinets and have
"been anything but indifferent to them; but I am
"certain that the Statesmen in past ages or present
"whom I reverence most for gifts or for honesty are
"not to me—cannot be to me—what the Sovereign
"is, even if the temporary possessor of the throne
"were not one whom I had cause to honour for
"personal merits. The Sovereign connects me
"with other times as well as my own; the Statesman
"may help to do that, if he is the counsellor of
"the Sovereign; on no other terms." The words
of an anonymous witness are worth very little,

The experience of an Englishman educated in republicanism respecting Monarchy.

except as they correspond to something in those who hear them. I have quoted them because I think there is something that corresponds to them in you, and because the circumstances and education of my friend makes him a crucial test of the way in which the monarchical part of our Constitution acts upon those who have no intellectual, no sentimental prepossessions in favour of it.

But at this time you will perhaps hear less about this part of our Government than about its Aristocratical element. You will be present at many discussions upon the desirableness of "a second Chamber." Do you really suppose that such arguments, if they are ever so cleverly conducted, will advance one step the settlement of the question whether England is or is not to have a nobility? I remember to have heard a distinguished man not many years dead, a Judge in one of our Equity Courts, expressing his opinion of Lord Russell's *Life of Moore*. "An amusing book," the Judge said: "I do not dislike the poet. He was a "terrible tuft-hunter no doubt. But what man or "woman or child in England, Ireland, or Scotland "has a right to cast a stone at him for that? There "is not one of us, you know, that can keep himself "from falling down and worshipping a lord when- "ever he has the opportunity." One laughed of course at the extravagance of this dictum. The speaker's own practice was I doubt not a refutation of it. But there must be something in such a remark which we cannot afford to forget. So acute

marginal note: The influence of Aristocracy upon all persons in this land.

an observer would not have pointed this out as our temptation, if it were not one into which we are all likely to fall. If that is so, there must be more in the existence of an Aristocracy than those have discovered who discuss the utility or the mischievousness of a second Chamber. For evil or for good it has penetrated into our social life; it affects our Social Morality. For evil certainly if it begets a base flunkeyism. But can you cure that by abolishing the Institution which has been an excuse for it? The disease may take a hundred forms, may be called forth by the most different objects. See whether you cannot counteract it by nourishing the temper of which it is the grovelling counterfeit. If you are loyal to the family sympathies which an Aristocracy represents—if you remember that you too have fathers and ancestors, let them be of what rank or reputation they may, whom it is in your power to honour or to disgrace—and you will find that an hereditary Chamber, whatever legislative functions it may exercise, need not depress, may do much to elevate, your national and therefore your individual life. The members of it may have temptations to which we are not exposed. If we are loyal to our common country we may find that what unites patrician and plebeian is stronger than that which separates them.

The cure of Flunkeyism.

I am not likely, as a Plebeian, to forget that part of our Government which stands in closest connexion with ourselves. Of course I desire that

The House of Commons.

<small>Lect. X.

What do our Representatives represent.</small>

it should be what it professes to be, that it should faithfully represent the mind of the English people. But that it may do this, there must be a mind to represent. Every one of us may be helping to form that mind. If we have any function here, that is our function. Our business is not to set England above other countries; to foster any national conceit. We are not to maintain that Nations are only good and true when they have a Sovereign and a House of Peers, and a House of Commons. But since this is the form of Government under which we have been nurtured, which has moulded the thoughts of us and our fathers, our loyalty to it will be the best security that we honour the institutions and desire the growth of every other Nation. Our judgments are apt to be arrogant, because we see but a little way. The hills that surround us and protect us may shut out the prospect beyond them. But when we reflect how much those hills are above us, how many generations have dwelt under the shadow of them, and have welcomed the sun as it rose behind them, humbler thoughts will take possession of us. We shall begin to understand that there may be other regions which lie under the shadow of their own hills, which are enlightened by the same sun.

LECTURE XI.

WAR.

LAW, Language, Government; all these it will be admitted have a certain worth. No one will say that a Nation can exist without them. Few will say that they are not precious to the Individual. But War—dare I speak of that as good either for the Nation or the Individual?

We do speak of it as good for both. The history of a Nation is often said to be in a great measure the history of its wars. Some of the most conspicuous individuals of every Nation have been its warriors. Artists and Poets choose them for their subjects. If we attribute that preference to a Pagan instinct, we are reminded that the books of Moses speak of war as well as the books of Homer; that Joshua and David fought as well as Miltiades and Alexander. If War is said to be the relic of an uncivilized age, we ask ourselves why it has called forth most enthusiasm amongst the people of Europe, which boasts to be most

Conflict of feelings respecting war.

civilised, most to have outgrown old superstitions? If it is pronounced irreligious, the question suggests itself why religion has produced so many wars? If it is said to be the produce of an Aristocratical rule, we can point to a number of instances in which Trade has been the great motive of it. If, as some of us were taught in the *Evenings at Home*, War is mischievous because it is costly as well as cruel, the children who learnt that lesson, the mothers who taught it, have discovered that speculations may be as costly as battles, that cruelties may be perpetrated by the ledger as well as the sword. If there have been in our day righteous and burning denunciations of the crimes of the Camp, there have been protests as righteous and as burning against the crimes which are engendered by a long peace.

It behoves us therefore to approach this subject thoughtfully. I might earn a cheap reputation for Morality by speaking to you of war as essentially and inevitably immoral, by affirming that it never had any good work to do in the world, or that it never can have any to do in the times to come. I believe that if I did so I should tempt you to great insincerity; I should lead you to think an admiration wrong in principle which you nevertheless cherish, and feel that you cannot help cherishing. I should teach you to think that the profession of a Soldier could not be a right and honest one; so if you engage in it, or if your friends engage in it, you will assist in

Marginal notes: Lect. XI. Peace has its own brutality and its own curse. Danger of denouncing War vaguely and rhetorically.

making it for yourselves and them what you account it to be. The confusion and mischief of that notion I hold to be incalculable. I mean therefore to shew you what I deem to be the morality of War, what its immorality.

I must begin by repudiating certain apologies that are often made for it. The first is this. 'Well, all you say against war as unchristian, or 'impolitic, may be true. But it is a necessary 'evil.' Were I to use this language I should tell you at once that a chair of Moral Philosophy is an absurdity and a delusion. Robbery, Murder, Adultery, are facts as much as War is a fact. If the fact that there have been wars makes them necessary, Robbery, Murder, and Adultery are also necessary. Calling them so—if by necessary I mean that I am not to labour that they should be punished as transgressions—I affirm that there is no order in the world, I canonize disorder.

Again, it is often said, 'There is a natural 'instinct of Self-Preservation in us all. I cannot 'let myself be killed or plundered; I must take 'the life of the man who threatens to kill or 'plunder me if I can. Why is it different with 'a number of men who form what is called a 'Nation? Why may they not obey the same 'instinct? Why may they not ward off blows, 'even if the lives of those who strike the blows 'are exacted as the payment for them?' There is a sophistry in this plea which ought to be laid bare, since it touches the first principles of Social

<small>Lect. XI.

An allowable instinct can never justify a deliberate purpose, far less a military organization.</small>

Life. No doubt there is an instinct in me which leads me to slay a highwayman. It is an instinct which an organized State is bound to *tolerate*. The verdict of justifiable homicide is one which is always accepted as reasonable. But that phrase implies that the act is *only* tolerated. Clear evidence must be produced that the life of a citizen had not been wantonly trifled with even under the greatest provocation. Suppose the injured man had chosen to suffer the wrong—even to be killed himself rather than to take the vengeance into his own hands—we might be sorry that a criminal had been let loose, that a just man had been his victim; but we could not say that the law had not been honoured—superstitiously honoured it may be, but still honoured—by the refusal to anticipate its decrees. How is it possible to assume such a ground for the deliberate act of an Organic Nation? How can it treat submission to a brute instinct as a justification for the calling together of an armed force expressly to fulfil the purposes of a Society grounded upon Law; to defend its existence? No natural instinct, nothing less than a moral obligation, can be an excuse for risking the lives of our own citizens, for threatening the lives of other men. Our admiration for soldiers, private men or leaders, means that we suppose them to have done a duty; our belief that any war is worthy of our sympathy means that we suppose at least one of the nations which entered into it to have done its duty. It is most important for the clearness of our own minds, as important for the well-being of our nation, that we should carry this conviction always with us and be ready to apply it in all cases. Let us try to consider it in reference to the different kinds of wars which we read of.

1. We cannot forget that every Nation now existing in Europe became a Nation through war. Britain was a part of the Roman Empire; a civilized province of that Empire; growing in luxuries. It was christianized when the rest of the Empire was christianized; it had its Bishops as well as its prefects. It rebelled frequently against its Masters; it was fertile, the saying is, in tyrants. It was not free therefore from petty wars by sea or land. But it was no Nation. By battles—to what degree exterminating or subversive of the previous civilization historians may dispute—but certainly by battles severe and bloody the Saxons established their supremacy here. It seemed to the old inhabitants mere destruction, a relapse into barbarism and Paganism. We say that a mighty blessing came out of this apparent relapse. It was emphatically *that* blessing on which I have been dwelling in this course of Lectures. First, a truer wholesome family life took the place of the corrupt family life which the Satirists of Rome describe and which passed from the capital into the provinces. Secondly, a people strong in the sense of neighbourhood, strong in the sense of personal existence, capable therefore of Law, of Government, bringing with them the roots of a vital native speech,

War changed Britain from a province to a Nation.

overthrew colonists in whom there was a feeble sense of neighbourhood, a feeble feeling of personal responsibility, who merely received Laws, Government, Language, Religion, from Foreigners. The Saxon wars destructive as they might be, yet were in the strictest sense the commencement of a new life in our island.

I take a very strong case; one which may be the more helpful to us because it does not enkindle any strong sympathies. We do not care about the details of these Saxon wars; we know exceedingly little of the men who took part in them. No heroical interest attaches to them; we assume them to have been guilty of innumerable violences. Yet we accept them as founders of our National Order; we believe that we should not be a Nation without them. What is true of England, is true *mutatis mutandis* of every state of Europe. And when I use those words *mutatis mutandis*, I intimate that each one was to be a distinct Nation, with distinct Laws, a distinct Government, a distinct Language, and that without wars often most savagely conducted, they would have remained an indistinct mass incapable of bearing any of the fruits which they have borne.

In saying that the more civilization advances the less we shall hear of wars, Mr Buckle may have asserted an important truth; but if the assertion is not analysed, if it is merely taken in the lump, it will utterly mislead us. There may be a Civilization which is destructive of Social Morality, of social existence. War may be—so far as we know has been—the only means of reforming it. There may be a Civilization which, like that of Rome, means a huge Camp, an enormous military System. The dissolution of such a System however effected, by whatever hard hands, may be the road to a truer peace as well as to a truer life.

2. Next come the religious wars of Christendom. In the third part of these Lectures I must speak of the Crusades as illustrating the conflict of two grand social principles—their historical importance in that aspect cannot be overrated. In another aspect the Crusades may be represented as an attempt to fuse together the different Nations of the West in a cause which was equally interesting to them all. But then we become aware of their weakness. The nations were *not* fused together. Each crusade exhibited more clearly the rivalries and conflicts between the princes and Barons of the separate Kingdoms. They had a field in Palestine for a Kingdom established on the maxims of Western Chivalry. It broke to pieces; there was only a repetition in it of Western divisions. If the object of these wars was to unite Christendom, they failed. If their object was to destroy Islamism, they failed. If their object was to eliminate from Christendom whatever elements of Islamism it contained within it, they failed. The Orders of Knights which these wars called forth were their most conspicuous feature; those Orders, not the Mahome-

marginalia: Lect. XI. — Religious Wars. — The Crusades.

tans but the Christian powers put down. Still more if their object was to consolidate the Papal authority in the West were they a failure. They gave rise to the bitterest complaints against Papal extortion and deception; they attracted popular sympathy to Frederick IInd and his house, the great antagonists of the Papacy. They were successful only as supplying a precedent for other wars of the same kind. If war was the best and holiest instrument for crushing Islamism in the East, it must be the best and holiest instrument for crushing heresies in the West. So Simon de Montfort went forth with authority and commission to extinguish the Albigenses; every crime under heaven being perpetrated by his hosts in the hope that the King of Heaven would reward them for breaking His laws and teaching men to regard Him as their enemy. The religious wars of the 16th and 17th centuries did not pretend to preserve the Unity of Christendom. They assumed that it was lost. But the Catholic League tried to make a united France; by the thirty years' war it was hoped to make a united Germany; the defeat of the Provinces it was hoped would have made the most Catholic Sovereign supreme. There was no want of genius in the Duke of Guise, the Duke of Alva, or in Wallenstein, no hesitation about the means for accomplishing their ends. Yet failure is stamped upon them all.

3. How would it be if men agreed to treat convictions about the invisible world with indif-

ference, only to busy themselves with visible interests? That is the next point to be considered.

I pass from religious wars to Trade Wars. The two classes may at one point be said to touch each other. The invasions of Peru and Mexico by the Spaniards professed at times to be undertaken for the propagation of the faith. No doubt their atrocities were sanctified in the eyes of the perpetrators of them by that notion. Still it is evident that they were mainly enterprises to satisfy the intense hunger for gold. Trade was their main inspirer, though the earlier chivalry of Spain must be credited with the valour and daring of the leaders. From that time onwards Trade has been a principal motive of Wars, a constant justification of them. Other ends no doubt were aimed at in the policy of Chatham both on the European and the American continent. The object of the Prussian Monarch was certainly not the advancement of Trade. But the establishment of our Indian Empire was begun by Tradesmen and maintained by them. The military genius of Clive was formed in the counting-house. The struggle to retain our Colonies was kept alive by the commercial cities of Great Britain; the loss of Empire was deemed ignominious, the injury to Trade calamitous. When the French War of 1793 began, the question about the opening of the Scheldt was most curiously mixed with denunciations of Republican and Atheistical principles. Mr Pitt made use of these

The Trade Wars of the last three centuries.

in his speeches, but he did not venture to rely upon them as the motive for commencing hostilities. Unless he could shew that there was an English Trade interest at stake he did not think that he had a sufficient *Casus Belli*. That feeling was interrupted by events of which I am about to speak; but it has resumed its ascendancy. Most of the arguments which are based upon the principle of non-intervention take this form: 'Suppose our 'Trade is attacked or is at hazard, there is a fair 'reason for threatening war, if not for making it; 'no other reason is adequate.'

<small>The Non-intervention doctrine.</small>

4. Burke protested against this mode of regarding the great controversy which the Revolution raised. He cried aloud for a war of principles. The monarchs of Europe adopted feebly, but they did adopt, his dogma. They proclaimed a Crusade against France. It was a Crusade against a Nation; the Nation had energy and might to repel it and defeat it. Then came the Crusade of Imperial France against the Nations. England considered long whether she had an adequate pecuniary interest in resisting that Crusade; or whether her interference could still be justified on the pleas which had been urged against the France of 1793. At length she heartily plunged into the war as one for the liberty and distinctness of the Nations. Then the heart of the country responded to the battle cry; then the best and truest citizens were the loudest in raising it. For this it was felt, and this only, makes a war lawful; that it is

<small>The first and second French War.</small>

a struggle for Law against Force; for the life of LECT. XI.
a people as expressed in their Laws, their Language, their Government, against any effort to impose on them a Law, a Language, a Government which is not theirs.

I believe this conclusion to be a sound one, Reluctant proselytes.
forced upon the minds of those who had the strongest natural aversion to war, who were the most suspicious of appeals to the ambition or the love of glory in their Nation, the most inclined by their habits and education to sympathise with any profession rather than with the military. I think that an experience of various kinds, obtained in very different circumstances, obliged them to account the arguments of those who pleaded for Peace at any price hollow in themselves, and fatal to the cause on behalf of which they were urged.

When these arguments turn upon the assertion The Christian arguments for Peace.
that Christ came into the world to establish a Kingdom of Peace for all Nations, I not only accede to the doctrine, but desire that it should be taken in its most strict sense. It is a Kingdom for all *Nations*. Unless there are Nations, distinct Nations, this Kingdom loses its character; it becomes a world Empire. I shall have much to say on that text hereafter; many terrible illustrations to give you of it from the history of Modern Europe. I shall have to shew you that herein lay the great contradiction of the Mediæval Church, that which produced its most monstrous

corruptions. It thought that it could exist without distinct Nations, that its calling was to overthrow Nations. Therefore the great virtues which nations foster, Distinct Individual Conscience, Sense of personal responsibility, Veracity, Loyalty, were undermined by it; therefore it called good evil, and evil good; therefore it mimicked the Nations whilst it was trampling upon them; therefore it became more bloodthirsty than any Nation had ever been. It could not maintain the Kingdom of Peace; it must introduce the sword of the flesh into the region which was only to be defended by the sword of the Spirit; it must practically deny that there is a Universal Church upon earth, because it chose to set up a Society which instead of including the Nations annihilated them. We have received this lesson as a legacy from our forefathers. It is a lesson respecting the special temptation of us who call ourselves Churchmen, and who feel that we are bound at all times and in all places to vindicate the name. If we are asked to vindicate it by speaking meanly of the Nation, we answer that we know what comes of that. When our convictions are earnest religious persecution comes of it, religious wars if persecution is resisted. When our convictions are not earnest, when we do not care for what we believe, we may talk about Peace and call it by what grand names we will. But Peace will mean laziness, luxury, self-seeking; whatever is most unchristian; whatever tends to the loss of moral fibre and purpose; whatever favours the growth of slavery; whatever makes Society intolerable and ensures its destruction by internal decay or outward violence.

Very soon the reasonings of the advocates for Peace at any price, which started from the loftiest principles, drift into an appeal to the lowest motives by which men can be actuated. The Sermon on the Mount is made the groundwork for the suggestion that men should not be such fools as to throw away their money or their bodies for such a merely invisible, imaginary cause as the defence of native Law and of an Order which they have inherited. 'Why need our native 'Law be better than any other? Why may not 'the Order that we say our fathers bequeathed 'us be advantageously exchanged for one which 'exists in a country equally civilized with ours? If 'we did become portions of some great Empire, 'would its rulers interfere with our Commerce, 'hinder the transactions in our shops, even, ex-'cept for a while, seriously affect the movements 'of the Stock Exchange? The real tangible 'blessings would be all preserved to us; only the 'intangible—the sentimental—would be taken 'away.' You may perhaps have read books in which these positions are formally, nakedly maintained. Would that they might be always put forward broadly, distinctly, in clear printed letters! Then they are comparatively harmless; then there is enough left of heart in most of us to hate the

Arguments for peace at any price.

LECT. XI.
Whence they derive their force.

lie that is hidden in them if we cannot at once detect it by our understandings[1]. The mischief of them is that they are mixed with much benevolent talk about poor creatures who are starved or killed for the sake of a phantom, with much religious talk about the wickedness of sending men out of the world sinful and unprepared; so that we are disposed to entertain them as respectable and highly sensible suggestions, such perhaps as we are not quite prepared to accept in their length and breadth, but as are worthy of our consideration.

Let me strip them bare of their plausible accessories. It *is* very shocking that the lives of poor men or of rich men should be sacrificed to phantoms. The question is, What are phantoms? Should any one say, 'The desire for Empire, for 'the annexation of territory is a grisly phantom; 'for that no lives of poor or rich ought to be 'sacrificed,' I heartily subscribe to his opinion.

---

[1] I received not long ago a tract issued, I believe, by the Society for promoting Permanent and Universal Peace, and intended specially for the clergy. It was on the text "Thou canst not serve God and Mammon." Feeling the force and awfulness of that position and knowing how much need we have all to be reminded of it, I beg to thank the person or persons unknown who forwarded it to me. If I had wanted other reasons, the lesson which it inculcates would be decisive in hindering me from joining the Society I have named. Its arguments seem to me alternately—or else indiscriminately—addressed to the servants of God and Mammon, and on the whole to assume the dominion of the latter as the established and legitimate one.

Should he say, 'The advancement of Trade— *even of a trade so advantageous to certain per- *sons engaged in it as that in Opium—is an ugly *phantom, for which the life of no Englishman, *of no Chinaman, ought to be sacrificed,' we are still altogether in accord. But just because I deem the invasion of a nation's freedom and laws for the sake of Empire, or for the sake of supposed pecuniary profit, to be an accursed crime, I hold the defence of the freedom and law of a Nation against such attempts to be a sacred duty. I tell the benevolent men who care so much for the poor, that they are slaying the souls of the poor by teaching them that freedom and law are only phantoms for them, are only realities so far as they protect the properties of the rich. I tell them that they are sanctioning a doctrine which leads to the trampling down of the poor by the rich, to the ultimate victory of mere force over right. And I tell the religious men that if they lead any whether rich or poor to consider objects unreal because they are invisible, because they cannot be expressed in the terms of the money-market, their religion is a phantom, the vilest of phantoms. Is it not a phantom also if they forget that for certain invisible ends men, rich and poor, are bidden to lose their lives instead of saving them? Do they explain away that language or resolve it into nothing, and yet call themselves disciples of Christ?

These points being settled, I may leave what

LECT. XI.

Civilization often the favourite plea for the most unjust wars.

I have said already about the number and the popularity of Trade Wars to answer the rest of those pleas which are not really *for* Peace, but *against* the sanctity of national life. If we yield to these arguments we shall have wars enough on our hand; we shall be continually drifting into them. For we shall have no standard by which to try their worth; and reasons of self-interest will continually occur to us why just in this case, and in this, we may use the force we have to crush some feebler power. Our civilization will be a great and continual excuse. And we shall exhibit this sign of barbarism, that we measure civilization by our own standard, and treat nothing as civilized which is not in conformity with our maxims[1].

I have tried, not by laying down arbitrary maxims or by making artificial distinctions, but by examination of facts, to ascertain what is the true ground of that admiration for the deeds of Soldiers which we all have cherished, and do

[1] Though I cannot feel the admiration for Chinese civilization which seems to be indicated by Mr Bridges in the very able article which he has contributed to the Essays on International Policy, I cordially recognize the value of his observations on the arrogance of our behaviour towards a people who on one subject at least have shown that their morality is better than ours. I would also express my thankfulness to him and his brother Essayists for the honesty with which they have maintained, in opposition to many current sayings, that the sins of our Middle Class on the subject of wars are quite as flagrant as those of the aristocracy.

cherish, as much in this day as in any former day; what turns it into falsehood. The inscription at Thermopylæ, 'These three hundred died in obedience to the Laws,' expresses briefly and grandly what seems to me the true conception of the warrior's life in the earliest ages and the latest. They go because the Law commands them to go; they stand and fall at the bidding of the Law; they are witnesses for Law against the brute force of Numbers. All discipline is included in that comprehensive praise, all the personal valour, which we sometimes foolishly set in contrast to discipline. The heart of Sparta was in those men whom Persia could kill but not vanquish; each was a distinct living man standing in his place, doing his work, dying his death. There is no blaze of sentiment, no flourish of trumpets. The name of Leonidas lives; his followers would have wished it to live, for they trusted him and obeyed him. Their names have perished; none of them would have cared for that. The Law did not command them to be remembered; only to keep the pass. That obedience to Law is the soldier's characteristic. Losing it, he loses everything. Whilst he preserves it we must reverence him even when we reverence least the cause for which he suffers, the rulers who have exposed him to suffer. But when, as in the case of these Spartans, subjection to the Law is inseparably combined with the defence of the Law against those who would have put a Tyrant Will in the place of it,

Lect. XI.

Death for Law.

Obedience always venerable.

there the sentiment of admiration has no drawback; we are bound to indulge it; we are ashamed of ourselves when in any degree or under any pretext we withhold it.

The endurance of the Soldier always a legitimate object of admiration; his ferocity never.

If we put the case before ourselves in that way, we shall not be confused by the question whether we ought to restrain our respect for the soldiers who followed Napoleon to Moscow or from it, because our sympathies may be and ought to be with the Russians who drove them back. They were engaged in an attempt to destroy the law of another people; the crime of him who aimed at that destruction was great. His followers died in obedience to the only law which they knew; if they yielded to the anguish of cold, not to sabres or guns, it is not for us to make that an excuse for refusing them any sympathy or honour. But it will in all cases be the readiness to endure, not the wish to inflict, misery which will extort from us either sympathy or honour. There is a brutal appetite for slaughter which is in the nature of every soldier because of every man—which war would probably call forth in each of us as much as in any of whom we read. But we have sunk into a very low state if that is what we like to hear of—still more if we can joke about it. Be sure that no brave man will do that; it is fatal to bravery if it once becomes predominant in any of us. And for civilians who are free from the temptations of the soldiers to indulge in it is pitiful as well as hateful.

I am not afraid that this appetite for slaughter should be strengthened by the scientific contrivances for effecting it of which our age has been prolific. The possession of terrible instruments does not of necessity stimulate the desire to use them; we may tremble, as Roger Bacon is said to have done when the force of gunpowder was discovered to him, at the powers with which we are entrusted. No gift of Science is itself a curse, though every one may become a curse. The pursuit of Science, if it cannot extinguish Savagery, certainly does not cultivate it. The real fear is that the Soldier may himself become a machine; that he may look upon himself as merely engaged to do works of slaughter. All efforts should be made to save him and us from that fatal calamity. You will not save him from it by telling him that it was a mistake of former days to treat his profession as a noble one; that it is in truth a miserable trade. He may all too easily be persuaded to think so; what a trade he will make it when he does, we know too well. Nor will the Tradesman have at all a higher apprehension of *his* calling. He will suppose that it is better than that of the man who carries arms, because it does more to increase the material resources of the country; the common weal will mean nothing to him but the aggregate riches of its citizens. All that is really to be admired in him, his industry, his forethought, his fidelity, will be only regarded as means to the great end of Success; that will be the god which

The danger not in machines; but in the loss of manhood, either in Soldier or Tradesman.

LECT. XI.
The Soldier and the Tradesman ought each to have a greater reverence for his own calling than he has.

he worships. No one portion of a Nation gains by the depreciation of another; the whole Nation gains when every portion of it is raised to the highest level which has ever been imagined for it. Let us have much higher thoughts of our soldiers officers and men, than we have ever had; let us do what in us lies that they may have much higher thoughts of themselves. In a former course of Lectures I referred to the tone in which some eminent military men had spoken of the common Soldier, as if he could not have an individual conscience, as if it was dangerous that the conscience in him should be appealed to lest he should prove refractory to orders. I maintained that the security for his obedience lies in the cultivation of his conscience, that if he does not think he ought to die at his post, he will not die at his post. I maintained at the same time that the security for a Tradesman's fidelity to engagements lies in the cultivation of his conscience; that as no dread of punishment or of public opinion will keep the soldier from being a deserter if the sense of personal obligation perishes in him, so no dread of punishment or of public opinion will keep the Tradesman from being a rogue and a defaulter if the sense of personal obligation perishes in *him*. Each maxim has its counterpart in the sphere of Social Morality. In the Tradesman the sense of personal obligation will disappear if the feeling that he is a citizen, the member of a Nation, disappears. In the Soldier the sense of personal obligation will disappear if the feeling that he is a Citizen, the member of a Nation, disappears. The Tradesman despising the Soldier because he does not contribute to the material prosperity of the country will cease to be a Citizen. The Soldier despising the Tradesman from any vulgar conceit that his pursuits are degrading will cease to be a Citizen. The recent Volunteer movement in England has been a most healthful sign of approximation between different classes, a recognition of the national bond which holds them together. I trust if the impulse which first led to this movement loses its power, a vital principle will take the place of it. Unquestionably it cannot depend for its permanence on any mere fashion or any sudden fear. But since we have a standing army—since the objections which were once raised against it have become weaker, since it is recognised by all parties as one of the Institutions of our country—it is most needful that all who belong to it from whatever class they come, whatever position, high or low, they may occupy in it, should learn to connect their profession with their English life, to think of themselves only as defenders of a life which has endured for generations, and compared with which the animal life of each man, precious and venerable as that is, should be regarded as a very light thing. The diffusion of this belief and this spirit will be the great security that the discipline of the English Army shall be a blessing both to itself and to the whole people; that both its courage and its machinery shall be used for our protection and not for our ruin. I do not enter upon the question what might be the employments of an army in time of peace. A friend of mine once wrote a pamphlet on that subject, which struck me in my ignorance as full of valuable suggestions. How far they could be applied must be left to the consideration of men who have experience and knowledge. If the Moralist tells them what it is that we want of them, I am satisfied there is among our officers abundance of skill and insight to devise the means of supplying it. Continually also they exhibit a sense of righteousness as well as of tenderness and humanity, which might make members of my profession and of other professions ashamed.

The Camp and the City subject to the same principles. Nothing is so mischievous to them as to us—for nothing is so false—as the assertion or the assumption that the Camp must be less under the dominion of law and of moral principle than the City. It is that doctrine which has produced the licence of Camps, and is sure eventually to produce the licence of Cities.

The Navy. But I cannot forget that in English eyes the Navy has a kind of reverence which scarcely belongs to the other service. I would say one word as to that.

Some may suggest that on moral as well as on economical grounds it might be far better that our Mercantile Marine should stand highest in popular estimation; that ships of war, if there must be such, should only be considered as waiting

upon that. The opposite opinion—that which
gives the naval officer an honour that is not
awarded to the hardworking man of peace, who
often encounters dangers as great, and needs an
almost equal amount of knowledge, belongs, some
will say, to a barbarous tradition which for us
ought to be obsolete. I am most willing that any
traditions should become obsolete which lower any
class of useful citizens, or which establish merely
artificial maxims of precedence. But it seems to
me eminently desirable—greatly for the interests
of Morality—that those whose profession is to
defend a Nation should be more valued than
those who merely contribute to increase the wealth
of its particular members. Let the mercantile
sailor have all the honour that can be given him;
but his honour will be greatest if there is a class
doing in a great measure the same work with him,
whose lives are devoted to the common weal.
They vindicate for him the right to say: 'I too
'am the servant of the whole land; these goods
'which I exchange concern not only him who
'sells or him who buys; they are the signs and
'pledges of the intercourse between my people
'and the other peoples of the earth.' Then look
at the results of the opposite policy—the one
which some would urge upon us 'Our navy
waits upon our Commerce.' Exactly, and therefore all the private grudges of commercial men,
all the jealousies of merchants whose language
and habits are unlike their own, become causes of

LECT. XI.
The Mercantile Marine—why it should not be preferred to the Navy.

national quarrels; the guns of England must be always ready to avenge injuries real or imaginary done to her traffic. There has been too much, I apprehend, of this subjection to the mercantile marine by the navy already; if we wish for Peace we shall diminish rather than increase it.

<small>A nation ought not to be suspicious; an Empire must be.</small>

The doctrine *Si vis Pacem para Bellum* is not the one which I have maintained in this Lecture, though in some of my statements I may have appeared to justify it. I do not ask England to be augmenting its armaments through suspicion of its neighbours. Such suspicion is almost inevitable in Empires—even in Empires whose motto is Peace; the defence of a Nation should have another ground. Every Nation should be an armed Nation, not because it regards any other with hostility, not because it imagines that any other has an interest in assaulting it, but because its own soil, its own language, its own laws, its own government are given to it, and are beyond all measure precious to it. Any contempt of foreigners, any notion that we are better than they, is so much deduction from our strength, so much waste in braggadocio of the valour which is needed for the day of battle. Reverence for the rights and freedom of every Nation is what we should earnestly cherish if we would be true defenders of our own. On the other hand, I cannot set much store by a man's profession of interest in the well-being of strangers who is indifferent about the land of his fathers.

Courage or Valour has been deemed in old times the characteristic of a man. I cannot hold that opinion to be obsolete, nor can I think that there will be valour in us if we are indifferent about the defence of our Nation. That is a duty which devolves upon us all in our respective positions. There have been times and countries when the professors and students of a University have heard the call to join an army which was to drive foreigners from their soil; when they have obeyed it with as much alacrity as any who had been trained to the service. But at all times and in every land the call in some way to fight for the nation is addressed to old and young, to rich and poor, to man and woman. We may all by grovelling habits, by low thoughts, by vanity and insolence, be working for its downfall; each one struggling with these in himself, strengthening his neighbour against them, may be as much as any soldier or sailor its champion.

LECT. XI.
The demand for Valour.

LECTURE XII.

NATIONAL WORSHIP.

<small>Lect. XII.
Reference to Domestic Worship.</small>
In the last Lecture of my course on Domestic Morality I spoke of Family Worship. I was not unwilling that you should give that phrase its most modern sense; I wish to remind you always that we are members of Families as much as Jews or Greeks or Romans were in the days of old. But I spoke especially of *them*. In opposition to the theory that Worship is primarily suggested by the wish to account for natural phænomena or to produce some change in them, I urged you to notice the most obvious characteristics of the Homeric mythology. Wherever the Gods dwelt, whatever regions they governed, they were husbands, brothers, fathers; they were the founders of families in Greece or Asia; they formed a family above. When you assume that men in an early stage of cultivation were busy about the causes of the appearances in the earth or sea or sky, you are bound to explain how such

curiosity was awakened; to introduce a 'law of Nature' is a clumsy expedient, which breaks down when you need its help most. If men are reminded continually by the facts of their own existence that they have some origin and some relations, may we not admit the Homeric evidence as to worship without gainsaying? May we not suppose that it was more difficult to explain whence the hero derived the qualities which enabled him to establish a house or do brave deeds without referring to some divine parent, than to account for the rain or an earthquake? Lect. XII. The Domestic and National conceptions of Divinity often at strife with each other.

I observed that in the Homeric mythology, though it had this primary domestic element, there were abundant traces of a national condition. I did not dwell upon these; closely as they were blended with the others, it was possible to overlook them. It will occur to you that there is often a positive tendency in these two portions of the legends to break loose from each other. Zeus the Lawgiver seems another being from Zeus the Husband and Father. The two characters modify each other. His justice is perverted by his affections; they must be cast aside when he gives the nod. Evidently the conceptions were hard to reconcile. In the traditions of an older Society which Zeus overthrew and for which he substituted a fixed iron rule, the contrast becomes direct and palpable.

Which was to be preferred? There was the dream of a golden age hovering over the first.

LECT. XII.

The old and the new Government.

Justice asserting itself above fondness and favouritism.

Physical Observations.

The gods were benevolent, tolerant, in sympathy with men. There was the sense of Order and Government about the latter. Wrong was forbidden and repressed; there was a demand for submission and dread; a throne above. Caprice was not excluded from this throne; he who occupied it might be vindictive. Still Right must be the ground of it. There must be a God of Right; there must be a supreme Justice. It was not only the philosopher who repudiated any conceptions of the Godhead which were inconsistent with Justice; the practical lawgiver, if he could not put them aside, if he was compelled to bear with them, was yet impressed with the conviction and sought to impress it upon his countrymen that there was a Judgment-seat not swayed by any of the motives which affected visible Judges; that there was one, whatever might be his name, before whom they must tremble, by whom their acts would be reviewed.

The mixture of observations and experiences respecting the outward physical world with those which concerned human Society introduced much perplexity into the national as into the domestic Worship. But as the belief in Law and Government became stronger, the view of natural phænomena became much changed. Those who had acquired the habit of recognising an Order in their daily transactions with each other were compelled to suspect an Order, and therefore some person or persons who administered it, in day and night, in summer and winter; therefore to suspect also some meaning and motive where they could discern no succession, where all appeared anomalous and incoherent. Thus we can understand a circumstance which our modern interpreters of ancient beliefs find very puzzling, that the thoughts about divine powers should not, as they would desire, be most conspicuous in barbarous periods, should not diminish as men entered into civil Societies, but should grow with the growth and developement of these Societies; should become complicated with their complications. It must be so if the demand for such thoughts is inseparable from the Law, the Language, the Government, the Conflicts of a people; if they become most earnest when a people has most feeling that it is a people—most sense how grand their fellowship is, how many influences are threatening to destroy it.

Worship not banished but developed by political life.

Before I speak of the way in which Greek idolatry enfeebled the belief out of which it grew and weakened the fibres of national existence, I will turn to that worship which was especially a protest against homage to any forms of Nature, to any likenesses of beast or of man. I said in a former Lecture that the revolution of which Mr Maine speaks as implied in the transition from patriarchal to National life is noted in the Jewish records with singular emphasis. The Israelites in the land of Goshen have become the slaves of

The Hebrew worship.

the most organised despotism existing in the world—a despotism upheld by a powerful body of priests and magicians who interpret the phænomena of Egypt and use their knowledge or their ignorance for the exhibition of various marvels. A lonely shepherd in a desert hears a voice commanding him to go forth for the deliverance of his countrymen. The voice proclaims to him first the old Name, the God of Abraham, Isaac, and Jacob. The God of his fathers commands him trembling and reluctant to face the Ruler of Egypt. But another more awful Name is joined to this. The I AM is speaking to Moses. That is to be the ground of the Nation's existence. In that Name he defies the miracle workers. In that Name he bids the Egyptian let the people go. In that Name he leads the herd of slaves forth; he gives them a Law. They become a Nation; they speak a common language; they have a Government. Jehovah is declared to be the King; the author of the Law, the ruler and judge of those who administer it. In this Name they enter into battle marshalled according to their families and tribes. In this Name they conquer Palestine and divide it.

All this history might be represented—so it has often been by divines—as one which only concerns a particular nation of the old world, and has no relation to the national life of England, or France, or Italy, or Germany. But by some means or other the book of Psalms, which em-

NATIONAL WORSHIP. 229

bodies all the characteristics of the Jewish national worship, which is national in its outward costume as well as in its essence, has penetrated into every one of these modern nations, not as a foreign literature, which may be contemplated with a certain interest and a tolerable understanding by antiquarians, but as the expression of the inmost trust and conviction of men and women utterly unacquainted with antiquities, in the most practical and tremendous moments of their existence. No difference of habits, no questions about geography or chronology, no doubts about the circumstances in which these hymns and prayers were composed, no blunders of translators, have hindered them from becoming the living possession of a divided Christendom; from being equally received and recognised by Greeks, by Roman Catholics, by Protestants, as their rightful inheritance. That being the fact in this nineteenth century as well as in previous centuries, it becomes interesting to look at some of the more obvious features of a book which stretches over a long tract of history—how long we may not be able to ascertain, but certainly a period during which the Nation underwent the greatest vicissitudes in its economy and government, during which it passed through every alternation of prosperity and humiliation.

Lect. XII. Their profoundly national character.

I. In these Psalms 'the God of our fathers' is everywhere the ground of confidence, the refuge from the darkness of the past, from the confusions

The God of our Fathers.

of the present. No image of Him comes before the eye; it is from images that the man flies to Him. So the family is linked to the nation; the solitary sufferer to both. Israel lives on from generation to generation amidst all changes; for a living Being, who was and is and will be, has given it a portion in His immortality.

2. The other Name which was heard in the bush stands forth in its awful personality, bound inseparably to this. In its presence the man dares to confess himself a person; claims whilst he trembles to be one. Not a Law written in stones but the Lawgiver speaks to him; He speaks in thunders, yet the voice delights him. For He who speaks is RIGHTEOUS; the assertor of rights; the deliverer of those who have no helper from the oppressor. Righteousness is not a quality, not the attribute of a Person. These Psalmists know nothing of attributes. They worship the Righteous Being; all that is not righteous is His enemy. Whether it is in the world or in themselves they can appeal to Him against it; they believe, in spite of the fear which continually besets them, in spite of all contradictory appearances, that He will put it down.

3. Since the root of all their faith and all their prayers is He whom they invoke as the living and true God, since they invoke Him not as the God of earth or sea or air, but emphatically as the God of Israel, as their God, you will not wonder at the prominence which the Covenant

with them and with their fathers assumes in these prayers. When we dwell chiefly on considerations of property when that becomes the standard by which all things are measured, the vulgarest transactions of earth, mixed as they are with chicanery and overreaching, determine the meaning of this word; they are transferred to the highest region. But thus the sense of these prayers is inverted; the Jew, like the idolators against whom he protests, is supposed to make the divine acts the image of his own. The Covenant, as the Psalmists conceive of it, is the ground of all Covenants between man and man. It is the ground of faithful, honest speech, of that which fails from among the children of men because each one is trying to deceive his neighbour and has a double heart. That insincerity is the horrible plague and curse which the Psalmists cry to the God whose words are pure words, who hates lying, who is the same from generation to generation. The man is aware of the temptation to this insincerity in himself. He asks to be delivered from it, whether he is the victim of other men's treachery or of his own.

LECT. XII.

The ground of all human Covenants.

4. I said that these prayers and songs belong to various periods of the commonwealth. Whether any of them were poured out before the kingly age may be doubtful; there can be no question that they extend to times when there were no kings, to years of captivity in another

Loyalty not dependent on circumstances.

land; to those when Judæa had rulers like Ezra and Nehemiah, whether they bore civil or sacerdotal titles. But Loyalty is one of their most conspicuous characteristics. It has seemed both to Jews and Christians so absorbing a one, that the name of David has in spite of chronology and direct internal evidence been associated with them all. A great truth has been concealed under that error. The Shepherd boy, the rival of Saul, the actual Monarch of Israel, is discovering his need of an invisible King, is learning by the bitterest experiences in all stages of his life that if there is not one to whom he may appeal in his weakness, from whom he derives his strength, he must be a victim of oppression or an oppressor, his life and his people's life must be a contradiction and a lie. Loyalty therefore must be in the King, if it is to be shewn to the King. He must confess a law which binds him; a law which does not bend to his self-will, which will assert its dominion over him and punish him if he sets it at nought. It is all very well to claim his people's obedience. It will not be rendered to him if *he* is not an obedient man. He may be the Lord's anointed; that does not mean that he can do what he likes; it means exactly the reverse of that; it means that he is not his own master; that he is only the people's master so far as he understands himself to be their Shepherd, raised up by One who cares for them more than he does, to rule them for their good. David and Solomon have all the temptations of Oriental Monarchs; gratify their lusts; multiply wives. The national Law does not prohibit these habits, mischievous as the history shews them to be. Something more than Law is needed for their cure. But it can do this. Whilst they long to be emperors, it reminds them that they are kings of a Nation; that if they trample upon Right, Right will prove too strong for them. That lesson survives for their descendants. The seers could be loyal when the monarchs were disloyal; loyal when all outward witnesses of the dominion of Law and a divine Lawgiver had ceased, when a man, exhibited in some Babylonian conqueror, appears to be supreme in earth and heaven. It is then that they enter into the very secret of Loyalty; then the past history of their land becomes dearer and more sacred to them than in their prosperity; then they are sure that the King who reigned of old is reigning still; then they are sure that He will reign for ever and ever. *The King lasts for ever.*

5. As the name of King of Kings lies at the centre of all these hymns, so does that of Lord of Hosts. The Psalms are eminently warlike; Israel is at battle in them with foes visible and invisible; its only hope is in a God who is fighting for it; who has called it to fight His battles. One cannot compel these writers to adopt the formula that defensive wars are justifiable, offensive never. The wars for dispossessing Palestine of its inha- *The Lord of Hosts.*

bitants were offensive; yet the victories of Joshua and his successors are subjects of thanksgiving. There is the strongest belief that those were wars of the Lord; that they drove out an utterly corrupt and debased people; that they established in their place a Nation which was to be a witness for Order and Right. Not that these writers boast of their countrymen as better than other men. The Psalms are full of confessions and complaints; full of anticipations that the same evils will, in every case, bring the same punishments, because a righteous Lord is King over all. But there is also a strong clear conviction that all the evils of the Israelites arose from their not believing that they were a Nation; from the covetousness and pride, the transgression of family order and civic order, which separated them from each other; which caused each man to think he had an interest apart from his neighbour. These habits of mind would assuredly bring invasions upon them from the great Empires round about them; they were mimicking these Empires; their monarchs wanted to have horses and chariots like the Babylonians; they were like them busy about guessing as to the future; they were trembling before powers of Nature; trying to find Gods in the outward world or to make Gods in their own likeness. They would have their way, and their way would bring ruin upon their land.

Such are a few of the notable features in a book which has taken hold of the thought and life of the Western Nations, of Nations prone to all the habits against which the Psalmists are praying and protesting; prone to disbelieve in a Righteous Being and to conceive of some capricious Power as ruling over Men and Nature; prone to falsehood in speech and in act; prone to forget the connection between Loyalty and Law; prone to fall into Wars for all selfish and unrighteous purposes, and then to affect a horror of war for any purposes. There is not a curse which threatens the life of England, of France, of Germany, of Italy as a Nation—not a disposition that has destroyed the individual strength and the reverence of neighbours for each other—which these Hebrew singers have not felt to be undermining the life of Israel and their own, against which they have not asked the help of the God of Righteousness. In spite of that fact—may I not rather say by reason of that fact —Englishmen, Frenchmen, Germans, Italians, have preferred those Hebrew devotions to any which have grown up among themselves, which have been shaped and coloured according to their customs and modes of thinking.

It has been strongly asserted in our day, by thoughtful and accomplished men, that there is in England an excess of what they call the Hebraic habit of mind, and that it ought to be qualified if not superseded by that which they describe as the Hellenic. I have shewn you already, that— little claim as I have to the artistic perception

LECT. XII. and refinement which characterise those who are imbued with Greek scholarship—I yet reverence at a distance the truth which discovers itself to me in the Homeric poems and in the Tragedies of a later age, as well as in the writings of the philosophers who sometimes complained of both.

<small>Hebraic exclusiveness, what comes of it.</small> So far as any persons undertake to magnify the Hebrew temper for the sake of disparaging the Greek, I think they are doing more injury to that which they praise than to that which they censure. They are denying that union of Jew and Greek in the complete man of which the Christian Apostle speaks; they are introducing that kind of Judaism which was his great antagonist. But am I honouring the Greek habit of mind by glorifying it at the expense of the habits which I have been describing? Rather I am eliminating from it that which has made it noble, that which has won the honour <small>Hellenic exclusiveness, what comes of it.</small> and affection of sincere men for it. They have felt that beneath all the corruptions to which Greek history and its literature bear such abundant testimony, there lay a belief in Law and Order, a sense of personal responsibility, a protest against falsehood, a loyalty, a patriotism, which no popular delusions and superstitions, no sophistry of rhetoricians could extinguish. They have felt that the Greek worship, however mixed with notions of supernatural caprice and baseness, did yet account the qualities which are opposed to caprice and baseness as the essentially divine. Because it did so, the art of poets and sculptors which was so

much interwoven with this worship could discover **LECT. XII.**
in the human objects that it contemplated, an ideal
which was above them though it did not interfere *The Arts of the Jew and the Greek.*
with their reality. The Hebrew, limited it may be
to two arts, music and poetry—since of his architecture we can only form guesses—used these to
express his sense of a perfect Truth and Unity, the
ground of all Truth and Unity in men. He sang
of a Lawgiver to whom each man was responsible,
of a God of the Nation who called on each man to
live for it and die for it. What do you suppose
would become of Greek life and art if all which
these Hebrews confessed were by some process
separated from them? You need not be at the
pains of speculating. You may contemplate that
life and that art when they had passed or nearly
passed into this condition; when Gods of caprice
alone were worshipped; when men recognised
them as their own creation and yet trembled before them; when philosophers laughed at such
service and practised it because it was good for
the multitude, and because the objects of it might
be as true as anything else. Is that the Hellenic *Hellenic Art without truth popular in old and modern days.*
habit of mind which we of the modern age are
to cultivate? Alas! the exhortation to cultivate
it is wholly needless. There is none which we
are so ready to adopt; no discipline is required
to perfect us in it. But whether, when we have
acquired it thoroughly, when all which resists it in
us is cast away, we shall care more for Hellenic
literature and history than for Hebraic may be

a question. I think it possible that we shall care less for English history, English literature, the English Nation, than for either.

What will pure Hellenism do for Science?

I have spoken of Art because we naturally associate that with Greece. But how will Science fare if all Hebrew elements are cast out of our minds and we are left to the influence of naked Hellenism? Then all the objections which scientific men raise against religious men for introducing an irregular and disturbing force into the order of Nature will be aggravated a thousandfold. For 'He spake and it was done,' 'He commanded and all things stood fast,' for the continual appeals in the Psalms to 'a Law given to things that they cannot transgress,' will be substituted endless vicissitudes, the likelihood of miracles at every moment. A habit of doubting whether anything is, whether all things are not the creatures of the eyes which behold them, would be far more than we now guess the prevalent one in our minds if we were left without that apprehension of a fixed government over ourselves which we do not derive from the Greeks, whatever else they may have taught us.

The horror of Sacrifices as bribes to the divinity Hebraic not Hellenic.

To the Jew again we owe that tremendous indignation and scorn which breaks forth in the Psalmists and the Prophets against those who fancy that the righteous Lord can be bribed by Sacrifices to alter His purposes or mitigate His Laws. These denunciations express the very meaning of the Jewish economy. It does not dispense with Priests and Sacrifices; they are parts of the national Order; they are declared to depend like all other parts of it upon the everlasting Lawgiver. But because they *are* part of the nation's Order, because they proceed from its Lawgiver, they cannot interfere with His order, they cannot be contrivances for escaping His judgments. They are declared to be His signs and pledges of reconciliation with His subjects; the worshipper gives up some dead thing as a witness that he gives up himself; that he repents of any acts which have had their root in self-will and disobedience. So the belief which was latent in the Greek Sacrifices is brought clearly to light, the falsehood which produced their direst superstitions and crimes—as it has produced the darkest superstitions and crimes in every age and country of the world—is also detected and exposed.

<small>LECT. XII.
They belong to the Nation's Order, which they cannot set aside.</small>

I shall be told that the interest in these Jewish devotions has nothing whatever to do with our English or French or German sympathies; that lonely suffering men conscious of their personal evils, caring nothing about the politics of kingdoms, are those who chiefly delight in them. My answer is this. An Englishman, a Frenchman, a German does not shake off the recollection that he is an Englishman, a Frenchman, a German because he is in a solitary chamber, because he is racked with personal suffering, because he is awake to evils which he has done. Much of his suffering, much of his remorse, will

<small>These Devotions would not appeal to individual if they did not appeal to national feelings.</small>

be connected with thoughts of fellow-citizens whom he has known, who have injured or neglected him, whom he has injured or neglected. The chains of neighbourhood may never be more keenly felt, may never enter more as iron into the man's soul, than when he seems to be most thrown upon himself. But suppose him by any artificial contrivances to have weaned himself from all national attachments — suppose him to be wholly wrapped up in the thought of his own felicity or misery present or future—or suppose him to look upon himself only as belonging to some school or sect, or only as a cosmopolite—then I say that if he mumbles these Psalms twenty times a day, they will be merely dead sounds to him; if he would extract any meaning from them he must reduce them into feeble allegories; he may talk about them, but they will not speak to him; he may try to think about them, but they will not express his thoughts.

So I apprehend it was with the Jew himself when he like the Greek became incapable of national life—*incapable* of it, I say; for when he had lost all the signs and pledges of it he may yet have longed for it, and then no utterances will have been more real and dear to him than those of the Psalms. But there did assuredly fall upon the most conspicuous men in his land—upon those who were highest in religious reputation, those who were so numerous a sect that a popular writer ridicules our ignorance for describing them as a

NATIONAL WORSHIP. 241

sect at all[1]—such a contempt for the people of the land, such a sense of their own superiority to the ordinary child of the Covenant as must have made them wholly incapable of entering into the belief of the Psalmist in a Lord God of Israel. They might glorify themselves for not worshipping the Gods of the countries in which they settled or with which they traded. They might, in the Reviewer's phrase, be "men of progress"—men who belonged to the present not the past, who had quite outgrown the pastoral or agricultural habits of a previous period, who believed in Commerce and applied a commercial standard to all their transactions with Heaven as well as earth. But the Law for them was one graven in stones; one to be exceedingly reverenced because it was *their* law—not a law proceeding from the mouth of a Deliverer whom they could trust. Words must have shrivelled into letters—as letters to be honoured and called divine. *Loyalty;* toward whom was that to be exercised? To the Priest perhaps, if he was of the proper sect; but chiefly to

The Pharisees.

Their respect for Law.

Their Loyalty.

---

[1] See the celebrated article on the Talmud in the *Quarterly Review*. The eulogist of the Pharisees clenches his position by saying, that it is as absurd to call them a sect as to call Roman Catholics a sect in Rome, or Protestants a sect in London. I do not see the force of the argument. I do feel the point of the sarcasm. That a Sect loses its venom by becoming large and powerful appears to me the most extravagant of paradoxes. That Protestants and Roman Catholics may be most sectarian when they are most large and powerful I sorrowfully believe.

LECT. XII.

Thoughts of a King and Deliverer.

the oracle of the Sect; to him who could best adapt old traditions to modern circumstances. A prince of the house of David might possibly arise; if the Herodian family was in the ascendant, the question how far it should be accepted as a fact or resisted by intrigues must be an open one. The Lord of Hosts might still be an object of wild irregular hope to the poor, a charm for some brigand champion to work with; the rich and comfortable would be thankful to the Roman Governor for quelling such disturbers. The Sectarian Morality in this case, as in all cases, was certain to extinguish the National Morality, unless that received some unlooked-for renovation; unless the prayers which Psalmists had poured forth for a deliverer of the Nation and of all Nations received an answer.

Such an answer might be as needful for the Conqueror of the Jew as for the Jew himself.

Roman Faith.

I said that I should have occasion to speak of the Roman faith as a political faith in the best and the worst sense of that word. You will not wonder now that I should acknowledge a "best"

Essentially National.

sense. A faith which is not political, which has nothing to do with Law, with Language, with Government, with Battles, is, it seems to me, not a faith in a righteous Being, a distinguisher of Right and Wrong, not faith in a Being who is true and who seeks truth in men, not faith in an object of Trust and Loyalty, not faith in a Source of Valour or Courage. Let it be ever so domestic—and I have said that the first element of Roman faith was domestic, the authority of the Father—let it make ever so much effort at universality, and we shall see hereafter how Roman worship in later days aspired to this merit—there will be in it no groundwork for that kind of character which we describe as manly, which was comprehended in the Virtus of the Republic.

LECT. XII.
Virtus.

Cicero is thoroughly sincere when he connects worship with Laws; when he does, though he may derive phrases or illustrations from his Greek teachers, he speaks as a Roman. As an Academician he could see certainty in nothing, least of all in any speculations about the divine nature. As a Citizen he felt the most unshaken conviction that there must be a ground for social life and social morality, that what is most right must be most divine. Fables about the Gods which he might accept or reject as a fit drapery for his belief did not touch the core of it; that was in a Lawgiver and Judge whom no fancy, no intellect could make or unmake.

Cicero; his sincerity.

But in his heart, as in the hearts of his countrymen, the profoundest insincerity lay hard by this honest and ineradicable conviction. There must be a divine ground of Law, said the inner conscience of the Nation and of the patriot. How necessary it is to *assume* such a ground that Law may be upheld, that men generally may respect it, said the lower nature of the man justifying itself

His insincerity.

by the calculations of a sordid expediency. We must make men observers of their words by feigning to recognise a God of truth! We must cheat men into loyalty, seeing how little there is to awaken it in self-seeking rulers, by threatening them with the vengeance of the Gods if they are disloyal! We must ask the augurs, scarcely able to refrain from laughing at each other as they meet, to invent supernatural reasons for rushing into wars or avoiding them; else how shall the soldier keep his oath to his commander, or not forget his discipline, or not shrink from the enemy when he should face him? Here was the hateful and accursed side of the worship, that which made it acceptable to the mere Magistrate, that which made it incredible to such men as Lucretius, who were sure that there must be in nature if there was not among men some order which was not based upon trickery and lies.

Not the philosophy of Epicurus but the dissolution of the Republic was to demonstrate the hollowness of such a System. A Nation cannot stand upon fictions. An Empire may demand them as its necessary supports. But an Empire introduces another division of Social Morality. The Battle of Actium signified not to Italy only but to Egypt, to Greece, to Palestine, to every country under heaven that Nations for a while were at an end. A world in which nations should be buried had been long preparing. It now came forth with the hero of proscriptions as its

Monarch and its God. That is the first form under which Universal Society presents itself to us in Modern History. We shall have to consider what Morality was implied in it, and whether any other Universal Society is possible.

LECT. XII.
Transition to the new Age.

LECTURE XIII.

UNIVERSAL MORALITY.

(1) *THE UNIVERSAL EMPIRE.*

<small>Lect. XIII.</small>

'I AM the member of a Family;' 'I am the Citizen of a Nation,' these are assertions which each of us confidently repeats to himself, about which he entertains no scepticism. Am I *only* the member of a family; *only* the member of a Nation? At a certain crisis in our lives this question, which has often been stirring within us before, is fully presented to us. This domestic circle has been unable to confine me within it. Can the Law, the Language, the Government, the Hostilities of a particular country confine me? Do I not belong to a larger Society, what is called a WORLD?

<small>Internal impatience of National boundaries.</small>

We have seen from the example of the first Social Moralist to whom I referred in these Lectures that this word is not necessarily a very comprehensive one. It denoted to Chesterfield, it has denoted to many, a peculiarly narrow Society; one the virtue of which consists in its narrowness. A

<small>The 'World' may be very small.</small>

number of other worlds entirely unlike that of Chesterfield, but possessing this characteristic, attract or repel us when we reach the verge of manhood. They offer a gratification to certain tastes which we are cherishing, a promise that we shall be associated chiefly with those who share the same tastes. We hear of a literary world, a scientific world, a sporting world, a religious world. Each of these worlds may have different hemispheres; those who dwell in one may not be able to endure the atmosphere of the other. The name therefore must receive rather a negative definition. It must signify that the inhabitants of these worlds are *not* admitted into them in virtue of any ties of blood or of country. The bond of their fellowship, whatever it be, is *not* this.

LECT. XIII.

Its negative definition.

Any one of these exclusive Societies may have a charm for us because it appeals to our choice. The family, the Nation, are given to us. Here is an opening into a region which we can compare with other regions, which we can adopt because it accords with dispositions or is likely to develope powers that seem to be specially ours. But though that which we select may be a world of its own, turning on its own axis or revolving about some sun which illuminates no other, the phrase 'man of the world' denotes one who is not a member of any such limited circle. We take him to be a person who may fall into any Society and feel no embarrassment in it, but who entirely refuses to be tied by the maxims, customs, beliefs of one

The 'Man of the World.'

or another. He floats at large—can adapt himself to the circumstances of every country or class, observes them acutely, perhaps with contempt, perhaps with pity, as far as possible with indifference, is entangled by no strong sympathies or antipathies, can use men to accomplish his purposes if he has ambition or avarice or any other passion to gratify, but can also dispense with them if he finds them inconvenient, or if other tools suit him better. That is nearly I think what we understand by a man of the world. There may be varieties of the species. The French man of the world may not be exactly like the English man of the world; may have fewer angular points, and therefore may fulfil the character more perfectly. No national peculiarities ought to enter into his composition; no family affections. They evidently weaken his forces, impair his completeness.

Such a model as this many set before themselves when they are approaching the age in which mere citizenship, as well as mere domestic ties become insufficient for them, when they are aware that they have grown not in thews and bulk alone, that the inward service of the mind and will has waxed wide withal and demands a wide society for its exercise. But to some who have reached the same stage, who are conscious of the same necessities, the question occurs, 'May not a MAN, perhaps, be more than a man of the world? If we can be thoroughly men shall not we enter more not less into fellowship with all people, and kindreds than he does? Shall we not have fellowship with what they *are*—not only as seems to be his case with the outside of them—with what they seem and are *not*? Having arrived by whatever process at that intercourse, shall we not understand better what *our* country is to us—what *his* country is to every neighbour, what our family is to us, what his family is to him? Shall we not be more thoroughly individual, be less lost in a crowd? These thoughts have worked and are working in us, side by side with the desire to have the credit and dignity of being men of the world. I apprehend that the chief business of a University is to ripen such hopes, to shew how they may be accomplished. If it does that—if it is, in the truest sense, a school of Humanity—it will also explain to its members how one may have a calling to this pursuit, one to that—how one may devote himself to Science, one to Letters, one to Politics, yet without being enclosed in an artificial, exclusive world, rather with the power of shewing how every study and work discovers some spring of life in man which without it would be closed.

We have always observed, thus far, that there is a correspondence between our own personal experience and the larger experience which makes up History. The transition from the patriarchal to the legal period—the shock which accompanies the transition, we noticed in both alike. To this amazing crisis through which we all more or less consciously pass, from the national to the universal condition, where shall we turn for a resemblance? If the remarks which I made at the close of the last Lecture are true, the point of comparison is marked enough. Just at the commencement of our era, at the moment in which Octavius Cæsar became lord of the World, did the age of Nations pass away with a great noise, did the universal age begin. What was to come of that universal age, whether nations were or were not in its womb, was to be declared hereafter; that it opened with the extinction of them, there can be no doubt. We have not to infer, as in the crisis spoken of before, some great revolution; nothing is more patent and notorious than the Revolution by which this the third period of historical development was inaugurated.

I do not, of course, limit the Revolution to the mere struggle of Antony and Augustus which brought it to its close. Figures far more striking and interesting than these had appeared in the earlier scenes of the Drama. Of old we used to speak of Brutus with some reverence; those who withstood Cæsar were thought to have been honest patriots if they took a wrong way of exhibiting their patriotism. Modern scholars command us to abandon such notions. Julius Cæsar, they say, understood his time as no one else did. His opponents were stupid pedantic worshippers of the past. His merits have been put upon another ground by his imperial biographer and panegyrist. Roman republican History, he says, exhibits only a conflict of orders. Julius Cæsar was the intelligent champion of equality; he was preparing the way for the only kind of government in which the Will of the Majority could become faithfully embodied and enforced. I submit to these authorities so far as the question is one which their learning or their practical experience is competent to decide. I accept the statement that Julius Cæsar had a remarkable, an unparalleled, understanding of his own time; that he was hampered by no traditions of the past; that he had no prejudices of any kind which hindered him from using any class of his countrymen for the object which he had set before himself; that he had a culture which placed him on the level of the highest orators, statesmen, even sages among Romans; that he had a capacity for government which made him able to manage the tempers and passions of barbarians; that he was perfect in the knowledge as well as in the temper which could win the confidence of the legions; that he was able to use the advantages of his birth or throw them aside if so he might conciliate the mass of citizens; that he thoroughly appreciated the decay of morality in Roman families; that he deliberately, as his greatest admirer declares, corrupted the matrons of Rome for the sake of his political objects. Being free from old Roman prejudices and principles, from all scruples of conscience, he did assuredly possess in a high, even in a transcendent

LECT. XIII.

Cæsar the champion of Equality.

His emancipation from all domestic and national restraints.

degree—the qualities of 'a man of the world;' he presented even a typical specimen of that character because he rose above it, because he had a geniality, a sort of half humanity, which properly forms no part of it. So far I yield to his panegyrists. I allow that the most profligate man in Rome had a clearer comprehension of what Rome had become than any of his contemporaries. I allow that he could not have used his profligacy so effectually, if he had not retained in the midst of it a nobleness which he did not derive from it. And I subscribe *ex animo* to the decision of a Judge who speaks not as a mere scholar, but (as he constantly intimates) from an observation of later times, that where Society has through a series of self-seeking plots fallen to the depths which Rome had reached during the civil wars, an Empire is its inevitable destiny.

Let so much be conceded. But when these Cæsarists further require us to reverence a man because he was without reverence for the laws of the household or the institutions of his country; when they require us to despise those who could not give up the dream, that there was an order which might be maintained—who could not accept the destiny of being subject to a military despot—we have a right to say, 'We will not obey you, whether you are scholars or emperors, for this is not a question which with all your wisdom you can decide for us. The question is whether it is a duty to worship success; whether we are to canonize triumphant wrong and to treat those as fools who struggled to the last for the right. We are not safe in doing that if all the historians joined with all the crowned heads in Europe to enjoin it.'

<small>LECT. XIII.</small>

The best justification of those who urge such a course upon us is undoubtedly this, that a man of a much vulgarer and baser character than Julius Cæsar ultimately achieved the dominion of which he was deprived. I have acknowledged already that such a result in the state to which Rome had fallen could not have been averted. I feel the fitness of the doom that the coarse and bloody hands of Octavius rather than the more graceful hands of his predecessor should have executed it. Nor do I, as I have shewn you already, look upon the change only as a degradation and a curse. The passage from the National into what I have called the Universal period, I hold in itself to have been an elevation and a blessing. Which words apply best to the Universal Society that owned Augustus as its founder I will now enquire.

<small>The actual Empire.</small>

1. I do not credit the Empire with the downfall of domestic life in the city or the provinces. I have accepted the testimony of a highly competent if a somewhat partial witness, that this had taken place already, that it was a most important and needful preparation for the Empire. I would only observe, that the precedent of the

<small>The overthrow of domestic virtues.</small>

illustrious Dictator was certainly not lost sight of by those who acquired the higher title. No angry language of Christian advocates, or of Pagan Satirists, should be invoked to establish that fact. Gibbon was certainly neither one nor the other, but an historian studious of facts, with a very fashionable, a most unpuritanical standard of morality. Certainly one would ask for no evidence that he has not accepted. I would rather that three-fourths of that evidence had never been produced or could be forgotten. Are we to conclude from it that there was no reverence for parents left, no affection between husbands and wives? There is enough in Tacitus to confute such a dark supposition, to shew how deeply he honoured such virtues; how convinced he was that they subsisted still among some of high birth like Germanicus and Agrippina, among some officials like his own father in law; how sure he was that they must be brought back through a barbarous race if they forsook the civilised world. His pictures may be treated by modern scepticism as merely fantastic. But whence came the fancy? That was not an imperial gift. It dwelt in a man who hated the Empire; who clave however hopelessly to the fallen Nation.

All protests against this decay associated with regrets for the Nation.

Law affirmed to be the Emperor's voice.

2. That Nation had stood on *Law*. Law was now declared to proceed from the mouth of the Emperor. He affirmed the Law to be his law. He knew inwardly that it was not his Law. He knew that he had received it from other ages.

The Jurisconsults, a brave and splendid race of men, did their best to make him and his subjects understand that the law was not of to-day nor of yesterday, that there were principles in it, which might be drawn out of it, formally asserted, applied to new cases. When they could not expand a law which was meant for a nation to suit all the demands of a world, they invented the notion of a Law of Nature—one which anticipated all formal law and applied to every race equally. What contradictions are involved in this conception Mr Maine has pointed out with his customary clearness and ability. With his customary candour he has shewn that there was a truth latent in the contradiction; that it was an effort to find some other basis for law than arbitrary will. The Roman Law unquestionably was able to reach the other countries of the world because they were under the Roman yoke. In that sense it may be said that the universal Empire conferred a benefit on them. But Law had itself a national ground; it was a silent protest against the principle on which the Empire rested; though it was obliged to tolerate that principle. We may see hereafter that it has only been a blessing to the nations of modern Europe so far as they are nations; so far as it has helped them to feel that the will of a man is *not* the source of Law.

Lect. XIII.

The Jurisconsults of the Empire practical protestants against it.

The Law of Nature.

3. From the phrase 'Augustan Age' which was so much used in the last century and has

descended to ours, it might be concluded that a new and brilliant epoch for the Latin language began with the establishment of the Empire. It is an obvious remark that the poets or historians who illustrated that age were all formed under the Republic, that Horace had fought, with however little distinction, under the standard of Brutus, that Virgil's experiences of the effects of the civil war in Italy were sufficient to account for his readiness to hail any one who could restore peace. Such observations would not account for the eminent writers of the, so called, silver age; for Seneca, Tacitus, the two Plinys, and Quintilian, or among poets Lucan, Persius, Juvenal. If the hearts of some of these were in the old time, they had unquestionably been subject to all the influences of the new. Seneca's philosophy had as little of a national impress as his life. He aimed at universality in the one; he was the parasite if he was the victim of his pupil. These accomplished men, so unlike each other, had yet one common characteristic which separated them from their predecessors. Cicero lived emphatically in his time; he recurred to the past for examples to guide the present; though he complained of the toils of the Forum, of the perturbations of parties, though he found a relief from them in letters and philosophy, he never doubted that his business was among them, that he had no right to stand aloof from them. The eloquent men under the Empire might still plead causes; if they were friends of the ruler they might govern provinces. But they were studying composition rather than frankly expressing themselves. The world around them chiefly supplied them with topics of lamentation or of bitter sarcasm. When that is the case with the wise men—the men of letters—there cannot be much communion between them and the ordinary citizen. Language cannot be that covenant of individuals and classes with each other which I have supposed it to be. So when we pass the bounds of the first century it is no longer to Latin that we turn for the truest and deepest expressions even of Roman life. Plutarch of Chæronea has more to tell us of the old heroes of the Republic than any who boasted descent from them, because he can compare them with Greeks. Philosophy, different aspects of which Lucretius and Cicero forced their own language to represent even if they sometimes complained of its stubbornness, no longer makes that effort. Even an Emperor thoroughly determined to be a Roman, yet finds that he can converse with himself best in Greek. If you reflect on these facts you will feel that the change which the Empire wrought in the feelings of its subjects respecting Law was scarcely greater than its effect on Language.

4. There is a great delusion latent in the expression 'form of Government' when it is applied to the Empire. It was not a change from Republican forms to a Monarchical form; Augustus scru-

pulously adhered to the old names, maintained the offices which were attached to them. He only drew the forms to himself, or round himself. He only said, 'I, the Imperator, claim all these forms 'as subject to me. They are nothing apart from 'me.' In other words he said, The notion of something permanent in civil Society which may not be set at nought by any temporary master has passed away. The General, the Head, and the King, he who commands the physical force of a Land and of its provinces, he is the Lord of all; whatever ancient titles he bears himself or tolerates in others mean nothing, if they are restraints upon his pleasure.

That is the imperial *doctrine;* I do not say that the doctrine faithfully represented *facts*. The ancient titles had a might which no decrees could annul. The loyalty which they once called forth could not be utterly extinguished in deference to brute force. The name of Consul lasted till the age of Justinian; it might be chiefly a sham and a mockery; but it had a signification almost to its final day. Besides the old republican forms imparted a shape to the provincial governments, teaching military Governors that they might be the authors of a civil order among barbarians. These forms were therefore checks, if ineffectual checks, upon mere arbitrary will; but to describe them as parts of the imperial System because it was not able to cast them off or make them absolutely its ministers, is surely monstrous. The

Oriental type was that which the Empire as such was always striving to acquire; in the age of Diocletian the aspiration was almost realised. The monarch of Nicomedia was not necessarily troubled with the traditions of Italy; he could encourage his colleagues in the West to shake them off.

<small>LECT. XIII.</small>

<small>Age of Diocletian.</small>

5. I approach the subject which all feel to be most important in speaking of the Empire. Its name, its origin, its continuance, all point to the function of the Soldier. He had been the defender of a Nation; wherever he had gone forth in wars of conquest, it was still to spread and glorify the national name. His discipline exhibited the submission of animal force to a commanding word, his courage the personal valour which is called forth in those who feel themselves bound by a common interest, united in a common cause. He had been taught in the civil wars—specially by the great darling of the Legions—that he had in his hands the weapons which could break down national barriers, which could make him supreme. The lesson was formulised by the Empire. The General was the chief not of a Nation, but of a World. The Army was a world power; all relics of national existence could not but look very paltry in its eyes. Yet they had a charm for it. The old oath, the traditional respect for Law, could survive great shocks. The Jurisconsults, whilst they saw the terrible force of the legions, did not despair of binding them with some of the withes and cords which in violent moments they had often

<small>The Legions.</small>

<small>The defenders of order becoming conscious of a power to destroy it.</small>

17—2

rent asunder. But restraints upon the army were in fact restraints upon the Empire. And it soon begun to be evident that the collision of *these* forces—the rising of the servants against the Master, their choice of some rival Master—would shew what the blessing of an Empire is. With great satisfaction the modern biographer of Julius Cæsar has dwelt upon the strife of orders in the Republic. Is there to be no sequel to that history setting forth in lively contrast the tranquillity of the military Despotism which displaced it?

6. Lastly, I come to the Imperial Worship. Wherein did it differ from the National Worship? No altar was displaced. The priests and augurs were what they had been; every god kept his place in the Pantheon. If there was a change in respect to foreign religions, it was on the side of increased toleration. The maxim that any kind of worship might be allowed and even encouraged which was not detrimental to public order and did not interfere with allegiance to Rome, must have become more fixed as the dominion extended, when it was confessedly a world dominion. Therefore so far as Worship consists of a routine of Services, the transition from the Republic to the Empire cannot have affected it. If there was a growth of Scepticism it was only a growth; the seeds were deep in the hearts of Romans when Augustus was hailed as their deliverer, their new God. Gibbon's dictum that to the people all religions seemed equally true, to the philosophers all

equally false, to the Magistrate all equally useful, is too epigrammatic, too evidently generalized from the experience of the 18th century, to be of much value. About the people he knew very little, either in his own time or in the time of which he wrote; his conclusion about the philosophers was borrowed from those who contributed to the Encyclopédie. The clause respecting the Magistrates may, however, be accepted. What a religion could do to keep up the dread of government in one tribe or another was the measure of its worth. If ignorant men and women trembled at the thought of Gods who might crush them, the trembling might be dangerous or helpful. The Divinity might be invoked by patriotic priests against the visible ruler; by dexterous management the priests might be converted into the servants of the ruler; the supernatural vengeance might be directed on the heads of those who defied him. Such calculations may have seemed highly reasonable to the conquerors of provinces in the former time. The difference was that the conception of a righteous and true Being, which had struggled with this policy during the Republic—which had been at the root of its worship—was necessarily banished from the imperial theory. The Emperor was the standard of Godhead. His power was the image of the highest, of the universal, Power. He did homage to heavenly powers no doubt. He wanted their aid. But he was to all intents and purposes the God of the earth. If

Lect. XIII.

Gibbon's celebrated dictum; how far true.

The Emperor the real God of the Earth.

the gods above protected him, he also protected them. They retained their authority by his permission. It would be a fair exercise of his prerogative that he should increase their number. He could not permit that any of them, more than any mortals within his dominion, should encroach upon his supremacy.

<small>Unbelief and Superstition working together.</small>

That the profound unbelief which was implied in such worship as this was compatible with gross superstition, with a reverence for enchantments, with an intense longing for tidings respecting the future, Gibbon, whose testimony on this point is open to no suspicion, has told us. On the other hand, that opinion which I quoted from him respecting the philosophers has the slightest possible application to the most eminent of them. Plutarch, so far from accounting all Religions equally false, spent much of his thought and time in distinguishing those which rested on the acknowledgment of righteousness and benevolence as characteristics of divinity from those which canonized Caprice and Terror. About Epictetus and Marcus Aurelius, as I shewed in a former course of Lectures, the statement is even more conspicuously untrue. To the latter I must refer again here, since it may seem to you that he, being an Emperor, must confute or at least weaken some of the remarks which I have made respecting the Empire generally. Retaining all the reverence I have expressed for him, wishing that I could give a more fervent utterance to it,—I yet look

<small>The Philosophers trying to restore faith.</small>

upon him as the strongest confirmation of the position that all the manners of the Romans, all that made them a great and noble people, came from an earlier time, that they derived actually nothing from the Empire but what was immoral and degrading. The Meditations of Marcus Aurelius exhibit a man who is striving by all means that he knows of—by the help of old traditions, of family attachments, of one or another form of Greek wisdom—to recover something which he feels has departed, or is departing from his country, from those who are governing in it, from those who are serving in it. The greatness of a battle conducted under such circumstances I cannot appreciate; if I dared speak of it in the language of some as a wonderful effort of unassisted reason, I should contradict my faith, should feel that I was blaspheming God. I believe the conscience and reason of Marcus Aurelius could not have been called forth—as I believe yours and mine cannot be—by any less divine Teacher than the one whom he confessed but knew not how to name. I feel that the more because I hold that he was dwelling under the pressure of an accursed and a doomed system, which brought forth its natural and inevitable fruits in his son's days and in the days that followed. I do not for a moment yield to the notion which Gibbon endorsed in a careless moment—when his customary fidelity to fact yielded to his passion for rhetorical

Marcus Aurelius.

His greatness does not diminish the darkness of the Empire, but makes it manifest.

Lect. XIII.

The notion that there was a specially happy period for mankind under the Empire wild and fantastic.

display—that the period from Trajan to Marcus Aurelius was one of the greatest happiness for the human race, while the period up to Trajan and after Marcus Aurelius was one of the most miserable. The acknowledgment of such miraculous influences proceeding from the government of men whose intentions were not always good, and when they were best could often effect very little, demands a stretch of credulity which sceptical historians have no right to demand of us. Niebuhr struck the extravagant dogma to the ground by noticing the plagues and pestilences with which this blessed period for the race was tormented in different portions of the globe.

Such dreams of the world's felicity may have haunted Seneca when in his comfortable gardens he was writing his book on Clemency and extolling the youthful perfections of Nero. I do not believe they ever visited the couch of Marcus Aurelius. He knew better what felicity was; and how little he could be the author of it to his people or to himself.

The contradiction in the heart of an earnest and true Emperor.

I have connected this remarkable man with the worship of the Empire, because he, unlike its other Rulers, knew that a Worship which was merely sanctioned by the Magistrate for its usefulness could not be useful, that what was built upon a lie must have the curse of a lie upon it. He had this conviction; it struggled with all motives and arguments of Policy in his heart of hearts. Yet he felt at the same time that he must any how keep alive the sense of religion which was perishing in the minds of the Romans, must permit them to hold fast—nay, must require them to hold fast—that which they had received from their fathers and had ceased to believe—rather than let a scepticism which seemed to him hopeless and destructive overshadow and possess them. One result of this conviction was that persecution which Mr Mill considers so great a deduction from the high character of the Emperor. I hinted before I could not join in the censure which comes with such weight from his lips. Why I cannot join in it I must explain more fully in the next Lecture, wherein I purpose to consider another form of Universal Society which appeared in the world contemporaneously with the Universal Empire.

LECT. XIII.

His motive to persecute.

LECTURE XIV.

(2) *THE UNIVERSAL FAMILY.*

LECT. XIV.

Under what conditions the Roman Empire is called a World.

WHEN I speak of the Roman Empire as universal—when I call it a world—you will not suppose me to affirm that it included all which was known of the earth at its fall or at its commencement. You know well that the Parthians disputed with it in the East; you will not forget the calamity of Varus which told Augustus what unconquered foes he had in the West. Nevertheless both the Latin poets and the writers of the New Testament speak of the dominion of the Cæsars as if it deserved the name which I have given to it. A world dominion it was. The boundaries of barbarous tribes, the traditions of civilised lands, did not determine its limits. The fortune of war might narrow or extend them. Emperors might decide what rivers or mountains their legions should not attempt to cross. Nor, whatever rivals it had, was there any where an organic Society which could be reasonably compared with it. There might hereafter arise in the East a compact Empire to resist and defy it. Parthians only half oriental—with customs and a faith derived from the Macedonian conquest—had no coherency in the least degree answering to that which centuries of conflict had shewn to exist in the Italian city. A grand future might be preparing for Germany; Tacitus might perceive those seeds of order in it which he thought were perishing in his own land: at present it was only a collection of warring tribes.

<small>No other organic Empire.</small>

I am now to speak of a Society which though it did not affect but disclaimed the title of 'a world,' was not more bounded by the divisions of countries or languages than the Empire, was not exposed to the vicissitudes of arms which affected the Empire, could not equally be restrained in its advances by the policy of its rulers. Beginning in the most exclusive of Nations, it appeared after the capital of that nation had been destroyed by Titus affirming that it was meant for all nations. Branches of this Society were found in all the great cities of the Empire. Divided from each other in place, often even by language, they were yet united by some secret bond of fellowship. They acknowledged an invisible Head or Lord. They were not content with saying that He was their Lord; they affirmed Him to be Lord all men. They did not urge the subjects of the Cæsar to revolt from their allegiance. They did say there was a Monarch above

<small>The Rival Society.</small>

<small>Its Monarch.</small>

him to whom his subjects owed a more complete allegiance; to whom he owed it. They said that allegiance to that King must affect all the acts of their daily life.

This Society not to be described as a Religion.

It is a perverse way of representing these facts to speak of a certain religion, called the Christian, as proclaimed in different parts of the Empire by a body of earnest teachers and devotees. The Roman Empire tolerated all religions. It could not have made a special exception to the disadvantage of a doctrine which, as its apologists assured their rulers, commanded abstinence from all violence, even from all retaliation of injuries. Yet the mildest and best Emperors —beginning from Trajan—felt that the Christian Society could not be tolerated, that the Empire in self-defence must trample it out.

It described itself as a Kingdom.

The reason is obvious if we do not substitute language which we have adopted from quite a different source for that which we find in the Gospels, in the Acts of the Apostles and in the Epistles of the New Testament. There we read nothing of a religion; we read in every page of a Kingdom. It is called a Kingdom of Heaven no doubt. But the first time it is spoken of we are assured that it is not in some distant region or in some future state. John the Baptist announces

Its character.

that it is at hand. The people of all kinds and classes in Palestine—the religious as much as the irreligious—are called to repent of their sins because it is at hand. So we learn that it is a

Kingdom over the man himself, over his thoughts and purposes, in that region which produces the acts whereof the Legislator takes cognisance but which he cannot reach.

<small>Lect. XIV.</small>

The Sermon on the Mount is occupied with this Kingdom. Christ speaks of it as the Kingdom of a Father. Multitudes are gathered from every quarter of the land. The poorest of the land are told of a Father in Heaven who cares for the just and the unjust, and the good and the evil; who cares for the lilies and feeds the birds and certainly will not forget to feed or clothe His children, but who has better things for them; who would make them like Himself, who would make them partakers of His own righteousness, of His own life. The Righteousness which these ignorant workmen are told they may possess, is of a different kind from that of the Scribes and Pharisees who were deemed the models of Righteousness by the Jewish people. It was nothing external. Their Father in Heaven would have them be righteous that they might do righteous acts. The tree must be good that the fruit may be good.

<small>The Sermon on the Mount.</small>

Such language has seemed to many a proof that the Morality of this kingdom is merely individual, that it is not Social Morality. The account of Social Morality, which I deduced in my first Lecture from the opinions of all who have written upon it, entirely refutes (as I remarked in that Lecture) this apprehension. It is with the ἦθος, the character which is the

<small>It sets forth a Social Morality.</small>

ground of social peace, that the Social Moralist is conversant; it is against the secret evils which make Society intolerable that he is contending. Is it otherwise with Him who spoke of Meekness, Mercy, Purity of Heart, with Him who denounced the roots of Murder and Adultery, leaving the crimes to the Lawgiver? He takes us at once from the solitude of the desert into a Society. A body of fishermen are gathered about Jesus. They are sent to preach of the Kingdom of Heaven in the most frequented neighbourhoods. They are warned that the Sects will always be their enemies. They are to address the children of Abraham as such, though they may be outcasts, though as farmers of taxes to the Romans they may seem to have forfeited their position as Jews. Jesus eats and drinks with those whom the teachers of the land deem accursed of God, who have often sunk into the worst evils with which they are reproached. He goes among them expressly to deliver them out of that condition, to tell them of a new life of which their Father in Heaven would make them capable.

It is as a King—the expected King of the house of David—that the Galilæans especially, amidst many doubts and hesitations, are disposed to welcome Him. He does not claim the honour, but His words are kingly and He exercises what seem to them the highest faculties of a King. He delivers them from the plagues and sicknesses which torment their bodies, from the powers which have obtained dominion over their spirits filling them with filth and madness. He appeals to something in the poorest man or woman which answers His voice, which believes in Him as a Deliverer. The Kingdom of Heaven He illustrated by parables drawn from the objects and relations with which His hearers were most familiar. So they were taught that He had come to open or unveil that divine life, of which the human life in all its social conditions and circumstances was the image; to the end that the lower might be reformed by the higher, not the higher debased and darkened by the lower. LECT. XIV.
Miracles and Parables.

The great scandal to the Jewish teachers was that He whom they called a Carpenter's Son spoke of God as His Father; said that He came to shew forth His Father's works to men. For that assumption he was condemned as a blasphemer by the Sanhedrim. But it was on the charge of assuming to be a King that He was brought before the Roman governor; on that charge He was condemned to the Roman death of crucifixion. To those who believed Him to be the Son of God, the King who was to rule for ever, such an end seemed incredible. The Gospels conclude with the announcement of His Resurrection. It is recorded in different words by each; in few and simple words by all. They assume the death to be the marvel, the victory over death to be implied in all that Christ taught, in all that He was. The Son of God.
The King.
The Resurrection.

LECT. XIV.

The gift of Tongues.

The Spiritual Society.

Its divisions.

Its expansion.

The message that the Conqueror of Death had appeared, that He had ascended on high to claim His rightful kingdom is that with which the book that we call the Acts of the Apostles begins. A sign is said to have prepared the people of Jerusalem for it. At one of their great feasts, where men were gathered from various regions, the Galilæan apostles begin to speak with tongues; each person in the crowd hears them in the dialect of the country wherein he was born. St Peter explains the meaning of the wonder. The Spirit of God has taken possession of their thoughts and lips that they may make known to their countrymen the deliverance which the God of their fathers has wrought for them, the King whom according to the promise He has given them. The words strike the hearts of some. A Society of men is baptized into the name of the Christ. The Uniting Spirit descends upon them. They do not claim the things which they have as their own. They confess God as their Father in Christ. They are brothers.

Divisions soon arise. There is a mixture of Hebrews and Hellenists in their new Society. The last think that they are neglected in the distribution of gifts to the poor. Stephen, a Hellenist, is one of an order which is appointed to meet the emergency. He first appears to perceive the full meaning of the Pentecostal sign. The King whom they have announced cannot be only the King of those who gave Him up to be crucified. He must be the Lord of all men. Some words of this kind made the Sanhedrim believe that the Law and the Temple of their fathers were threatened. Stephen defended himself, and in a popular frenzy was stoned as a blasphemer.

The book goes on to record how Peter was brought out of his Jewish prejudices to believe that men of another nation might hear the tidings which he had preached to his own; how a fierce young Pharisee who had taken part in Stephen's death was convinced, not by argument, but by an overwhelming discovery to himself of the Lord whom he had resisted, that the Jew was not better than the Gentile, that both alike needed a deliverer from their own evil, that both alike possessed one.

The incorporation of Gentiles.

The battle of the circumcised people against the acknowledgment of a common Lord for them and the uncircumcised, with the establishment of Churches in such cities as Corinth, Ephesus, Philippi, Thessalonica where they were mixed together, is the main subject of the book. In each of these Societies the strife reappears. The Jew who accepted Jesus as the promised Deliverer and Ruler of his land yet cannot bring himself to believe that he has not some advantage over those who have been idolaters. The Greeks bring into the Churches a number of their idolatrous habits, a number of notions derived from their political and philosophical factions. The

The elements of strife.

treatment of these controversies becomes the leading purpose of St Paul's letters. The principles of his Social Morality, of his Moral Theology, are developed in reference to them. The efforts on each side to separate were struggles against a Spirit who was working to bring men into one, to overcome the animal tendencies, the narrow notions, the spiritual enemies which were tearing them asunder. This Spirit of moral purification raises men to know that they are spirits; to confess a Lord of their spirits who took their nature and bore their death that He might deliver them from sin and death, that He might unite them to the Father from whom He came, whose express Image He was, whose Will He came on earth to do. The Will therefore to all good—the Will manifested in Sacrifice—is the ultimate ground to which the Apostle refers the fellowship of human society, the virtues of every man who is a member of it.

The Name into which all the members of the Christian Church were baptized was according to the Apostle the reconciliation of his nation with all other nations; the Universal Sacrifice which is commemorated by the Eucharist was the deepest basis of a Human Morality, the meeting-point of a fellowship between the Father of all and the children of men. The Apostles of Jerusalem who contemplated the Christian Church less in its various departments, more as a whole expanded out of the Jewish Nation, were set in contrast to

St Paul by the Jewish and Gentile factions, the first claiming Peter or James or John as their champion, the other the tent-maker of Tarsus. He indignantly repelled the injurious honour in speaking of the school among the Corinthians which thrust it upon him. *Their* Catholic Epistles shew that they foresaw, as he did, the utter shaking and overthrow of their own nation, and sought as he did, in the divine Name, for the foundation of a Unity which should be liable to no accidents or limitations of space and time. The last book in the Bible purports to set forth the Revelation or unveiling of the Righteous Lord of Heaven and Earth, the discomfiture and overthrow of the powers whether in the Jewish or Gentile world which had divided them.

<small>LECT. XIV.

Their external diversities and essential agreement.</small>

A Society starting from these principles and aiming at these results could not be very alarming to the Roman world while it appeared as one of the Jewish sects, whilst the really powerful sects in Judæa, in the Greek cities and in Rome, could treat it as an insolent disturber of their dogmas and traditions. The impartiality and indifference of the Roman judges towards all questions of opinion had many opportunities of exhibiting themselves when the Nazarenes were brought before their tribunals. The Roman magistrate at Ephesus ridiculed the notion of interfering even on behalf of the Goddess of the City, the market for whose shrines had been injured by St Paul's preaching. When the proconsuls of Cæsarea were

<small>How long the Church continued harmless in Roman eyes.

The Empire its frequent protector against Jews and even Greeks.</small>

inclined to favour the Sanhedrim at his expence he could appeal to the Emperor. Suppose the story of Nero's torches is true, it does not prove that he was the least alarmed at the progress of a body, the very name of which was mistaken by him and his biographer; it was only an act of imperial wantonness or a desire to conceal his own crime. After the fall of Jerusalem we begin to hear of some enquiries made by Domitiam respecting kinsmen of Jesus who might be pretenders to the Jewish throne. If St John's deportation to Patmos took place under that monarch or before him, it was probably suggested by some notion that he had spoken of a Kingdom which would overthrow the Roman. But it was not till the beginning of the second century that anything which deserves the name of an imperial persecution commenced.

What I have said may shew you that that name 'Persecution,' if it is supposed to indicate a departure from the maxims of toleration which had been habitually recognised in the Empire, is altogether misapplied. The motive which influenced Trajan was clearly not zeal for any set of opinions or mode of worship, dislike to any other set of opinions or mode of worship. If the organised society which he found in his different provinces had any reason for its existence—if it did not repudiate the reason given in the books which it accepted as authoritative—it was based upon principles utterly at variance with those of the Empire, principles implying that the principle on which it stood was false. These principles could not be concealed. The Christian Society was bound to proclaim them; its members must endure any punishments rather than be silent about them. What could the Emperors do if they meant to maintain not the authority of the gods but their own? They were not bewildered by notions into which modern times have fallen. They knew that the Christian Kingdom in whatever sense it was not of the world came directly into contact and collision with their world. Those who spoke of it dwelt upon the earth, addressed men who were engaged in the common occupations of earth, sought to regulate their behaviour in their earthly transactions. It was as little possible to evade this conclusion because the Christians preached everywhere that their Master had risen from the dead. He had risen, they said, to claim His kingdom over men. His Resurrection was a witness that Death was not the Lord of the Universe, that One who had overcome Death was its Lord. By faith of the operation of God who raised Him from the dead, they rose, so they affirmed, to a new life here. If these words have lost their meaning for those who repeat them now, Trajan and his successors could not treat them as without signification then. The words might sound most foolish in their ears; but they had an influence which wise statesmen could not disregard.

As little could they be affected by a notion

The Christain Society affecting the government and business of the earth.

The Resurrection.

which has become popular in our day, that the Apostles expected, and taught their disciples to expect, that the Son of Man was coming speedily to destroy the earth and its inhabitants; therefore that the polity of the earth was of no concern to them. The Apostles unquestionably expected the end of an Age. They said that if the Son of Man had indeed come to claim a Kingdom, He would prove by some tokens that He was King. They looked therefore with awe and trembling to the downfall of that City which was dear to them above all others—which they deemed to be emphatically the holy city—but which had become an accursed city, the home of furious sects, hateful to man and God. Its fall was to them, in the fullest sense, the end of the Jewish or separate age, the discovery or unveiling of the Universal King. Suppose the Apostles were so flagrantly inconsistent as to expect the destruction of a Universe, which they affirmed that Christ had redeemed and reclaimed from its destroyers—suppose they treated human politics as indifferent when they were announcing a polity for men—the Churches had survived the crisis to which they looked forward, were composed of Hebrews, Greeks, Latins, Barbarians, were declaring that they had a commission to be the salt of the earth, to be the lights of the world. In that character they were endangering not the religion of the Empire only but the entire fabric of it.

What might strike us as an assault upon

its religion was in truth an assault on its existence. Ignatius, the overseer or father of the Church in Antioch, denounced in language which sounded to Trajan very monstrous and ridiculous, the Demons whom he and his subjects worshipped. Christ his Lord, he said, had come to deliver his disciples from the Demons. The instinct of the Emperor enabled him to perceive in such phrases, however he might laugh at them, the tokens of a perilous revolution. If he had known more of the ground on which the old teacher rested his assertion his alarm would not have been diminished; he would have felt it to be most reasonable. Man, it was affirmed, could throw off the service of Gods half human half divine—having the benevolent and malevolent caprices of human creatures—because One had appeared on earth and had ascended on high, in whom perfect Humanity was united with Godhead; in whom men might claim fellowship with their Father in Heaven. Such a doctrine struck at the foundation of that which I have described as the worship of the Empire. The idea of essential actual Right being eliminated from the conception of Godhead, there remained as a comfort to the affections, as a refuge from the terrors of the Conscience, these half beings who might change their aspects every hour according to the state of the worshipper's temper or of his digestion; frightening him to occasional acts of service, cheering him with occasional hints of patronage.

Lect. XIV. Ignatius of Antioch. Demon worship. To overthrow it was to undermine not a form of worship, but the imperial worship as such.

The man clung to them chiefly in the vague hope that they might shield him from the Highest of all whom it was terrible to contemplate. Not the most profound Unbelief could drive out these demons; Unbelief must endure them, and make certain compacts with them. But if the Highest of all was declared to have revealed Himself as the Father of men, to have entered into fellowship with them, that He might draw them from the adoration of all creatures to the adoration of Him; then indeed the homage of demons was shaken to its centre. It was inevitable that Trajan, feeling the continuance of the Empire to be involved in the continuance of some worship of this kind, should not treat those who were overthrowing it as he would have treated any ordinary fanatics, but as Atheists and traitors. With his desire to indulge the inhabitants of Rome in the amusements which they liked best, it was natural that he should expose Ignatius to the beasts of the circus.

Thus the distinction between a *Religio licita* and one that must be dealt with as disloyal and destructive, had a clear justification in the minds of those disposed to the broadest toleration. Anything or nothing might be true about the unseen world. All guesses about it, all modes of expressing the guesses, might be legitimate. But the Christians were interfering with the visible world, and at the same time denouncing uncertainty in the invisible. The line between religion and politics has been found a difficult one to draw in every period; I do not think it was drawn less accurately by the ruler of Rome than it has been by any later rulers, or than it would be by the most liberal men now.

With Marcus Aurelius policy was not the sole motive for punishing the Christians: a dread of weakening reverence in his subjects for what might be divine, must have mingled with the obvious necessity of putting down a rival—however feeble a rival—of the power which he was appointed to exercise. It cannot be doubted that he threw more heart and energy into the cause than Trajan or any previous ruler. The deaths in Gaul during his reign may be ascribed to the zeal of proconsuls, may have been only sanctioned by him. But Justin suffered in Rome, apparently through the agency of men about the court, favourites of the Imperial Philosopher. Justin's life would seem to have been a singularly blameless one. If he had any affectation it was that of being himself a philosopher. He had pleaded earnestly and eloquently for a thorough examination into the principles and conduct of the body to which he belonged. The condemnation of such a man by one so habitually just and humane as Marcus, is the most decisive proof which can be given that there was a necessary and inextinguishable hostility between the Universal Empire and the Universal Family which no individual merits on one side or the other could mitigate. The

Justin; his martyrdom probably due to Marcus Aurelius himself.

LECT. XIV.

Bad Emperors generally the least impatient of the Christian Society.

safety of the Church may be said generally—there were exceptions—to depend on the carelessness of the Emperors in upholding the dignity of their position. A brutal gladiator like Commodus was likely to indulge its members—at least not to treat them worse than his other subjects.

The Image of the Emperor.

Sacrifice to that the test of allegiance.

In a short time a test was discovered which clearly separated the Christians from those who had merely preferred certain demons or customs to others. Would they sacrifice to the image of the Emperor? That was a trial of political fidelity. If they accepted it, no objection would be taken to any early or midnight meetings for special acts of homage to their own divinity. Only let the Emperor be acknowledged as the King of kings and Lord of lords; the reserved rights of any unknown gods would not be challenged. There was a curious felicity, I ought rather to say, a stern logic, in the demand. It *was* the image of the Emperor to which, under the name of Jupiter or any other, a majority of his subjects were offering their sacrifices. A dominion bounded by no law, brute force in its fullest development, force which could inflict any amount of mischief if it pleased, and which probably might please to make this or that man or people know what it could do, this was becoming more and more the concentrated Godhead before which the world trembled. That there should be weak men and women to say, 'For no tortures or fires will we sacrifice to such an image—be it of a visible or an invisible power'—was the wonder of the age. To endure pain and death was an ordinary phænomenon. Soldiers could do that; their business was to do it. But to endure pain and death because they would not submit to an act which seemed to most a mere form—which was to many a reality because it expressed what they felt—that was Christian martyrdom.

LECT. XIV.

There is no need to dispute about the number of the martyrs. They may be reduced to Dodwell's estimate or below it. Still they will explain the essential character, the radical opposition, of the two Polities; how one stood on force, the other on sacrifice; how the capacity of inflicting death was the measure of the force; how trust in One who had conquered death—not as some fancy the vision of garlands and crowns after it—was implied in the Sacrifice.

The diagnosis of the two Polities.

There are many notorious events in the history of the early Church which may have reasonably diminished the dread of it in the Roman Ruler, because they seemed to confute its boast of Universality. The disputes in the Churches over which the Apostles presided between Jews and Gentiles, if they became less obvious after the fall of Jerusalem, took forms more various not less fatal to peace. Opinions evidently derived from the Synagogue clashed with opinions which were as evidently the offspring of idolatrous customs. There were aspects of the Gospel for all Nations which touched the spiritual conceptions of

The perils and weaknesses of the Christian Family.

Heresies.

Syrians and Egyptians; Christian teachers who mixed with either brought these points into prominence, gave them an exclusive character, and,—whether through their own fault or the suspicions of men trained in another school it does not concern us here to enquire—became separated from the fellowship of the Church. Latin and Hellenic diversities became equally and very soon conspicuous. Churches excommunicated each other because they could not agree about the time of keeping the festival of the Resurrection. One illustrious Apologist of the Church, the African Tertullian, having acquired the habit of contemplating the Christian as a rival religion to the Pagan, and of defending it with legal acuteness and ferocity, asked himself how closely he could draw the lines of his religion: at last they were found to exclude the great body of those who bore the Christian name. One of his successors in the same Church, Cyprian, was a far more genial character, full of impartial kindness to Pagans and Christians when they were suffering in the same pestilence. But cases of apostasy by men under the terror of death, which had been condoned at the intercession of confessors who were themselves about to incur it, led him to lay down tremendous canons respecting the 'lapsed;' to distinguish very sharply between the Clergy and the Laity; to question the validity of Baptism when administered by those whom he counted heretics. He proclaimed by the whole course of his acts, whether in themselves reasonable or foolish, that comprehensiveness was the peril of the Church, exclusiveness its security. In his own Church especially, but to a great extent in all the Churches of his time, a passion for government was evidently developing itself. The union of the Christian family could be secured, it was thought, by the frequent gathering together of Councils, which often raised the questions discussed and apparently settled in them into causes of separation.

<small>Passion for legislation.</small>

Meanwhile another passion was appearing which threatened the social life of the Christian Society. It had been proclaimed in the most rich and corrupt cities of the Empire. It had established itself in them. The Christians in Egypt, to escape either from enemies of their bodies, or from enemies of their spirits, betook themselves to deserts. The hermit life was no invention of theirs; there were precedents for it among Jews and Heathens. It was altogether a strange graft upon the New Testament stock; yet no one could say that it would not grow upon that stock. If it was anything but a graft, if it assumed to be the original Christian principle, it must subvert the practice as well as the doctrine of the Apostles.

<small>The flight from cities.</small>

Somewhat allied to this tendency—yet in one way most unlike it—was another that appeared in the same region. The Alexandrian Church was of all that existed in the Empire the most learned, the most inclined to profit by Hellenic as well as Rabbinical wisdom, the least timid in acknow-

<small>The Alexandrian Church.</small>

<small>Its Learning.</small>

ledging obligations to Pagan philosophers. In one sense appealing much more distinctly and boldly to human sympathy than the Church of which Tertullian and Cyprian were the lights, the Alexandrian teachers were much less capable than they were of entering into the ordinary habits and pursuits of the earth; were much more disposed to cultivate an exalted mysticism. They felt strongly that Christ had come to be the Redeemer and Head of men, not of a sect of men. But they found it difficult to recollect that men had bodies as well as spirits; that the common earth had a sacredness of its own and was not merely a picture or parable or prophecy of an invisible state. In spite of their learning, therefore, they had affinities with the hermits who despised it.

Its mysticism.

If ecclesiastical historians appeal to these different impulses and aspirations as proofs of the many-sided character of the message which the Church had received—as proofs that it could not sink into the dead uniformity of the Empire so long as a quickening Spirit animated it—they shew a sense of the grandeur of their subject; they can imitate the honesty of the Scriptures in exposing the partialities and wrong doings of their heroes. But after all we may justly apply the words of the Satirist respecting Cicero's verses,

These inclinations made the Church less dangerous to the Empire.

> Antoni gladios potuit contemnere si sic
> Omnia dixisset,

to the cases of which I have spoken. The Church

needed not to fear any disturbance from the Emperors, if it had been content to quarrel about Easter, to fraternise in particular notions or conceptions, to try how many it could exclude from its ranks, to play at legislation, to organise a sect or school, to hide itself in deserts, to eschew the common earth. There were Emperors—the heartless and odious Philippus Arabs was one, the amiable eclectic Alexander Severus was perhaps another—to whom the Church presented itself merely in this light, who fancied therefore that Christians might be safely trusted with offices under the Emperor, even that their Lord might be adopted as one of the objects of imperial patronage. The feebleness of such experiments soon made itself manifest to the more vigorous rulers like Decius. The Society was maintaining its coherency and its claim to universal diffusion in spite of the efforts of its teachers to reduce it into an ordinary Sect organisation defined by tests of opinion. It would not submit to the manipulations of its ablest and acutest doctors. It was evidently intended for the people. Being so intended it was a continual defiance of the Empire. The hostility was felt most strongly when Diocletian realised the true conditions of an Empire, when he perceived that it must be Oriental, that the old republican ligatures must be thrown off. Since Rome, with its manifold traditions, was a great hindrance to the accomplishment of this purpose, it must no longer be the recognised centre; there must be

Lect. XIV.

But it continues to give signs of popularity which cannot be overlooked.

different heads of the world to encounter in closer conflict the various powers which were threatening to rend it asunder. To Diocletian and in general to his subordinate Cæsars the Christian Society appeared the most formidable of these powers; an effort was made to crush it which for system and completeness had no parallel in the earlier times. This ten years' attempt at extermination immediately preceded the determination of Constantine to ally himself with the Church, and to establish a new Centre for a Christianised Empire. The effect of that alliance on Social Morality I shall consider in another Lecture.

Lect. XIV.

The Diocletian Persecution.

Constantine.

Before I enter upon that subject which will lead us over a tract of a thousand years, I wish you to observe how the morality of this Universal Society is related to that of the Family and the Nation as it presented itself to us in former Lectures.

The Morality of the Universal Family.

According to the Christian Creed the Authority of a Father, the Obedience of a Son, lies at the root of the Universe, is implied in its Constitution. In a living Spirit the Authority and the Obedience are for ever united. After this image it is declared that Man is created; the perfect Humanity is in the Son of God; the Spirit guides men to see in the Son of Man the Son of God; in His Father their Father. Absolute Faith or Trust in His Father is declared to be the characteristic of Him who took men's nature upon Him; such faith or trust, exalting men above themselves, makes

Its foundation.

them partakers of the true human life. The Son of Man is announced as the Brother of all men, one who has entered into the conditions of the poorest, the most suffering of them, one who has endured their death. Men are proclaimed to have a Universal Brotherhood in Him. Lastly, the principle of the Kingdom of Heaven is said to be, that the Chief of all is the Servant of all; the King of Heaven having become in very deed a Servant of His creatures. Here is the announcement of a foundation or underground for that ἦθος which we found to be demanded by all the relations of the Family.

<small>Lect. XIV.</small>

<small>The Universal Foundation of Domestic Morals.</small>

I have carefully pointed out to you that National life was in suspension or abeyance during the period which we have been examining. We are reminded of that suspension in the conditions of the Church as much as in those of the Empire. The awkwardness which the writers of these centuries exhibit when they come into contact with the common earthly records of the Jewish history —which yet they could not help regarding as the starting point of their own—their eagerness to resolve honest facts into flimsy allegories—indicate the atmosphere by which they were surrounded. But the question is not how far they understood the characteristics of national life; it is whether the Universal principles of which they were bearing witness were incompatible with it, or were such as might restore it.

<small>Was there also a foundation for National Morals?</small>

I have said already that the Christians, just

19.

as much as the Imperialists, recognised a Will, a supreme and Absolute Will, as the ground of life and order to man and to the Universe. Was it an *Arbitrary* Will? If it was, Law was a fiction which might be tolerated, might be necessary; it was only another name for physical force. I have endeavoured to shew you, that the deadly opposition between the Empire and the Church had its root in the fact, that the latter preached to the world of a Will which was not arbitrary, of a Will which was essentially righteous, of a Will to make men righteous. Because the image of such a Will was before the Christian Martyrs they could not do sacrifice to the image of the Emperor.

The sign that a Universal Church had come into existence was, so the members of it declared, a gift of tongues. A Society with such a belief could not attach any special sacredness to one language, were it Latin or Greek or Hebrew. But it might keep alive the belief that there was a dialect for each race; it might nourish the seeds out of which organic languages should proceed. The acknowledgment of a Spirit who rules over the speech and the thoughts, who makes speech the real expression of thought, must have been felt by many as the promise that such seeds would be ripened by a divine culture. And since this Spirit was declared to be emphatically the Spirit of Truth, the Spirit who guides into Truth, just so far as He was believed in, the reverence for veracity, the horror of lies, would have its deepest root, its strongest security. *Lect. XIV.*

The belief in an invisible and righteous Government, a Government over men, over the earth, was involved in the original idea of the Church. If at any time the teachers of the Church lost their faith in this invisible government, they became eager to define their own rights and powers; so the sense of Service was lost; so the domestic character of the government was lost. But while they lived in the confession of an actual King over men they were witnesses for the authority of lawful kings in the former days and in the days to come; of kings, I mean, who should not reign after their own pleasure. *Actual Government of Heaven over Earth.*

Since the belief in God as the Reconciler of Mankind to Himself, of Sacrifice as the instrument of Reconciliation, was one which expressed itself in all the life, acts, institutions of the Christian Society, it may be thought that the old name of a Lord of Hosts which was so dear to the Psalmists must have lost its force; that the Prince of Peace must have banished war from the thoughts and language of those who confessed themselves as His subjects. Yet no book of the Bible is so full of Trumpets of doom, Vials of Wrath, of Earthquakes and Revolutions, as the last; the one from which the Church derived its permanent imagery as well as some of its most practical lessons. So long as there is wrong and oppression on the earth, so long that book as *The Reconciler.*

19—2

well as every previous one declares that there will be war in Heaven against these destroyers; that the powers of Nature as well as human instruments will be employed against them. That book said as emphatically that those who drew the sword would perish by the sword, that those who brought others into captivity would go into captivity. It promised victory to patience; they who followed Christ must conquer as He did, by giving up themselves to die, not by seeking power to kill. These warnings have remained for the Christians of all ages; but they cannot be separated from the others. If the Universal Family seeks to prevail by persecution and bloodshed it becomes a world Empire. But World Empires are overthrown by the arms of Nations; Humanity—and therefore those who believe in a Son of Man—must rejoice in their fall.

Much has been spoken and written about the 'secondary' causes which may have contributed to the triumph of a Society so weak as the one that was proclaimed by Galilæan fishermen. Perhaps we are not quite settled in our minds about the *first* cause. If we suppose it to have been some supreme power which could dispense with the laws of the Universe, we may account for an Empire, we cannot account for a Society which uses the Lord's Prayer, which starts from the belief of a Father in Heaven. If we assume Him to be the first cause of the Society, we shall of course admit secondary causes—I adopt the phrase because it is given me, not because I deem it a philosophical one—provided they are homogeneous with the character of Him who has established it and with the character of the Society itself. Believing in a God who has constituted families, who has constituted Nations, we may ask whether there is any Universal Human Constitution which is in harmony with these; for which these may prepare us. We may joyfully admit that Judæa, that Greece, and that Rome had the preparation of these secondary causes; that without them the Christian Society would have been utterly unintelligible to those among whom it first appeared. If we do not acknowledge their worth it will be unintelligible to us; the most incredible of all anomalies.

What their character must be.

You may say to me perhaps: 'But there must be a certain ἦθος which is characteristic of the Universal or Human Society as such; it cannot be merely the support of the subordinate Morality.' Yes! the old doctrine of Cardinal Virtues I have no doubt is a sound one. I may have something to say about them hereafter. Here I will only repeat the sentence, "And now abideth Faith, Hope, Charity, these three; but the greatest of these is Charity."

The Human ἦθος.

LECTURE XV.

THE UNIVERSAL FAMILY SUBJECT TO THE UNIVERSAL EMPIRE (CONSTANTINOPLE).

LECT. XV. WHETHER Constantine was or was not taught by a vision—as he affirmed in his latter days—that he would conquer if he took the Cross for his sign, there can be no doubt that he had some reason to despair of conquest unless he could find some other weapon than any which was supplied by the Roman armoury. The Empire had lost its Unity. Through a trial of ten years the Church appeared to have preserved its unity. A man of less foresight and enterprise than Constantine —in less difficult circumstances—might have asked himself whether he could have more cordial friends than men whom he had suddenly delivered from a great persecution. No one has pretended that he began his toleration with any strong faith in Christ. Eclecticism had diffused itself among philosophers; it had many attractions for intelligent soldiers who were used to

The Edict of Milan; what it meant.

measure the claims of divine Persons by the Lect. XV.
strength which they imparted to those who served
them; it might easily associate itself with the
old Roman indifference to particular forms of
worship. That the Edict of Milan, like any
other, was not a mere offspring of a man's
will, that the Emperor was *not* the King of kings
—those who hold the Christian faith must, of
course, maintain. That the ordinary motives of The motives of Constantine in publishing it. selfishness and ambition were concerned with the
publication of it, those who hold that faith are not
the least obliged to deny.

It is far more important to consider the Why it could not issue in mere toleration. inevitable effects of this step. Impartial permission of Christian and Pagan worship was all that
Constantine at first dreamed of. The impossibility of stopping at that point was not evident to
him with all his sagacity, with all his knowledge
of the deadly battle between the two Societies
which had lasted for more than two centuries.
Facts soon proved too strong for him. Other
rivals being crushed, his colleague Licinius became
the champion of Heathenism. Constantine must
become the avowed patron of its opposers.

In taking this course he seemed to be departing as widely as possible from the policy of He fulfils the purpose of Diocletian. his predecessor. He was really aiming at the
same objects as his predecessor. The ingenious
scheme of saving the unity of the Empire by
giving it different rulers had been tried and
failed. But all the reasons against allowing Rome

to remain the centre of an Oriental Government were as strong for Constantine as they had been for Diocletian. And if a new capital could be found, how much more effectually might it be stripped of old Italian associations if it could start with new temples, with a new worship. The discerning eye of the Emperor fixed upon the best site in the world for the experiment. For a thousand years Constantinople was to be the theatre for it.

When one talks of an *alliance* between the Empire and the Church, there is much danger of misconception. No terms were arranged, no agreements concluded. The Emperor remained what he was. All powers that belonged to his predecessors rested in him. He was able to adopt new titles of Eastern origin which old Romans knew not. He was able to cast away many restraints and limitations which impeded the action of a military despotism that had been developed out of a Republic. The Eastern Empire was precisely what Augustus or the most arbitrary of his successors might have wished to make his own if he had been able. There were no vestiges in Byzantium of a People; no Orders; officials were officials merely. Domestic life was less sacred, more directly insulted, in the new court than in the ancient. The records of Constantine's family are bloody records. The worst creatures of Eastern despotism were soon the guardians of the palace, specially of its women.

Where then was the Christian Family? Its

presence was indicated by the name of Patriarch. He stood near the Emperor in the capital. Each city had some one higher or lower in office who bore a name kindred to that, *suggesting* domestic associations. These ministers of the Christian body had the honour of being officials of the government; had privileges and exemptions which distinguished them from ordinary men. The Emperor and his court performed Christian rites in temples dedicated to Christ or to one of His apostles. The Emperor could summon the Bishops or Fathers from different lands to discuss questions in Theology which were producing strife. He could preside at their deliberations; if he pleased, he could enforce their decrees. That was the alliance. Those who were baptized into the name of the Invisible Father the Creator of all things, of a Son who had redeemed mankind and established His Kingdom over all men, of a Spirit who worked in men to overcome their enmities and bring them into fellowship with each other, paid practical homage and worship to a visible Emperor, acknowledged him to be the Lord of Men. The contradiction of these Kingdoms remained just as real as it had been in the previous centuries. But Constantine had won a victory which his heathen forerunners had failed to win. The rulers and officers of the Christian body performed that sacrifice to the imperial Image which the Martyrs had suffered death for refusing.

It is impossible, as every reader of Gibbon

Importance given by Gibbon to the Church controversies.

must have perceived, to separate the history of the Empire from the theological controversies in which the Church was engaged. Indifferent as the historian might be to the subjects of these controversies, his conscience as a narrator of facts obliged him to give them prominence. No one on the whole has done the Christian teachers in the Greek world so much justice as he has done. The figures of Athanasius, of Gregory of Nazianzus, of Cyril, of Chrysostom, which in most purely ecclesiastical narratives are dry skeletons whether they are chosen as subjects for applause or condemnation, acquire in his pages flesh and blood; we feel that they were not doctors in a school, but human beings exercising a powerful influence on the life of society. The nature of this influence, and how it was compatible with the dominion which the Empire undoubtedly claimed over the body that had been taken under its patronage, we have now to consider.

Athanasius.

1. Perhaps the most full length and remarkable portrait in the *Decline and Fall* is that of Athanasius. The historian had many excuses for representing him as a divine who was ready to embroil the universe for a single letter. On a closer view he discovered in him sound practical ability and common sense; even a willingness to overlook distinctions which he deemed important if they did not concern his main purpose; along with these qualities a marvellous power of enduring the opposition of emperors and ecclesiastics rather

than desert his cause. It has been a wonder to most readers that such a man should for such a cause pass through incredible hardships, the loss of property and reputation, the risk of death. If the contest as they have supposed was for a subtle school question, not concerning any common living interest, not affecting human progress, the wonder would be to me incredible.

^{Lect. XV.}
^{Was his battle for a school Dogma?}

To many Bishops at the Council of Nice who were very vehement on either side of the controversy, to many amiable and devout men who were anxious for the settlement of a dispute which was evidently the cause of bitter feelings and of many unchristian acts, to Constantine himself looking at the subject as one which was disturbing his government, it bore no doubt this aspect. To Athanasius any denial of the Unity of the divine Father with the Son meant the restoration of demon worship— Christ being on that hypothesis only one, if the most important, of human creatures. It seemed to him, therefore, that he was asserting the existence of that Kingdom which the Church had proclaimed, the union between Earth and Heaven of which it had borne witness. We may find as we proceed that this Kingdom might be denied, this union set at nought, by many who accepted the formula of the Nicene Council. Perhaps all who in that age or any other accepted it merely as a formula,—who supposed that the relations of God and Man could be determined by the votes of a Majority in an ecclesiastical assembly—rejected the principle for

^{The principle involved in it.}

which Athanasius contended, as much as any Arian could. I may fully admit that he was unable to perceive how many recognised his principle who did not understand his formula. Like all men of his time, as of later times, he was bewildered between the feeling that he was the steward of a spiritual treasure for which it was worth while to die, and the feeling that circumstances had placed not far from his reach a material force which he might use to kill those who dissented from him. Happily for his character, this force was not generally *within* his reach. He had through the greater part of his life to experience the weight of it directed against himself. He was taught by hard blows how little the decrees of a Council can avail to maintain any cause which it is worth a man's while to stake his existence upon; how ready he must be to withstand ecclesiastical powers as well as secular if he would do any work for mankind. It seems to me that he *was* doing a work for mankind; that if that work had not been done, the Empire, garnished with Christian notions and ceremonies, would have been more perilous, more crushing to Humanity, than it had been in any former day. The question whether there was any other Universal Society than the Imperial—whether all thought, belief, hope, which belongs to the invisible was not to be crushed under the hoof of a visible Despot—was the one at issue, that which Athanasius often almost alone, was called to face.

2. I am not delivering a course of Lectures on

THE CHRISTIANIZED EMPIRE. 301

Ecclesiastical History—but on Social Morality; I am contemplating all topics simply in reference to that. There is another subject, deeply concerning Social Morality, which the life of Athanasius brings distinctly before us. He fled from cities into the desert of the Thebais. There he found a set of monks who welcomed him when most of the dignified ecclesiastics had deserted him. Gratitude might have been reason enough for regarding them with affection and reverence. But they had other attractions for him. In his life of St Anthony he expressed his admiration, endorsed their claims to miraculous powers, recorded their conflicts with unseen enemies who took visible shapes. So this form of life with all its accompaniments in that and subsequent ages, comes before us with the imprimatur of a man for whose wisdom as well as his zeal I have professed so much respect.

Lect. XV.

The Monks of the desert.

His admiration for them.

I cannot separate this phenomenon from those of which I have spoken already. When there is a Court like that of Constantinople—when it assumes a Christian name and uses Christian teachers as its instruments—there will be, I believe there must be, this kind of protest against it, this savage war in the name of Christ against a corrupt civilization which usurps His name. No two men can be much more unlike in their characters or their beliefs than Athanasius and Rousseau; but the manners of Constantinople or Alexandria in the fourth century were not unlike those of Paris in the 18th. The disgust for them

They were protesters against a corrupt civilization.

LECT. XV.

His reasons for believing in the miracles of the Monks,

must have been deeper in the mind of the Bishop than of the Genevan philosopher; if the former could find the life of the woods connected with what seemed to him an earnest faith he may have accepted it with the like enthusiasm. He had been wont to think of the miracles of our Lord on earth, and of His Apostles after His departure from earth, as signs of the dominion of the Son of Man over the powers of Nature to which men had bowed down. Coming from a Society in which visible things alone were really reverenced whatever phrases might be used to express a reverence for the unseen, he would be likely to recognise any wonders which the monks were said to have enacted as proofs that Heaven was not hopelessly separated from earth, that Christ still asserted His rule. Above all he would have felt that the wickedness which he saw in so many concrete and dispersed forms in the great cities must be traced to a root in some powers of spiritual wickedness of utter darkness. If he found Monks who were shut out from participation in the follies and crimes of the external world declaring with deep earnestness that they were brought into direct combat with these spiritual principalities, there would be I apprehend in his reason, as well as in his conscience, much that would respond to their testimony and that would make him unwilling to examine it with any sceptical suspicions.

and in their conflicts with evil Spirits.

Looking at all these questions with the light of fifteen centuries reflected on them, we may observe, as I did last week, that the desert life was borrowed not from the example of Christ who preached the Gospel of His Kingdom in the most frequented places, not from the example of His Apostles who marched straight into the most commercial and luxurious cities and formed flocks out of the inhabitants of those cities, but from such examples as were familiar in Egypt, as are still most common in Hindostan. We may perceive that the monkish miracles appealing mainly to the sentiment of surprise in those who beheld them, claiming to be divine *because* they were irregular exercises of power, coming forth as frequently and effectually in the form of curses as of blessings, were in all respects unlike those acts of Christ which awakened faith in an abiding Ruler and Deliverer, which were done to exhibit the character of His Father in Heaven, which were to restore health, to prove that disease and death are not the laws of God's creation but the violations of its Law. They resembled therefore much more nearly the miracles of the magicians who resisted Moses and of those who resisted the Apostles. We may see that if the Monks who performed them had at first a thoroughly honest purpose— if they felt that they were putting forth a divine energy not an energy which they could claim as theirs—they were continually tempted to confound their own glory with God's, and then to think that they were honouring both Him and themselves by falsehoods. And it may become more and

Lect. XV. Contrast between this life and its accompanying miracles and the life and miracles of the New Testament.

St Anthony's temptations.

more terribly evident to us that while the temptation of Christ in the Wilderness as a preparation for His conflict with the sins of cities was a witness that Good is mightier than Evil; those conflicts in the wilderness which were not such a preparation suggested the thought that the power of Evil is indeed the mightiest of all, and can only be resisted by some specially trained recluse or devotee. Out of which terrible notion a scheme of Demonology issued which has afflicted mankind frightfully in all ages, the Evil Spirit gradually losing both his characters, moral Evil being changed into physical deformity, a Spirit passing into what is most palpable and material. Of such facts and consequences every Moralist who does not separate Morality from History is bound to take notice; to omit them would be to leave some of the darkest passages in human experience untouched. But I should be cowardly if I pretended to think that modern conclusions upon these topics are not liable to be as confused, as mischievous, even as superstitious, as those of the Alexandrian Bishop. In the lofty wisdom which looks down upon the seclusion of deserts, we may be fostering the corruption of Cities; even boasting of it as a proof of our advanced Civilization. Then assuredly we shall have our retribution; not only in the growth of the vices we have loved, but in the appearance, under the most unhealthy form, of the refuges from them which we have abhorred. We may refuse

to believe in the power of men over nature be- LECT. XV.
cause we crouch to it and deny our human rights;
a state of mind which must issue at last in a
despair of Science and of all mechanical inven-
tions. We may be thinking that powers of Evil Modern
have no terror for us or influence over us, and may logy.
find suddenly—not indeed that we are fighting
them but—that they have become our gods; that
we confess no other. In the midst of fopperies we
may be cultivating a most contemptible Demonology; the devilish may be the more supreme
over us because we have ceased to acknowledge a
Devil.

3. These observations are not really a digres-
sion from the story of the Greek Empire. The main The dis-
characteristic of it was a frivolity which could find Constan-
an occupation in any thing, which did unhappily tinople.
find one of its principal occupations in theological
disputes. These amused the people in the Circus,
these took their turn with all other ways of killing
time or men among the inhabitants of the palace.
I may agree with the Comtists in regarding Julian Julian.
as a fanatic who dreamed of restoring what had
passed away; I may call him, as Strauss does, a
Romancer on the throne of the Cæsars. But I
cannot wonder that he should have been intensely
disgusted with all that he saw and heard in the
Christianised Capital, that he should prefer the
poorest Athenian Sophist, the most extravagant
of Egyptian hierophants, to the Orthodox or Arian
disputants who dwelt under its shadow. And I

certainly see in the two years' dominion of Paganism which he established, and in the much longer and more persecuting reign of the Arian Valens, a far greater blessing to those who accepted the teaching of Athanasius than in the victory which they won when Theodosius became master of the world. Great as was the temporary advantage to mankind of being subject to an honest and able man not born in the purple but trained in poverty and hardship, it could scarcely compensate the mischiefs which arose from the insolence of such Bishops as Theophilus of Alexandria, who believed that they were worshipping the true God because they were demolishing the temple of Serapis, and who shewed what kind of faith they would substitute for that of which they destroyed the external emblems by their malice against some of the truest and best men of their own order. The Episcopal champion of orthodox Christianity conspired with the miserable successor of Theodosius and his wife to hunt into exile and death Chrysostom, a faithful witness for a Gospel to the poor, and therefore of course an offence to the Court of Constantinople. Even in the better days which preceded the reign of Arcadius, Gregory of Nazianzus, a man scarcely less eloquent and not at all less sincere than Chrysostom, who had suffered for his orthodoxy under Valens, lamented, as Gibbon will have told you, the degradation and loss of strength which he experienced in being permitted to enter the capital in the imperial train as the representative of a successful opinion; he lamented even more bitterly the odious temper of Ecclesiastical Councils in which he discovered the Spirit of the Devil rather than of God.

4. I would willingly linger over the tragedy of Chrysostom's life; it illustrates so strikingly the moral of the whole history. But you may read it for yourselves in Gibbon, if you have not leisure or inclination to study original documents. Chrysostom was emphatically an opposer of tyranny; he believed that the Kingdom of Heaven was a Kingdom over men and for men. The people of the City looked up to him as their friend and champion; the officials of Arcadius, whether lay or clerical, felt towards him as an enemy. But though he could be a sufferer for justice and truth, he could not be in any effectual sense a Reformer. The very means which he deemed the best for the renovation of Society indicated its incurable decay. Bands of women under the guidance of himself or some other priest might give themselves to the service of God, and even to good works for their fellow-creatures. They were flying from a detestable society; they were vindicating high duties for their sex. But they were combining with the court to suggest the belief that domestic life is an essentially unholy one; that women were only in their right state when they lived apart from the other sex, subject to a Confessor or director of the conscience who was likely, even if he were a good

LECT. XV.

Influence of the Church.

man, to confuse rather than elevate their standard of character and duty. The Church in the lower Empire could not cease by its Creeds and by the acts of its better priests to remind men of a Universal Family—the express contrast to an Empire. But the Family caught the image of that against which it was the protest, and became itself the antagonist of the household. Still less could it rekindle any national life in those who spoke the language and preserved the memories of Themistocles and Demosthenes.

Eastern Civilization.

5. You must not forget that literature, so far as it can be divorced from life, had still a home in Constantinople and the great cities which were subject to it. So far as all antiquarian knowledge went, the care and study of MSS, the Arts which ministered to luxury and amusement, the East was becoming more and more markedly contrasted with the West. I reserve all considerations of that for the next Lecture; but I must remind you here that it was subject in the days of Honorius and Arcadius, and throughout the fifth century, to inundations of the tribes which seemed for a while just as likely to overwhelm the Greek Empire. They rolled over that Empire leaving it much as it had been; rather with an increased persuasion that it was the centre of Order and Civility to the Universe. That persuasion reached its highest point in the reign

Justinian. of Justinian, when the Goths of Italy and the Vandals of Africa were subdued by the arms

THE CHRISTIANIZED EMPIRE. 309

of Belisarius; when Arianism was crushed by LECT. XV.
a Ruler who yet had his own theological fancies
and was suspected of heresy; when he could
command old Rome to yield up its laws that they
might be organized by his ministers and receive
their authority from his sanction. A time no The grandeur and degradation of his age.
doubt very grand for Imperialism, when it put
forth its most gorgeous fruits, when it seemed to
strengthen its roots by the mixture of a soil that
was not its own. A grander time also than ever
for disputes about theological terms and the
colours of horses; for intrigues against the most
faithful generals; for intolerable female profligacy
in the highest places. A preparation for another
time which was at hand, for a proclamation utterly strange, tremendously startling to Rulers and
to people.

6. That proclamation issued from a cave in Ara- Mahomet.
bia while the monarchies of Greece and of Persia
were engaged in a struggle no less terrible, but
far more equal than that between Alexander and
Darius. A poor and solitary fugitive declared
that there was a God actually ruling in Heaven and commanding men to serve Him upon
earth. That was the awful and amazing news
which overthrew one of the two contending
Empires and robbed the other of its choicest
provinces. The addition 'I Mahomet am His Power of his message.
prophet' would have diminished the force of the
message, would have only added another sect
to the multitudes already in existence, if it had

not meant 'I proclaim war against all your idols of wood, stone, paper, in the name of this God. He lives, and is calling you to account for your worship of other Gods.' That was a sound before which the monarchs trembled, for it reminded them that they had professed a faith in this living God; that they had been debating about Him in all modes of their speech, with all fury in their acts; and that after all they had not believed in Him as their Ruler and Judge. When Temples and Cities, whether Persian or Christian, fell down before the armies of the Prophet; when places most dear and sacred to Jews and Christians owned their sway; when the first City of the Christian Empire was itself threatened; then indeed Christians felt and understood that with no Arabian Sect were they engaged, that One of whom all their Sects spoke was come down to fight against them.

7. No such series of events is merely stunning to those who are the witnesses of it. The defence of Constantinople shewed that a spirit had been slumbering in the people which could be awaked. The movements of the Emperors for breaking the images which they and their subjects had worshipped testified to the effects of the Islamite denunciations. But never more remarkably than in this iconoclasm was the essential contradiction of the Empire made manifest. Leo and his successors imitated Hezekiah and Josiah in their acts. But *they* were Kings of a Nation;

witnesses for the invisible Ruler of a Nation. The Isaurians were witnesses for their own right to dictate the faith of their subjects; whatever invisible Power they might in their hearts confess, their own power was what they seemed to the monks and people of Constantinople to be asserting, what they were in fact asserting. And *this* power the faith which they had trampled upon was able to defy. The Image meant what was more deep, more living, more righteous, more unseen, than the arms which broke it in pieces or punished the adoration of it. First in Greece, afterwards more completely in Italy, the iconodulists questioned, even set at nought as impious, a dominion which till then they had owned as sacred. A great Western Revolution—the birth of a Western Empire—was the consequence of the movement. In the East the monarch undid the acts of those predecessors and bowed to the images which the people had refused to abandon.

8. The dream that Constantinople might be the centre of the Latin as well as the Greek world which had been cherished by its founder, almost realised by Justinian, was now over. Could not the Family at least maintain its universality? No! Language and difference of customs seemed to affect this Society as well as the other. Latins and Greeks found reasons for anathematising each other. The common faith was the very plea for separations. In the ninth century the enmity of the Churches was declared, in the eleventh reconcilia-

LECT. XV.

Tyranny involved in it.

Defeat of it.

The Eastern and Western Churches at open war.

tion appeared to be hopeless. Then began that new fanaticism among the Mahometans who were in possession of the Sepulchre which stimulated the powers of the West to combine for its recovery. The Grecian Empire felt the increased terror of the Crescent, was inspired with still greater terror by the advance of the soldiers of the Cross. It tried to repel both forces by cunning; it shewed both how weak it was in the midst of its magnificence. The lesson was not lost upon Venice, which knew the East better than the rest of Europe, and for which a rich and commercial city offered a dearer prize than Jerusalem The fourth Crusade in spite of the threats of Innocent III. was directed against the city of the Cæsars. He received its homage from those who had disobeyed his commands and incurred his excommunication. For a few years the bishops of Rome could appoint Patriarchs over the heretic Empire, and were acknowledged by its civil rulers. To endure such a yoke was impossible. All there was of religion and of native life in Greece rose against it. The conquerors themselves, lay and clerical, felt their position to be untenable and ridiculous. If Greeks and Latins were to be united it could not be by compelling either to adopt the habits and ceremonies of the other. So a most instructive and precious lesson respecting the distinctness and sacredness of native life was borne in the heart of an Empire which had done all that was possible to extinguish it.

9. Not by Latin hands was the predestined doom of the city to be accomplished; not by Latin hands was it to be averted. The early Saracens were full of passionate zeal for the *faith* which had taken possession of them; but the Islamite *polity* was never realised—never presented to the world—as it was by the Ottoman Turks. When they appeared it was manifest that the destroyer, however his march might for awhile be retarded, was on his way. The two divisions of Christendom might by degrees awake to the sense of a common danger, to ineffectual efforts at reconciliation. They might ask themselves like men in a dream whether a Christian Family ought not to be at one; why it could not be; why it could not resist an enemy whom it deemed the enemy of Christ. There was no answer except the dishonest cabals of a council, that could split hairs and tell lies, but the members of which had no belief in each other or in themselves or in God. The best and only answer came from the Constantine who died before the gates of his city as the Mahometan victor entered it.

How that fall affected the Society and the Social Morality of the Latin kingdoms I must consider in another Lecture. I contemplate it now as the necessary catastrophe of the Constantinopolitan history, as the true interpretation of that history. For a whole millennium the question was tried under the most favourable conditions whether a Christian Empire is possible; whether the idea

LECT. XV.

The destined Conqueror.

The Council of Florence.

The Fall.

The Moral of it.

LECT. XV.

The impossibility of a Christian Empire demonstrated.

The change to Ottoman Rule a reason for thanksgiving.

of it does not involve a flagrant contradiction. Every new passage in the story has helped us in the examination of that problem; here is the final solution of it. Such a revelation of the name and character of God and of His relation to His creatures as the Christian's Creed and the Lord's Prayer take for granted cannot coexist with an Empire such as that which Augustus established, which Constantine transferred to a new city and consecrated with new names. All who adhere strongly to the Polity which is described in Scripture as the Kingdom of Heaven must be in hostility to this Kingdom, must, however little they may aim at that result, be working for its subversion. Such an Empire nevertheless demands some invisible basis for its support; cannot exist without it. The Mahometan Creed, the announcement of a God who merely commands His creatures, who stands in no living relation to them, supplies this basis; it is a firmer one than a shifting sand of words notions and ceremonies like that on which the Christian Emperors tried to build their palaces and their temples. I cannot conceive—History gives us no warrant for conceiving—that an Empire like the Turkish can exist in its greatest vigour without the accompaniments of Turkish life—polygamy and that dread of a brother's succession which leads to his murder. But even if these are recognised as necessary elements of the Society, it is less hideously insincere, less intrinsically immoral, than that of which I have been speaking to-day. One should never contemplate without awe the departure of such an Empire from the earth; but it was an incubus from which men must have been delivered before they could be convinced that Truth and not Falsehood is the Lord of the Universe.

LECTURE XVI.

THE UNIVERSAL FAMILY A LATIN FAMILY (ROME).

<small>Lect. XVI.</small>

In my last Lecture I may seem to have spoken of Constantine with less honour than he deserves. If I have erred it has been in good company. That the puritan poet Milton should have thought slightingly of him might cause you no surprise. But the language of the Catholic theologian Dante is even more vehement. The poet finds Constantine among the blessed indeed, but if he has been saved himself 'he has brought ruin on the world.'

<small>Del Paradiso, Canto xx. lines 55—60.</small>

What this ruin was in Dante's judgment we learn from his *Inferno*. He supposed Constantine to have made a donation of lands to the Bishops of Rome. That donation, it seemed to him, had been the cause of unspeakable corruption to them and to the Church. Had Dante been aware that no such donation was made, that the story of it was a fiction which wise men in the 9th century disputed, which was afterwards to be thoroughly exploded; *his* special reason for bitterness against the

<small>Dell' Inferno, Canto xix. lines 115—118.</small>

<small>Dante's reason.</small>

first Christian Emperor would have been removed. Naturally enough he contemplated all subjects from a Latin point of view. He describes Constantine as founding his city in the East, that 'he might give the Shepherd room'—in other words, that he might leave the Popes in possession of Rome.

Constantine makes room for the Pope.

That mode of interpreting History is not so unphilosophical as to our Protestant eyes it might at first appear. The great contrast of the two portions of the modern world from the beginning of the fourth century to the middle of the 15th, is that an Emperor had dominion in the one—an Emperor *plus* a Patriarch; that one claiming the name of a Spiritual Father was *the* Ruler of the other; Emperors when they existed often challenging a rival authority, but always paying homage to his. The fourth century from the conversion of Constantine to the end of the reign of Theodosius may be looked upon as an intermediate period during which this new authority was beginning to make itself felt, often checked by the presence of an Emperor in his own capital. When Honorius left Rome for Ravenna—when Alaric sacked the old city and shewed a reverence only for Christian priests and Temples and for those whom they protected—then it became a question whether this reverence would be sufficient to hold in subjection rude tribes which certainly would not bow to any material force that could be sent against them. When the little Augustus disappeared from the stage, and the temporary anarchy gave place to the

The sacking of Rome.

The fall of the Empire.

sway of the Ostrogoths, there was the dawn of a national life for *Italy;* there was no longer any *Roman* monarch who could dream of contesting with Constantinople for Universal Empire. The Popes might sometimes turn to the Empire for protection against heretical neighbours; quite as often the Emperors and their ecclesiastical dependents were the heretics whom they confronted with their own decrees. Justinian's victories might be welcomed by them for a while. But the Lombards came—perhaps by Greek invitation. The Bishops of Rome knew not whether they or the Exarchs of Ravenna were least to be trusted. In the utter desolation of Rome Gregory the First shewed himself the true father of it. He realised the might of that name. He had faith to expect that a European family would gather around it. His Popedom was the inauguration of such a Family.

What were its limitations? The Patriarch of Constantinople, John the Faster, said that he who claimed to be a father should be a Universal One. Gregory's humility trembled to usurp the name; his Greek antagonist would not concede it to him. But he could not frankly *disclaim* it. Was not the Family which Christ established a Universal one? Could he on whom the duty had devolved of bringing men into it dare to confine it by any geographical boundaries? Yet must it not have a common worship; and if that, a common language for the expression of worship? If there was that unfortunate Greek tongue, if it had been turned to rather sacred uses, if the wretched Jews boasted of their language as entitled to a certain veneration, what were these facts to the tribes which Gregory longed to reclaim and unite in a divine Society? They were clearly committed to Latin Guardianship; in Latin habits they must be clothed; in Latin songs and prayers they must pour out their deeper thoughts; they might talk of their farms and their merchandise in what dialects they found convenient. So did this excellent man seek to mould the West according to his conceptions; so to the degree that his conception prevailed, did he convert what in his inmost heart he believed to be a Universal Family into a Latin Family.

To the extent that his conception prevailed; how can we determine that extent? Certainly by no measures of ours. We can only perceive that two principles essentially hostile were contending in European Society, contending in the same minds lay and ecclesiastical, male and female; contending in the Bishops of Rome themselves. It was not merely the notion that the sacred world was a Latin world in conflict with a belief that a Son of Man had appeared for the redemption of all people and kindreds. Inseparable from this was the perplexity between the Father of Heaven to whom prayer was offered, and the Father who dwelt in a house, perhaps a palace, upon earth; the perplexity whether there was a King-

Whom it affected.

dom of Heaven governing the earth, or whether Heaven and earth were hopelessly separated, and only a mimicry of one could be exhibited on the other. Most practical was this perplexity for those who inhabited cities and were concerned with the occupations of men; not less so for those who dwelt in solitudes or religious societies, trying to raise their thoughts from the visible to the invisible, believing that the true home of their spirits was in the last. Every one who repeated the Lord's Prayer or the Creed had some sense of this confusion; it beset doctors of divinity when they recollected that they were human beings. Gregory's own dream could not have been fulfilled if men learnt to believe chiefly in him. He hoped to make them trust One whom he trusted; it was his calamity if he interposed himself between the worshippers and the object of their worship.

Islamism in the West.

The proclamation of Mahomet followed the work of Gregory the Great. It was the proclamation of a Universal dominion, of a God who bade all men submit to His invisible rule. The soldiers of the Crescent had no thought of bounding their conquests by continents or by languages. The old province of Africa stooped to them, they subdued the Visigoths of Spain; they entered France. But in Western Europe Islamism encountered not an Empire but a Christendom; a Society based upon the Family principle under whatever contradictions that principle might be exhibited. The Invisible Father stood in contrast to the mere

Christendom.

Sovereign; the confession of one in whom Divinity and Humanity were united confronted the denial of all fellowship between them. These conditions involved others, which the Popes could not understand. The message of a divine Fatherhood and of a Son of Man had gone forth among tribes distinct from each other. The Ostrogoths in Italy had begun to develope a national order, laws which, if affected by those of Rome, were not imperial. The Lombards impressed a far more distinctly national character upon the land. There was clearly a kind of morality in them which Churchmen did not manifest at all in the same degree. Humanity was not the characteristic of these tribes, nor forgiveness, nor humility. Respect for veracity and justice, however passion might interfere with it, was. The same qualities, accompanied probably with a stronger domestic feeling, a deeper honour for women, dwelt in the Anglo-Saxons to whom Gregory proclaimed the Gospel of Christ. In them, as well as the Franks, these qualities might sometimes be cultivated by the lessons of Christian priests, sometimes stifled; but the elements of them existed before those lessons were imparted; if that had not been so, we have no reason to suppose they would ever have penetrated into the social life of our ancestors. I believe the *foundations* of that Social life were discovered by those who spoke of the Family for all mankind. But their imperfect announcement of that Family, their circumscription of it within Latin

<small>LECT. XVI.</small>

<small>The Latin parents surrounded by troublesome children.</small>

<small>The Clashing of the particular families with the general Family.</small>

limits inevitably made them jealous of the nations which they were nurturing, incapable of perceiving what need there could be for them. Many of the habits which were to be characteristic of the Nations, industry in tillage of the land, the invention of useful arts, the honour of letters, the cultivation of the man himself, had distinguished the Monasteries of the West from those of the East. From these proceeded many of the brotherhoods which were so beneficial in the infancy, which may perhaps under new conditions be more beneficial in the maturity, of Trade; which contributed to the organization of towns. The Monks of the West, as Count Montalembert has shewn, undertook also splendid labours for the evangelisation of different European countries and for the reformation of their manners. But they shared with their Eastern prototypes the inevitable disease of seeming to be protesters against family life as gross and secular, witnesses that the sexes will be most holy when most separated. The excuses for such an opinion lie upon the surface of history; the accidental and occasional benefits of the separation cannot be gainsaid. But even if it had been limited to the orders, even if Celibacy had not become the universal law of the Latin priesthood, it must have shaken to its roots the feeling of a connexion between the Universal Family and the particular Family and have reacted most injuriously upon the former.

The effects of this reaction became specially

manifest when those events happened which separated the Western from the Eastern World. The Bishops of Rome, quarrelling with Emperors of Constantinople on the subject of Images and dreading the Lombards, invoked the aid of the Franks. They appealed not to the Merovingian kings—the *Rois fainéants*—but to the Mayors of the Palace. As the reward of their services they were constituted monarchs of France by the Popes. When the Lombards were overthrown Charles received the iron crown. He made the donation of lands to the Roman Bishop, with which Dante credited Constantine. He was consecrated by that Bishop Emperor of the West.

The Popes rewarding their defenders.

The foundation of this Empire notwithstanding the endless questions respecting spiritual and secular Jurisdiction to which it gave rise, is hailed by some modern philosophers as the commencement of a Social Life for Europe, and through Europe for America. It is strange that these philosophers should be the great champions of Fact against all metaphysical and theological conceptions. A conception, partly metaphysical, partly theological, was involved in the establishment of a Western Empire; to be the rival of the now heretic Greek Empire; to rest upon the authority of the successors of St Peter, yet to inherit the traditions of Augustus, Diocletian, and Constantine. Men intoxicated with mysticism may lose themselves in admiration of a phantom which combined so many fragments of the past, which exhibited Pa-

The Empire of Charles the Great.

A theologico-metaphysical conception.

ganism and Christianity in such a beautiful mosaic. The disciples of 'positive' fact ought to remember that the Empire of Charlemagne, though it had a founder so able and brilliant, so capable of appreciating the worth of Legislation as well as of education, yet fell to pieces on his death; his laws, his Education, since they were not buried in its ruins, helping to invigorate the Nation which it would have extinguished.

I do not, of course, forget that this holy Roman Empire was to have a revival in the tenth century. That fact is very important: but instead of connecting it directly with the experiment of Charlemagne, we must trace its origin and necessity to the social bewilderments of which that experiment was the source. Was the Western Bishop the creator of the Emperor, or was the Emperor the Patron of his spiritual father, the real source of dignity to the Pope? That was the question to which the circumstances of Charlemagne's elevation gave birth, or at any rate which it forced upon the consideration of the West. It was a most practical question—one which was certain to involve the most practical results. It must as far as possible be kept out of sight; if nothing else could be done the secular patronage must be thrown back to a distant age. The Gallic Monarch was dangerously near; if the first Christian Emperor could be supposed to have acknowledged a spiritual supremacy already attested by the decrees of various Councils in the Roman Bishop—and to have endowed him with a permanent territory—there was a sacredness about the dominion which at least would diminish the obvious incongruity of it with his pretension to be a Universal Father. It was needful to forge the ecclesiastical decretals as well as the imperial donation. A monk believed that he should be doing God service in undertaking that task; his compilation was accepted and endorsed by a succession of Popes. But it was not unchallenged. Hincmar, one of the greatest ornaments of the Gallican Church, denied that an Italian had ever been exalted to absolute supremacy over all other Bishops. A quarrel began between Cismontanes and Ultramontanes which has not terminated in our day.

<small>LECT. XVI.</small>

<small>The Gallican Protest.</small>

This dispute concerns my subject chiefly as it illustrates one specially weak point in ecclesiastical morality. It has not the same general interest as those frightful abuses in the Italy of the tenth century which produced the German effort for Reform. The Empire of the Othos was not called into existence by the Popes to save them from extinction. It was sullenly accepted as the only means of introducing something like order and morality into the election and the conduct of the spiritual Rulers. To that extent it was successful. Some scandals were abated, a higher moral standard recognized. But then came the great reaction of the eleventh century. Hildebrand arose to declare that none could reform the Church

<small>Empire of the Othos.</small>

<small>Totally unlike in its nature and object that of the 9th century.</small>

but its spiritual fathers; and that they had also a right to reform, govern and depose Princes. A Western Empire coming to its birth under such circumstances and encountering in its cradle such an antagonist might be useful or mischievous; but it would bear a very slight, chiefly nominal, resemblance to that which passed under our review in the last Lecture. The hands were the hands of the Roman, but the voice was the voice of the Teuton. Arminius was clothing himself in the robes of Augustus.

The conflict which ensued between these powers down to the time when the House of Hapsburg became supreme in Germany is of profound interest. No one can deny that the conception of Hildebrand was a grand one. He would be content with no Latin dominion. The dream of an imperial derivation for his authority was hateful to him. The father of Christendom must be a Universal Father. Not the Emperor Constantine but the fisherman Peter must be the rock on which his rights were founded. Was not the humbleness of his progenitor his glory? What was the glory of princes in comparison with it? Holding such a position, could he tolerate the beggarly ambition of ecclesiastics who would sell their heavenly offices for the paltry lucre of earth, who cared for the delights of marriage, the honour of transmitting lands to their heirs? They must be hindered from this low trafficking; they must be roused to consider the amazing spiritual power which they might exercise if they were indifferent to such trumpery prizes. He would shew them how a man conscious of celestial prerogatives could mock and defy those to whom they were looking up for patronage or protection. National Kings, what were they but servants whom he might use or cashier at his pleasure? Emperors who dared to talk of Rome as if it were theirs—who had thought they could make and unmake their divinely appointed Master—let them kneel at his feet, or try whether they could withstand the bolts of the Almighty which would be hurled against them. It is impossible to listen to such words without a certain admiration for the man who poured them forth, especially when he proved that he was able to endure punishments as well as to threaten or inflict them. Hildebrand had assuredly a deep and inward conviction that a Universal Family had a divinity which did not belong to a Universal Empire; had an honest contempt for that because it seemed to claim a divinity for brute force. And yet perhaps the chief claim of Hildebrand upon the respect of the Social Moralist is, that he brought into clearer light than any less earnest and resolute man could have done the contradiction that was latent in the ecclesiastical scheme to which he was imparting so much new energy. The conflict with the Empire shewed how much of imperialism the Papacy itself embodied; how much the Father must be transformed into an Emperor if he would be the rival of the Emperor.

Lect. XVI.

Defiance of Monarchs.

His effort to be different from them a failure.

328 UNIVERSAL MORALITY.

Irony of his position.

His separation of the priests from the people mischievous to both.

He held his office by descent from St Peter; perhaps so; what inheritance did he take by the descent? Was he a Servant of Servants in virtue of it, or a King of Kings? Hildebrand would fain be both; one because he was the other. But to be King of Kings he *must* have some dominion such as Kings had. The imaginary donation of Constantine, the real gift of Charlemagne, had attached such a dominion to the See of Rome. Did it seem to Gregory a humiliating mixture of earthy dross with the heavenly treasure which the Apostle had bequeathed? If it did, he must submit to an increase of the humiliation. The piety of Matilda greatly enlarged the Church's patrimony. He who claimed to set his foot on the neck of Princes is himself a Prince. How insoluble this knot would become by human fingers, how many efforts would be made to cut it, future ages were to declare. Hildebrand was not without a bitter foretaste of the perplexity.

Nor could he be wholly content with the result of his domestic legislation, many excuses as there were for it in the irregularity of the Clergy, in their neglect of their proper duties, in their servility to lay patrons. Great as these evils might be, did their separation from human ties bring no contempt upon those ties in the flocks which they were to guide, did it create no perilous arrogance in themselves? It gave them a 'detachment' from common mundane interests, which might in some cases leave them more free to think and speak of the Kingdom of Heaven. Might it not also tempt them to set up a kingdom for themselves which was not heavenly at all, which is exactly the reverse of heavenly if spiritual pride is the special attribute of the devil?

LECT. XVI.

The Crusades in some degree abated the strife between the Holy Empire and the Holy Church. They had a more important effect, it has been observed, in turning the thought of the West from Rome to Jerusalem, from the Vicar of Christ to Christ. The Orders which devoted themselves to the recovery of the Sepulchre were bound to an invisible chief; the symbol of every warrior suggested One who had conquered by suffering. However many influences were hostile to these and at last swayed the hosts more completely, one must never forget such signs in estimating the character of an age and the impulses by which its acts were determined. I have dwelt in a former Lecture on the failure of the Crusades to accomplish their primary object, as well as on the absurdity involved in the conception of drawing swords to prove how much better the New Testament method of propagating a faith is than that which is sanctioned in the Koran. But while we take full account of these inconsistencies and treat them as indispensable helps in judging of the mediæval ἦθος, it would be a great blunder to overlook the other not less obvious side of that ἦθος, all which was implied in the reverence for weakness by men whose temptation was to glorify

The Crusades not on the whole favourable to the Papal ascendancy.

The reverence for weakness by strength.

strength. I have shewn you that I am not disposed to exaggerate the graces of Chivalry; that I regard even its special grace, the homage to women, with a kind of suspicion. Taking that homage however in connexion with the whole life of the Knight—with his manifold inducements to ferocity—I cannot but hail it as a great step from the purely virile into the humane morality. Chivalry had its self-exalting and therefore its degraded side. It might foster the pride of birth; it might injure women by making them idols. But it bore witness against dogmas which both the Greek and the Latin Church were hallowing. The boast of Apologists that Christianity has elevated the condition of women may be open to dispute; much which has been called Christianity in all divisions of Christendom has degraded them. If any opinions about Christ hinder us from regarding Him as the Centre of the Humanity which is common to both sexes, those opinions must lower both. Chivalry, however imperfectly, did counteract some of these opinions.

There is one aspect of Latin cultivation in which it was markedly contrasted with the Greek; *curiously* contrasted, since it was indebted to Greeks for the divergence. I have remarked how carefully the study of the letter of the old classical books was pursued by those who were elevated above the vulgar at Constantinople, how a kind of antiquarian taste must have been diffused through Society. The Latins with the most imperfect means of understanding the old Philosophers—with bad translations of Aristotle made from a corrupt text—nevertheless received an impression from them, specially from him, which had nothing that answered to it among those who could converse with him and with Plato in their own tongue. This fact has been represented to us in words that convey a very confused notion of it, and which make it simply miraculous. Aristotle, it is said, became a supreme dictator in the schools of the West, because they needed a philosophical dictator as well as one in theology. Why did they ask for a philosophical dictator, and why did this one offer himself to them when there was everything in his Pagan reputation to alarm them, when Popes had openly denounced him? It was not first as a dictator—it was in precisely the opposite character as the awakener of the subtlest intellectual questions—that he attracted and subdued them. Greeks would have ridiculed the mediæval Latins—moderns have ridiculed them—not for their willingness to embrace any conclusions which were given them, but for their restless anxiety to solve riddles which men who are busy with the affairs of the world find it convenient to pronounce insoluble. How the words we speak are related to the thoughts which they express, to the things which they indicate—this doubt tormented them; they could not dismiss it. They could learn the forms of Logic while it was unsettled; they could not satisfy themselves about the use or sig-

Marginalia: Lect. XVI. What was the power of Aristotle over them? What have words to do with things and thoughts?

nification of Logic. And was not Logic intertwined with all the subjects upon which it was possible to discourse? did it not mean Discourse? Aristotle, the great Logician, had also discoursed about Ethics, Physics, the Soul, Being, all things in Heaven and Earth. Christian Theology lay a little out of his sphere; but must it not be mightily influenced by all that was within his sphere? A multitude of quibbles were mingled with these thoughts; triflers could entertain themselves with these, feeling so much the more zest in them because they were evidently on the borders of the gravest controversies that men could be occupied with. But we shall be triflers more vain than they were if we treat the questions which the Nominalists and Realists debated in the schools as beneath the notice of intellectual men. The fault of the schoolmen was that they were far too intellectual; they were always striving to sound the depths of the human intellect; to ascertain its capacities. A time came when such enquiries became utterly exhausting to those who were engaged in them; when the heart and flesh of men cried out for some more nourishing food. Nevertheless it is true that the relation of words to thoughts and things is not less important to the nineteenth century than it was to the twelfth. However contemptuous we may be towards those who felt themselves compelled to study these relations, we may, before we are aware, be embarrassed by them while we are studying the courses of the planets, or the intrigues of cabinets or the fashions of drawing-rooms.

There was a movement in the beginning of the 13th century which ultimately affected all the pursuits of the schools, but which began by affecting the people much more. The Mendicant Orders were witnesses that the Church was meant for the poor; that it failed utterly and denied its first principle, if it had not a message for the poor. Retirement into cells for the sake of holiness might be good; the Franciscan and the Dominican felt that their primary vocation was to act upon the unholy. It might be very honourable for priests to sit in high places and receive the homage of princes; another kind of honour was claimed by the Apostles; the circumstances of later times had not made it obsolete. What was Property in the eyes of the Fishermen? They gave up their goods, they had all things common. If the fallen were to be reclaimed, if the complaints of heretics were to be answered, the new preachers like their prototypes must be servants not masters, beggars instead of lords.

The Mendicant Orders.

Their principle and object.

The project was formed in the days of the Pope who possessed most of worldly power, who exhibited the most of worldly sagacity. Innocent III. exercised the dominion which Gregory VII. claimed, but exercised it with the full persuasion that he could only trample upon princes by resorting to the arts of princes. A career, on the whole, of marvellous success—of success, as in the case of

The time of their appearance.

the Latin conquest of Constantinople, when it could have been least expected, when it came by disobedience to his own commands—was drawing to its close. He had sanctioned the horrors of the Albigensian war; could he be quite sure that he had taken the divinest way of vindicating the cause of Christ? He was a Ruler over both divisions of Christendom; had he any real authority over the hearts of his subjects in either? The proposition to turn enthusiasts loose upon the world was contrary to his maxims of Policy. But might not enthusiasts, however unpalatable to wise men, do a considerable work among fools? The lofty politician accepted the help of the beggars; they soon justified, and more than justified, his calculations. They did acquire the dominion over the vulgar which seemed likely; they acquired also a dominion over the learned which would have seemed most improbable; in a little time they became the most effectual champions of the Papacy in all lands against the national spirit of those lands.

For this becomes now a far more important conflict than that between the Empire and the Popedom, though in many ways entangled with that. The Italian Cities, in their efforts for emancipation, so full of various interest, so broken by quarrels with each other and by intestine conflicts, sometimes call forth the wrath and tyranny of the Empire, sometimes secure a strange patronage from the Papacy; not seldom link themselves first to one then to the other, always having a reasonable excuse for distrusting both. Their experiments in government; the talents and the arts which they develope; their commercial activity; their manifold crimes and bitter disappointments; exhibit a most striking picture of what may be called naked civilization; that is to say, the civilization of *Cities* without the stability, the comparative dulness which belongs to the land, to a people that has land for the basis of its interests. In the other parts of Europe, as I hinted in my first Lecture, the growth of nations cannot be identified with civilization of this kind. The towns were to be all important elements in them; without a municipal order they would have been at the mercy of rude and tyrannical proprietors; but the two, country and town, were not separately, but together through collisions, or through the dependence of each upon the other, to work out a distinct native life. In the Western world these silent processes went on without much disturbance from the Holy Empire or the Bishop of Rome; not however without many and opposing influences from those who called themselves the servants of the last. The priests of the town left to themselves were generally fostering the native habits, contributing to the unfolding of the native speech; the monasteries, though essentially Latin, were producing Chronicles which were often vehemently patriotic. But the Friars in their character of Reformers were essentially Cosmopolitan, which meant at last essentially Roman; defenders of the Papal

[margin: Difference between the Italian Republics and the rest of Europe.]

[margin: Ecclesiastical influences in the various nations, some favourable some obstructive to their growth.]

power as the only sacred and divine power. The dignified Ecclesiastics, on the contrary, were often much more attached to the native King of whom they held the lands than to the distant Priest from whom they received their pall. And the Universities, however devoted to general Latin cultivation, often resisted the intrusion of the Mendicant Orders into their government, often nourished the temper which those orders were seeking to crush.

<small>The Friars altogether Roman.</small>

<small>The result.</small> Thus the different representatives of what I have called the Universal Family under a Latin limitation, were working either by encouragement, or by an opposition which was even more effectual than encouragement, to call forth that national life in different lands which the Popes desired to extinguish. The blessing of that awakening, the elements of Social Morality which we owe to it and which were perishing for the want of it, I have considered already. I shall not repeat what I said on that subject in the second part of this course. But I must beg you to notice one or two points which concern us especially here.

<small>The conflict between Property and Communism.</small> 1. I have said that *Property* is one of the characteristics of a Nation, that the sense of Property appears in us along with the sense of Law. I have said also that the refusal to call anything which they had their own was one leading characteristic of the Universal Family on its first appearance in Jerusalem. No law had affirmed or could affirm such a principle; the Apostles uni-

formly treated it as lying wholly out of the range of law. But the adoption of this principle as the governing one of their lives unquestionably gave the Friars their great power in all lands; *they* seemed to have caught the mantle of the Apostles while most of those who were called the successors of the Apostles had envied the purple of the Cæsars. The shock was therefore tremendous when these orders were found to be willing agents in collecting revenues from the national Clergy to increase the Papal Treasury; when subtle questions about the limits of general property and individual property divided the disciples of Francis; when religious mendicancy appeared to be cultivating covetous habits in those who gave as well as in those who asked. These discoveries, of which our earliest English literature is full, embittered the feelings of the yeoman and tradesman against the Friars. Though we know that there were noble specimens of moral excellence as well as of theological wisdom among Franciscans and Dominicans—they began as orders to be regarded with detestation, not by those who disbelieved the Creeds of the Church, but by those who clung to them; by those who cried like the writer of *Piers Plowman's Visions* for a living God, and felt that the popular teachers were separating the people from Him. It cannot be too strenuously repeated, that the movement among the middle classes in England during the 14th century against the Friars was in the strictest sense an assertion of Englishmen's

The communism of the Friars a chief secret of their power.

Their traffic made them hateful to devout men.

right to be members of the Church of Christ; a vindication of it as a Church for the Nation. There was no denial of the Universality of the Church; there was a denial of the attempt to make it a Latin Church, and to disconnect its morality with that of the ordinary Citizen. There was no denial of its claim to be a Family under a Universal Father; there was a suspicion that the Universal Father must be nearer to His children than the city of Rome was, that he who dwelt there must have taken a title which was not his.

2. The prestige of that City had been great. If a Universal Family was to succeed a Universal Empire, and if there was to be an earthly Father of that Universal Family, no one can wonder that this should have been regarded as his proper throne. It was startling then to hear that a Pope who had specially exulted in his dignity, who had proclaimed a triumphant fête to all Nations in the eternal city, had been driven from that home by French Lawyers, and that his successors had abandoned it for Avignon. No amount of humiliation for a servant of God would have seemed strange to those who read the Apostolic records; but humiliation following such boasts as those of Boniface VIII., followed by such flagrant and open contempt of Morality as that displayed in the Court of Avignon, did startle the people of Europe, all the more because they were beginning to recollect what manner of men the early Ministers of the Church

had been. It is impossible by any cold study of the past to measure what these scandals were to those who were living among them. A number of passages in our own literature as well as the letters of Petrarch, who visited Avignon and felt the departed glory of Rome, may help us in some faint way to realise them.

3. Then came the greater and more amazing scandal which is denoted by the name of the Western schism. That was a battle between two and three bad men—a battle waged with every spiritual and every carnal weapon to decide which was the Vicar of Christ, the father of the Universal Family. When the evil became intolerable, when every nation was rent asunder by it, the University of Paris by the mouth of Gerson and other illustrious doctors declared that the knot must be cut, that a Council must be summoned, that it must decree who were the pretenders to divine authority, who was the appointed Judge and Dogmatist of Mankind.

The Western Schism.

Every one must have felt the force of the argument, that if such a Judge and Dogmatist existed the pretension of a Council to be above him involved a strange contradiction. Gerson and his friends were aware of the contradiction. They resolved to face it. Events for which they were not responsible, which they could not control, had produced a state of things which was flagrantly monstrous. The remedy might be dangerous, the disease must be fatal. Some have thought that

The pretensions of Councils.

nothing came out of the Councils which were summoned at that time except the murder of Huss, with the justification which it afforded for the strifes between Emperors and Ecclesiastics, seeing that when they were agreed it was to commit a scandalous breach of faith, as the prelude to an enormous crime. I should not undervalue that result since I look upon Huss as a martyr for truth, as an asserter of national righteousness against both the enemies of it. But the Councils produced other and wider, if not more important consequences than this. The reasonings in favour of their interference, and in opposition to it, forced the thought on Europe—"Popes then and Councils, these you 'think govern the Universe, separately or together, 'as friendly or as hostile powers. The Holy Em-'pire you suppose is meant to use its sword in 'obedience to them. You have deliberately, dis-'tinctly settled that God has left the earth to 'these rulers, that He takes no further charge of it. 'Then the Creed which you have taught us to 'utter, the Lord's Prayer which you give us indul-'gences for repeating, clearly mean nothing. They 'are mockeries.' So men in many a shop and household—in many a lonely monastery—were beginning to speak. The speech might be deep not loud; it was the more perilous for that.

4. The principle of a Universal Family then had maintained itself in the West under very different conditions from those which we examined in the last Lecture. It had not been merged in an

Empire; had not generally been in alliance with one. It had not shrunk before the Mahometan proclamation; it had defied that proclamation. It had met the announcement of an Absolute Despot in the Heaven with the assertion that there is a union between Heaven and Earth in a Son of God. All the order of the West had borne testimony to this difference. There was no dead uniformity in Latin Europe though Churchmen had tried to create one. Nations had started out of the Family; the Church in each land had assumed national characteristics. But it seemed that the offspring must destroy that from which they had sprung if the Family was only Latin; if it could not really make good its claim to be universal. In the midst of these doubts and speculations—when the Father of the West was once again holding an insecure seat in the old City—came the news that the other City, the city of Constantine, was ready to fall. I alluded in my last Lecture to the efforts of the West—feeble and dishonest efforts—to avert that fall. When it actually came Nicholas V., a man of sincere purpose and high cultivation, trembled for the whole of Christendom. Could not he do something to repair the calamity? The Greek and Latin Churches had never been able to unite. Might not Greeks and Latins together constitute a commonwealth of letters; the first bringing the wisdom which was banished from its original home; the second, through their spiritual Ruler, diffusing human culture as they had once

Lect. XVI.

Contrast between the East and West.

The crisis for both.

diffused divine doctrine? Dean Milman's clear historical instinct perceived in these thoughts of the Pope, and in the events which issued from them, the crisis of Latin Christianity. What Christianity was to succeed that we must consider in the next Lecture.

LECTURE XVII.

THE UNIVERSAL AND THE INDIVIDUAL MORALITY IN CONFLICT.

NICHOLAS V. was unlike his most eminent predecessors. He did not aspire to convert barbarous tribes like Gregory I.; he did not dream of setting his foot on Kings like Gregory VII.; he did not suppose that the world could be held together by webs of policy like Innocent the Third. He did not appreciate the Mediæval divinity or philosophy, or the speech in which they were expressed. He accepted the signs of the times. He mourned over Constantinople as if it had been not the centre of a doctrine or ecclesiastical government opposed to the Latin, but as the centre of a culture by which Latins might benefit. He did not think that old Pagan learning would unchristianise Christendom. He hoped it might do much to humanize Christendom.

 His aspirations—if they were of this kind—had ultimately, it seems to me, a higher fulfilment than

_{LECT. XVII.}

_{Nicholas V.}

_{His aims and hopes.}

he expected. Whether they were fulfilled during his own century, by what is called the Renaissance or the Revival of Letters, you will hear different judgments from persons eminently qualified by their knowledge and ability to pronounce a judgment. Mr Roscoe, himself a merchant, felt an honourable sympathy with the Medicean Family, believing that it had converted Trade from the pursuit of personal pelf into an instrument for civilizing Italy and Europe. Mr Hallam, uniting the man of letters to the constitutional politician, hailed with joy the time when students ceased to pore over questions about the relation of words to things, and busied themselves with the orators, poets, statesmen who had used words gracefully and effectually to explain things and the relations of men to each other. On the other hand, you will read in Mr Browning's subtle and vigorous verse, in Mr Ruskin's eloquent prose, many an exposure of the external affectations, of the inward heartlessness, of this brilliant time. And if you turn from these native critics to the patriots of Italy, you will hear still more fervent denunciations of Medicean princes and popes who trafficked with the liberty of Florence, and ratified a code of political morality that debased their own land and all lands for more than a century.

If you reflect on these testimonies and steadily recognise the facts to which they appeal, you may gain a lesson from them all; you will not be overpowered by any of them. You will thankfully ac-

THE REVIVAL AND THE REFORMATION. 345

knowledge what innumerable benefits we owe to Greek literature; how Greek art has taught us to reverence the actual form and countenance of human beings; what a new impulse, what a sense of common fellowship Philology has imparted to the thoughts of men; what treasures of political experience are contained in the histories of the old Nations. Without that movement of which I am speaking, these gifts, and many that were to proceed from these, would have been hidden; the schools must have persevered in working mines in which gold had been found, in which little was left but rubbish. But precious as it is to know what men thought and what they were in the ages before the existence of a Universal Family for mankind was proclaimed—little as we can understand what that proclamation means if we treat these ages with indifference—it is impossible for Mr Browning or Mr Ruskin to exaggerate the habit of lying which was diffused among cultivated men by their efforts to reproduce the manners and tone of thinking in the old world. To call *such* a revival of the past *Progress*, is surely to indulge in the most ridiculous and the most mischievous of fictions. No popular superstition was really subverted; the people were encouraged to amuse themselves with all delusions, the most immoral and destructive. The refined men—sanctioning them in their intercourse with the world at large—had another set of superstitions older than these with which they trifled; not attaching any

Lect. XVII.

Blessings of the new learning.

Falsehood of modern Paganism.

meaning to them, liking them *because* they were unreal. Nicholas V. had probably no anticipations of such a calamity. Some of his successors welcomed it and adapted themselves to it. Some of them resisted it, not in the interests of morality but of their own paltry local ambition. Alexander VI. strikes us as a monstrous figure to stand at the end of the century of refinement and revival; but Macchiavelli, a most competent eye-witness, regarded him as the type of the princes and the policy of his time. If Europe was somewhat startled by what it heard of his iniquities, those who followed him exceeded other monarchs in the lust of conquest, excelled all in intrigue. From those whose main object was to win some paltry principality issued the spiritual decrees, the examples of spiritual wisdom and character which the Universe was to obey and copy. For Greece was Mahometan and America had been discovered. The Pope who used the Sultan to do murders for him, bade the most Catholic monarch take possession of the new world in Christ's name. What kind of life and government the Spaniards would exhibit to those who had worshipped the gods of Mexico and Peru, might be conjectured from the authority under which they conquered, from that specimen of life and government which they deemed the most sacred and divine.

But it is not possible to test the Morality of an age by looking at its more glaring transactions.

The Dialogues of Erasmus lead us from the acts of Emperors and Pontiffs, from the victories over a Continent, to the inner life of small circles of ordinary men, not in some foregone time, but in the very time which produced scholars of such ripe culture, of such exquisite faculties, as Erasmus himself. A more brilliant and in another sense a more dark picture than those dialogues give us of a time 'in which prophets were prophesying lies, and the priests bearing rule by their means, and a people were loving to have it so,' it is not easy to imagine. Practices which debased Society—which lowered the heart and bewildered the judgments of individuals—come before us stamped with a holy sanction, recommended if not enjoined as opiates or stimulants to the conscience, submitted to—it might be with grumbling with a half sense of their vanity—but still submitted to; for what other schemes had an equal chance of turning out useful hereafter? And these pictures are not drawn by some prejudiced fanatic, by some rebel against the existing order of things, by some malignant infidel. They are sketched by a humourist remarkable for his clear manly sense, by one who disliked innovations, who thought Leo X. might restore the age, by an earnest student of the Scriptures and of the fathers. Erasmus suffered much from external difficulties; but he was not tormented by internal struggles; he had the temper of the revival; he was what was called then, and has been called

LECT. XVII.

The Dialogues of Erasmus.

The picture of Social Morality which they present.

since, a Humanist rather than a Theologian. With the dogmas of those days he had little quarrel; what he lays bare is its want of ordinary Morality—social and individual.

No one, I think, proves more clearly to us that a Reformation could not come from the quarter whence he looked for it. Leo X. might fully appreciate the jokes of Erasmus, might call himself a humanist, might claim, beyond all question, to be one, if humanity consists in spending money upon works of art. But if Humanity has a connexion, as we sometimes fancy it has, with Man, with his well-doing and well-being, then Leo was not a humanist; for on that particular creature he had no leisure to bestow any thought, except so far as it had a capacity of hewing stones out of a quarry or of moulding them into certain shapes. Did Erasmus sincerely hope that any one of the scandals which he had charged other priests with promoting would be checked by this Pope? that it would not receive his fullest imprimatur if it would add a shilling to the treasury which he wanted for the purpose of enriching his city or glorifying his name? If the poor Scholar entertained such a dream it was soon to be scattered.

The story of Leo's sale of Indulgences and of the way in которой Tetzel proclaimed it in Germany has been told so often by authors writing in what is called the Protestant interest, that it becomes difficult to remember what profound moral interests, concerning all nations and all men, were

marginal notes: Was Leo X. a Humanist? · Sale of Indulgences.

involved in it. To me it seems the most momentous practical question ever presented to the consideration of human beings; one which never can be obsolete, with which every Protestant of the nineteenth century is engaged, not when he is refuting Romanists, but when he is examining his own deeds and principles. The watchwords of Luther may be repeated in England or Germany by those who in spirit are on the side of Leo. The maxim on which the Pope acted was this. He assumed that men in his own age and in every age must desire to escape the punishment of the evil deeds of which their consciences accused them, that for the chance of such an escape they would be willing to pay much. If there was a growing Scepticism about the papal power as well as about all other invisible influences, that scepticism might be rather favourable than damaging to an experiment grounded upon an accurate calculation of the ordinary motives of human conduct. A general feeling of uncertainty —a notion that all things may be true because nothing is certain—leads men to make ventures for objects which they feel would be desirable supposing they were possible. There may be a hundred blanks in a lottery, still the one prize tempts to a moderate, even an immoderate outlay. Popular preachers could persuade the vulgar that the promised pardon would be an effectual one in the courts above. Their rhetoric might not affect the more educated, but would they grudge a sum

<small>LECT. XVII.</small>

<small>The Calculation on which it rested.</small>

<small>General Scepticism favourable to its success.</small>

which *might* bring a reversion of profit to themselves, and which would be spent on the restoration of St Peter's? Suppose the accomplished prelate had any misgivings—very likely he had none—about so obvious a method of raising funds, the end to which they would be devoted must have soon comforted him. The event justified Leo's hopes. The age believed, as it had been taught by the highest examples, that money is the great power in the Universe. Crimes were rife in all classes of Society. Princes and peasants had an equal interest in getting them condoned. They had a good chance of eluding the vengeance of the Law on earth—it was powerless enough in most countries against ordinary thieves, still more against feudal brigands. But might it not pursue them into the other world? Princes and Magistrates declared that they had no jurisdiction there; that they could set aside no divine sentences. The Pope said that *he* had jurisdiction there also; that *he* was endowed with powers to remit the divine sentences. Tetzel declared there was no limit to that power; the papal treasury of pardons was infinite. Were his hearers mad enough to refuse the needful price for such a blessing?

There was but one answer to these pretensions that could be effectual. *Was* it a blessing which Leo offered? Martin Luther declared that it was not a blessing but a curse. For a man to escape from the punishment of his crimes was the worst misery that could befal him. It would be worth while for any one to spend a fortune if it would avert that misery. A man carries a plague of evil about him, which goes forth in crimes against his fellows. If he can be delivered from this plague—from the guilt, the guile, by which his conscience is tormented—if he can be made a right man—that *is* the blessing of all blessings. That is the blessing which he claims when he says, 'I believe in the forgiveness of sins.' Indulgence, remission of penalties is saying to a man, 'There 'is no forgiveness for thy *sins*. They cannot be 'sent away from thee to Hell. They must go with 'thee there.'

Forgiveness the opposite of Indulgence.

This was the spirit of the famous theses which Luther fixed on the door of the Church at Wittenberg. If they are construed into a mere denial of the Pope's power to do what he professed to do, their moral force is lost; their moral force and with it their effect on the Society of Europe. Luther as little asked God to let him escape from the punishment of his wrong doings as the Pope. He *had* asked for that gift in unutterable agonies. He had found that it *could* not be granted him. What matter was it where he was, in Hell or Heaven, if he was still the same? But if He who punished him was One in whom he might trust, who punished him that he might cease to trust in himself or to seek any good in himself—then indeed he might enter into the freedom of a man; the accuser and tormenter who was always near him could be answered and overcome.

Luther's Belief.

LECT. XVII.

Luther's recurrence to the old Creed.

This was that faith of Luther which assuredly did not seem to him a new one, introduced into Europe or Germany by him in the 16th century. He declared vehemently that it was the old Creed of his fathers, that he wanted no language to express it in but that which had been current in Christendom for centuries, that which children were taught in their nurseries. To that Confession he had had recourse in his own personal conflicts; as he studied the Hebrew Psalms and the Epistles of St Paul he had come to apprehend, in some small measure, the meaning of it, though he never expected to fathom its meaning. He was thoroughly sincere in these assertions, his whole heart was thrown into them. Why then was he at variance with those who used this Creed, who declared that it expressed what they believed and wished all men to believe?

How he became separated from those who repeated it.

The first answer is, that they commanded men to believe *implicitly* on the authority of others that which he exhorted men to believe *directly* for themselves. The belief in Christ he said was an escape from his own opinions and from the opinions of men. It was trust in One who could teach a man better than all mortals could teach him, or than he could teach himself. The second answer which is implied in the former is, that Luther claimed for all men, even the most sinful, the right to believe that they might become righteous; whereas faith, as it was generally understood, was either a necessity to which men must submit under dire penalties or a privilege which certain men might exercise, if they had by previous discipline entitled themselves to it. The third answer I have hinted at in the title of this Lecture. A Universal faith, a faith for the whole Church, for the whole human family, might at times seem to Luther a great gift. He might rejoice that he and his German countrymen had inherited it. But the formula of the Creed is '*I* believe.' That was strictly Luther's formula. He had fought for this faith in his closet. It had come to *him* as *his* deliverance. He was the champion of an individual life, an individual Morality. He inaugurated a time in which individual Morality was to engage in a very strange kind of battle with that Morality which had associated itself either with the Empire or the Popedom. The nature of this conflict we should try to understand; then perhaps we may have some hope that principles seemingly hostile will be reconciled not by superficial agreements or hollow compromises, but through a fuller discovery of that which is involved in each of them.

The Individuality of Luther's Faith.

Mr Clough sings in his remarkable *Amours de Voyage*,

Clough's Poems, Vol. II. p. 304.

Luther they say was unwise; like a half taught German, he
    could not
See that old follies were passing most tranquilly out of re-
    membrance;
Leo the Tenth was employing all efforts to clear out abuses,
Jupiter, Juno and Venus, Fine Arts, and Fine Letters, the
    Poets,
Scholars and Sculptors and Painters were quietly clearing away
    the

> Martyrs and Virgins and Saints, or at any rate Thomas Aquinas:
> He must forsooth make a fuss, and distend his huge Wittenburg lungs, and
> Bring back Theology once yet again in a flood upon Europe:
> Lo you, for forty days from the windows of Heaven it fell; the
> Waters prevail on the earth yet more for a hundred and fifty;
> Are they abating at last? the doves that are sent to explore are
> Wearily fain to return at the best with a leaflet of promise,
> Fain to return as they went to the wandering wave-tost vessel,
> Fain to re-enter the roof which covers the clean and the unclean.
> Luther they say was unwise; he didn't see how things were going.

So many have said, and more have thought; the description is vivid, dramatic, and suggestive. Leo's mythology is admirably contrasted with Luther's theology; the popularity of the first in its own age and later ages with the cruel German deluge by which it was for awhile overwhelmed. If Jupiter, Juno and Venus, the fine letters and fine arts, had only shewn a man how he could have a clear conscience the deluge might have been averted. The dove will go out of the Ark and return again and again, now, as of old, without much avail, if she can bring no leaflet of promise to that. Yet I would not have you suppose that the individual Conscience alone was benefited by this flood. He who 'employed all efforts to clear out abuses' sanctioned as the Vicar of Christ an abuse which struck at the root of all national law. If he could sell indulgences, he could make void the efforts of Statesmen and Legislators; he could teach the people to think that there was no sanctity in any prohibitions. Those who defied them might be exposed to

THE REVIVAL AND THE REFORMATION. 355

present risks; every robber and murderer of course incurred risks in the pursuit of his business. But it was merely that; a higher authority could set him free from future risks; could secure him against much more serious contingencies than any to which he was liable if he were clumsy or unlucky enough not to evade human justice. From that hour to the present every organised society has experienced this peril; the papal dominions most. Can you wonder that Nations should be thankful to Luther, the theologian, for proclaiming that the doctrine of Indulgences is not divine but devilish? *Nations therefore interested in the Reformer's protest.*

I am illustrating a maxim which I announced in an earlier part of these Lectures when I point out this sign of fellowship between the individual and the national Morality; when I say that Luther vindicated the one because he vindicated the other. It is a confirmation of that truth not an exception from it, to say that when the teaching of Luther gave birth to a Lutheran Sect or Society, much confusion was introduced into States and Nations, a new element of discord among men. Just because Luther proclaimed again the "I believe"—just because all his discoveries in theology were the discoveries of an individual man —realising truth for himself before he announced it to his fellows—the effort of putting these discoveries into shapes and moulds for the purpose of argument against opponents, still more for the purpose of testing the allegiance of disciples, led to the most unsatisfactory results. It seemed more *But not interested in the establishment of Protestant Sects.* *The Individual faith also suffered from them.*

and more as if those who called themselves Reformers could not unite, as if their symbols of fellowship were in fact symbols of division. The States which were most disposed to accept the news that the Bishop of Rome had no commission to rule over their kings or set aside their laws —which felt that they must assert this liberty and struggle for it to the death—yet suffered exceeding inconvenience and mischief from the dogmatic temper of the Reformers; from their inability to content themselves with the old Creed which Luther valued so dearly, or to frame one from which there would not be a number of dissentient voices among themselves. So although the circumstances of Germany and its princes obliged the Lutheran divines to frame the confession of Augsburg—though the men who were chiefly concerned in the composition of it were both learned and moderate—it could not become a uniting bond for Christendom; it was not one for the Reformers in Switzerland or for England or even Germany.

The most powerful monarch in the world found himself embarrassed in every one of his dominions by the tumult which a Saxon Monk, the son of a miner, had raised. As chief of the Electors of Germany Charles V. found himself in conflict with Princes who supported Luther. In the towns of his native Flanders he saw the infection spreading among tradesmen, even among nobles. The religious troubles interfered with his plans in Italy, made his relations with the Pope contradictory

THE REVIVAL AND THE REFORMATION. 357

and hypocritical. Francis could intrigue with the Protestant subjects of Charles, though he was bent upon crushing Protestantism among his own. Even in his hereditary kingdom the most Catholic Monarch of Spain and the Indies could not be sure that there was not a leaven of disaffection at work, or that he had any power to expel it. But in Spain the armour was to be forged for resisting the Reformers which its ruler did not possess.

The Catholic Champion not the Catholic Monarch.

When you hear of the Jesuits you think of a society diffused through all parts of the globe, exercising a mysterious influence everywhere. The impression is a true one. I wish to shew you how true it is; how strictly they belong to the subject of *Social* Morality with which we are occupied. But that I may prove my right to speak of them I must leave Society for the lonely chamber of a wounded knight, a knight who was exchanging the dreams of love and conquest for real struggles with his own soul. Very unlike the birth and education of Luther and Loyola were; directly contrasted the results at which they arrived. Yet there was this resemblance between them. Neither was occupied with dogmas, or opinions, except accidentally. Both were occupied with the problems of their own being. Both owed their power to exercises through which they passed in hours when no eye but God's was upon them. They had this further resemblance. Both spoke much of death; not of a death to take place at a certain hour when the body should cease to breathe, but

The Society of Jesus.

Its foundation in the struggles of an individual.

of a present death; a death which a man enters, as the caterpillar becomes a chrysalis before it emerges into a butterfly. The anguish of this death each might describe in his own way, the Spaniard with not less intense conviction of its necessity than the German. But here begins the difference between them to which all others were subordinate. Luther deemed the death an accursed state, out of which the man by trusting in a Deliverer arose a new creature. Loyola held that the disciples of Jesus were not faithful to Him, unless, by all their studies and meditations they produced this death and cherished it when it was produced. What would be the fruit of this process? The individual being slain the Society became all in all. The member of it had nothing to hinder him from paying the most absolute submission to its commands. Whatever it bade him do, he would do.

Loyola's a faith in Death; Luther's in Resurrection.

The result of the former, absolute submission to a Society.

What *it* bade him do;—but was there no one to give the 'it' a living personal force? Were men to obey an abstraction? Loyola had no such idle fancy. Beginning in romance he had become sternly practical. Of course the decrees of the Church must come through the Pope; of course the notion of resisting him which the Reformers had encouraged—pretending their duty to obey a higher authority—must be dismissed as a mere device of self-will. But the Pope himself though very valuable as an expression of authority that *might* be exerted, of decrees that *might* be issued through Christendom, was too apt not to exert

The Society how represented.

The Pope and the Superior.

THE REVIVAL AND THE REFORMATION. 359

authority, not to issue decrees; even to use his authority first on one side then on another, to issue contradictory decrees. For a practical man like Ignatius Loyola the Church of other days was by no means a complete or satisfactory Society. The Society of Jesus must compensate its deficiencies. The Superior of that Society must be obeyed as the Pope had never been. The members of the Society must present such models of individual death, of purely social vitality, as the members of the Church certainly did not present. *[The Society of Jesus overshadows the Catholic Church.]*

How dangerous such a Society might become to the one which it was created to protect, many of the Popes who witnessed its vast progress were painfully aware. They made their dislike of it evident; they used the old orders against the intruder. But the Jesuits became mightier and mightier. They could gather the most enterprising and devoted spirits about them; they could invade countries which the Church had not subdued; they could reach the lowest and the highest in all lands; their three instruments, the pulpit, the school, and the Confessional, were reclaiming women, children, and men from the Protestant sects, were bringing them under the yoke of the Papacy. Could it afford to disown such services? Could it deny that a new machinery had been invented exactly fitted to cope with the temper of the times, because it was ready to discard as well as to defend the habits and maxims of an earlier time? *[Some of the Popes rebel. But in vain.]*

It was indeed a *Society* which Ignatius Loyola

had called into existence. If a Society reaches its perfection when the life of the individual is crushed it may be called *the* Society of the Universe. None that preceded it did, none that are to follow it I suspect will compass this end so completely. Framers of philosophical Systems may set the same object before them; their means of realising it look very feeble and contemptible by the side of those which the Spaniard of the sixteenth century called into play. We must not forget that he *was* a Spaniard of the sixteenth century. Though his disciples penetrated into all lands—made themselves familiar with all classes in all lands—though no order had done so much to break down the distinction of Nations, still the image of Spain was stamped upon their acts, still it was at least as much the dominion of Spain as of Rome that they were extending. That might not be the case in the following century; but while Philip II. reigned, the Jesuit principle—the Jesuit resolution to crush individual life—was paramount in the mind of the Monarch, paramount in every plan which was directed against the insurgents of Holland, against the Huguenots of France, against the Queen of England. The skill of generals, the discipline of armies, the craft of monarchs, all these would have been ineffectual if Ignatius had not taught men to regard death—not physical but moral death—as the highest result at which the most devout men, by persevering struggles and by divine grace, could arrive. Men who knew nothing of the exercises of Ignatius, men worn out with self-indulgence—exhausted by fruitless efforts to determine which of different opinions was the least improbable—having tried all the resources of self-will—heard with delight that their highest duty was to abandon the search for truth, the dream of finding any illumination respecting the divine purposes. Only by submitting to the judgment and the will of a fellow-creature could they obtain the slightest satisfaction of their discontent. When they had submitted, it would vanish away. Was this a hard death to die? Multitudes in that day, multitudes in all days since, have said that none was so easy, that it was like the death of the philosopher in the bath, the veins slightly opened, the blood trickling quietly away. And then how quickly the rewards of this death follow! You have not to wait for them in a future state. All goes on so pleasantly here. Give yourself into the keeping of one who has a right to direct you and how tranquilly business may be done and leisure enjoyed!

Popularity of the suicide recommended by the Jesuits.

If the word *Faith* was Luther's, *Obedience* was Loyola's. Grand names both. I put the last first when I spoke of a Father's Authority as the foundation of Domestic Morality; I have put it first also in speaking of the Universal Morality; since I have said that the Will of the Father in Heaven, the Obedience of the Son, takes precedence of other principles in the Revelation of Christ. But you will have observed that this is not the

Character of Loyola's obedience.

Obedience which Loyola enjoined. The domestic relation has nothing to do with the Society of Jesus; the Universal Relation, however essential as a dogma, just as little. The obedience which it exacts is to a *Superior*. The Pope is the Superior expanded and weakened. Thus the belief in Paternal Authority, which is expressed in the Creed of Christendom, after struggling for centuries with the acknowledgment of a visible Latin Father whose authority consisted in his right to say what men should think and believe, received its greatest shock from Jesuitism. So far as the principle of this Society penetrated the minds and hearts of men, the Pope's dominion no longer presented even the faint image of this authority. But more effectually than ever it helped to make the Lord's prayer unintelligible. When you hear of Jesuit obedience you must keep this distinction in your minds. It must not be forgotten, on the other hand, that the Jesuit had a power which the Lutheran did not possess. The first started from a higher ground. One spoke of the solitary creature in her weakness and evil flying to a Deliverer; the other began with a call on all men for submission to a Ruler, who, if not absolutely omnipotent, yet appeared to represent omnipotence on earth. If some felt intensely their need of such an emancipation as the German spoke of, there were far more who felt that they and all their neighbours needed government; was not the Spaniard's message then one for them?

THE REVIVAL AND THE REFORMATION. 363

No! answered another voice; the voice not of a German, of a Spaniard, but of a Frenchman; 'just because you demand a Ruler, an absolute 'Omnipotent Ruler; just because each nation re-'quires such a Ruler and each man, you cannot 'be content with the rule of the Pope; you must 'renounce that rule utterly and for ever; you 'must pronounce it accursed and hateful. The 'Pope's Church is no Church. God Himself is 'building His Church, is calling us into it. We 'stand upon His election. He can make us know 'what that is. We want no other.' So spoke John Calvin; and numbers in France, in Holland, in Scotland listened to his words. The wars in France were wars of the Calvinistical principle against the Catholic. The deliverance of Holland from Spain was the work of Calvinists. The formation of the Scotch nation and the overthrow of Mary Stuart was the doing of men possessed by the Calvinistical conviction. A Principle which produced consequences so mighty, that which was the counteracting force to the Jesuit force, must demand the earnest attention of the Social Moralist. Without it Social Morality would, as I think, be feeble and imperfect.

In his Essay on Milton, Lord Macaulay dwelt with a young man's eloquence on the power of this faith, as it was exhibited in the lives of the English Puritans. In his mature years he illustrated it far more strikingly in the character of William the III., the central figure in his history.

The records of our civil war and of the Revolution which concluded them are, as he felt, unintelligible, if we treat with indifference the belief in an Unchangeable Personal Will which not only governs the course of events, but which, first of all, chooses out individual men to fulfil its purposes. The strength of Cromwell, Mr Carlyle has shewn us, lay in the conviction that he was a called and elected man; the strength of each man in his host depended mainly on the sense of his own vocation to be there for death or for life. What was true in the following generation was true of those whom William the Silent gathered about him, was true of those who were inspired by the preaching of Knox. The teacher whose name they all reverenced was a great dogmatist. He had the love of system which belongs to Frenchmen; he had no impatience of the fetters of Latin when he was most opposing himself to the Church which had consecrated that tongue to its service. But his dogmas, his systematic gifts, his Latin lore, however they might be prized by his disciples, would have stirred no armies to battle, no people to rebellion. A living God higher than all dogmas and systems was heard, not by the schoolman, but by the hard-handed seller of cloth, by the rough ploughman, speaking in no school tongue to him, bidding him rise and fight with himself, with monarchs, with devils. The Jesuit told him that his salvation hereafter depended on his submission to the decrees of the Pope and the Church. Let the soldiers of Philip and Alva yield to those threats. He dared not. He must defy them. What were the Pope, or the Church, to him? They were fighting against the God who had called him out of death to life.

The war a deadly one.

In such a warfare there could be no compromise and little compassion upon either side. My heart and soul sympathise with those who were engaged against Alva and Philip. I hold as much as any one can, that they were struggling for freedom to act, and think, and live; for the right to be men. I hold that unless that right had been asserted, the meaning of the words mercy and justice would have been lost for us who have followed. But I dare not pretend that except in rare instances where feelings derived from other sources modified those which were characteristically theirs, they did or could display those virtues towards their enemies. To stamp out Papists as enemies of God was, they deemed, their vocation. They did not differ from the early soldiers of Islamism in that respect. They were both equally Iconoclasts, both equally destroyers of those whom they accounted worshippers of Images.

The Calvinists give no quarter and ask for none.

Since I did not scruple to speak of soldiers of the Crescent as witnesses for a Truth, against which the Imperialism of Constantinople with all its surface Christianity could maintain no permanent contest, you will not suppose that I can withhold my homage from those who regarded Christ as their supreme Lord. John Knox, we are told, died with the Apostles' Creed on his lips, wishing that those about him could understand it as he did at that moment. He had always rebutted with indignation the charge that he worshipped a mere Sovereign instead of an essentially Righteous Being. Perhaps when he was leaving the earth the name of Father which he had pronounced so often came before him with a new vitality, deepening and expanding his thoughts of a supreme Will. It was not to be expected that he or his followers, whilst they were in the midst of a deadly struggle, should suppose that this Name had anything to do with those who hated them and whom they hated. When the struggle was over, when the Calvinists settled down in Holland or Scotland as dominant ecclesiastical bodies, or elsewhere as organised sects, the dogmatic and negative elements of their belief almost inevitably became predominant over those which had a quickening and inspiring influence on them in the sixteenth century. They suffered their children and men in general to say the Lord's Prayer; but it was in an unreal sense; they would have done more honestly to forbid it altogether.

In speaking of the Lutheran, the Jesuit and the Calvinist, I have alluded to Germany, to Spain, to France, to Holland, and Scotland; only by accident, in connection with the Puritans and William of Orange, to England. For England, under the Tudor Princes, exhibits an aspect of the struggle

THE REVIVAL AND THE REFORMATION. 367

between the Universal and the Individual Morality which is peculiar, and should not be confounded with what we read of elsewhere, though the phenomena here can never be understood apart from those on the Continent. Through all the Plantagenet period the strongest princes were maintaining a national position against the claims of the Pope to universal dominion. The issue upon which the controversy turned, was the dependence of the Clergy on the native Sovereign or on the foreign Bishop. There were Beckets among the native Clergy; there were such men as the Bishop of London whom he excommunicated; insurgents against royalty in the name of the Pope and the Universal Church; servants of the King in the name of the National Church. In the reign of Henry III. the suspicion of Roman ascendancy and of its supporters the Friars became strongly developed among certain of the Clergy. It grew as the national language grew. It became associated with a vehement protest on behalf of individual morality under Wycliffe; of individual morality united with domestic morality. The Friars were denounced as the foes of practical honesty, even of chastity. The prelates were denounced as luxurious and simoniacal. Under the Lancastrian princes the Wycliffites lost their sympathies with the royal power; the monarchs united with the prelates to persecute them; the prelates in recompense paid homage to the Sovereigns and submitted to many restraints upon

Lect. XVII.

Circumstances of England.

The National King and the Universal Bishop.

Wycliffe national.

The Lollards not national.

LECT. XVII. intercourse with Rome. The abominations of the Ecclesiastical Courts vexed people of all classes; the Monasteries were suspected of indolence and of various crimes; there were cries for Reformation; for a political Reformation, for a moral Reformation. The right of the people to a Bible was proclaimed as it had been ever since Wycliffe's days; it was denied more vehemently than ever when it was seen that the Bible would be accepted, not as a document for other ages, but as a message to that time about its evils. The rage which Henry VIII. conceived against Luther arose from the belief that he was stirring up the people against their rulers, civil as well as ecclesiastical. The renunciation of the papal authority by the same Henry was not merely the gratification of a private indulgence; it was prompted by the instincts of an English Sovereign determined to assert his own position, able to assert it more completely than his predecessors had done. For a large portion of his people went with him, hailing him as their representative; a large portion of the most zealous, learned, youthful of his Clergy went with him, feeling that he would deliver them from the power which had granted indulgences, which interfered with direct faith, which exalted itself into the place of the highest Will. That is to say, the intensely individual feelings to which Luther and Calvin had appealed co-operated with the old national feelings of Englishmen, and accepted the Sovereign as their cham-

The Sovereign and the Reformers beginning to understand each other.

The fruit was an English not a sect movement.

pion. When they did not, when they simply proclaimed themselves Protestant, King Henry persecuted them; he had no notion of allowing sects in his Kingdom. On the same principle though to an opposite effect, Edward VI. claimed the land as Protestant, and persecuted Romanists; whatever is not national must be put down, was the maxim of both. When Mary gave herself up to the Spanish alliance, when she besought the Pope to accept her again as his subject, the Protestants were treated as rebels; they must be punished as the Christians under the Roman Empire were punished. They endured as those Christians endured. The refusal to acknowledge the supremacy of the Pope was for them what the refusal of sacrifice to the image of the Emperor had been for the former. They looked up to the Christ whom they had confessed in the Creed to preserve them from reverence to His vicar at Rome. But it must be said, at the same time, that they were not like the Martyrs of the olden time, maintaining the reality of a Family for *all* nations. They were doing a work, it seems to me, as necessary; testifying for the sacredness of *their* nation's life, testifying for the relations of the family against those who were undermining them in the interest of a society boasting to be spiritual and universal. I cannot think our gratitude to them can ever be exaggerated, but it should be placed on its right ground; their influence on subsequent history will then be fairly appreciated.

The worst and best tendencies of the Tudor period National not Catholic.

The Marian Sufferers.

LECT. XVII.
The Elizabethan age.

In the next reign England was brought face to face with Spain and the Jesuits. They laboured more to overthrow our Queen and Nation than to effect any of their purposes. They felt that for this end all contrivances were lawful. Numbers were ready to risk death themselves if they might inflict it on Elizabeth. This discipline, I conceive, was exceedingly salutary to us. That our Statesmen were led to commit a number of falsehoods in contending against falsehoods; that in such experiments they had generally the blessing of being outwitted; that the Queen was perplexed and vacillating in her own humours; that the Clergy in their eagerness to be national often crushed the witness for a Universal Family, which amidst all contradictions the Romanists were bearing—often crushed the witness for individual life which amidst all contradictions the Puritans in their own body were bearing; that they were sometimes slavish in their devotion to Royalty, sometimes arrogant in asserting their own prerogatives; this I am far from denying. But somehow, through the errors of all parties and by means of them all, England was learning a lesson practically which the latest school of French Philosophy is attempting to teach theoretically; that there are two bodies needful for the good order of every State, one a governing, one an educational body; that if the last assumes the province of the first it must fail, that if the first assumes the province of the last it must fail;

Benefits which England derived from the conflict with Philip and the Jesuits.

that they must work co-ordinately if the nation is not to become feeble through want of external law or of internal life. The distinctness and co-operation of these two factors of national existence we commonly express by the phrase, 'Union of Church and State,' which may be abused to many sectarian purposes and receive many perverse interpretations, but which, when it has been purified of the baser elements that have mingled with it, will be found, I think, to express the secret of English stability. We should as frankly acknowledge—for history demands the confession— that unless the individual election of the Calvinist, the protest for Universality by the Romanist, had worked continually by the side of this national principle—each threatening at times to extinguish it—a habit of feeble compromise, of insincere profession, of satisfaction with mere negatives, would have prevailed both among our Churchmen and Statesmen. They are reminded by the presence of those who ridicule their fellowship or condemn it as wicked, that they can only prove it to be good for anything by shewing that it gives a higher tone to Statesmanship, a more practical direction to the thoughts and acts of the Churchmen. Not producing these fruits it carries within it fatal signs and seeds of dissolution.

marginalia: The Union of Church and State; is it a reality or only a watchword?

marginalia: Has not been sufficient for English life though the strength of it.

Oftentimes the Union of Church and State is represented in very different language to this. It is supposed that the State, requiring the aid of a spiritual Society, provides the funds for its use without which its operations would be ineffectual. Dogmas of this kind seem to me strikingly at variance with history. The Universal Church instead of suffering from want of funds, has been in perpetual danger from the overflow of them; its rulers have been continually tempted to turn them to their own account. In different lands the cry of Simony and Extortion has been raised against its teachers; the most notorious acts of States—especially of our State —have been designed to hinder the accumulation of revenues in ecclesiastical hands, to prevent the misappropriation of them. Sometimes this has been done honestly and beneficially; sometimes injuriously, because the State has thought that only outward and material enjoyments were of any worth to its subjects. Even in such instances the spiritual body may have derived great good from the lesson; its guides may have been led to ask themselves whether they do not exist to testify that outward and material interests are not the most important of all to a Nation; and *therefore* that Money cannot be their chief agent. There may often be much insincerity in the taunt that rich Churchmen profess to derive their lineage from poor fishermen. But we cannot afford to dispense with the admonition, be it sincere or insincere. For Money, as we learn from the instance of Leo X., does very easily commend itself to men in ecclesiastical positions and at a time of high civilization as *the* good thing, which all Morality may be sacrificed to obtain. If Statesmen remind us with a sneer that the Universal Family was established in the world by men who did not count that which they had as their own, we must not dispute or qualify the assertion. I cannot believe that there will be a true Universal Morality which does not in some way give effect to that principle, or a true National Morality which does not reconcile it with the possession and administration of Property in the hands of individuals.

<small>LECT. XVII.</small>

<small>The Church may be the greatest witness for or against Money Worship.</small>

The subject which I have been considering throughout this Lecture suggests this puzzle to us continually. The Individual and National Morality bore a noble protest against the Money Worship of the Church which professed to be Universal. That was the beginning of the protest, and never ceased to give it vitality. But individuals and Nations are the conservators of property; *they* cannot shew us any *human* basis for Society which can prevent Property from being accepted as the basis of it. Where is this human basis to be sought for? Who can tell us of it?

<small>The great puzzle of the age.</small>

These questions began to occupy men's minds when the weary battles between Romanism and Protestantism, which the 16th century had called forth, were approaching to a close.

LECTURE XVIII.

ATTEMPTS TO DEDUCE THE PRINCIPLES OF HUMAN MORALITY FROM OBSERVATIONS ON HUMAN NATURE.

<small>LECT. XVIII.

The new age.</small>

I COME now to the seventeenth and eighteenth centuries of the Christian æra. What lessons have these centuries contributed to our enquiry concerning the basis of Human or Universal Morality? I believe that we owe them much precious instruction. And when I say we owe it to *them,* I mean to teachers in those centuries who differed altogether from each other, who seemed as if they existed to confute each other. I think each of them has told us something which he had ascertained for himself; I think he has left us the task of considering how it is possible to reconcile the principle which seemed to him all sufficient with principles which he rejected as untenable. That we may see from what point the philosophers of those centuries started, I must recall to you some of the observations which I made in the last Lecture.

We found ourselves encountered by a strange paradox. The men, women and children in all parts of Christendom were repeating still—as they who went before them had repeated—a Creed which implied the belief of a Divine Humanity; a Prayer which implied that all men had a Father in Heaven. The most eminent Christian Teachers, Lutheran, Jesuit and Calvinist adhering to these forms, inculcating them on their disciples, yet amidst all differences seemed to agree on this one point, that Humanity was not divine, that the majority of men could not call God their Father. It seemed as if they had arrived at this conclusion in spite of efforts against it. Luther felt intensely that what was true for himself, a sinner, must be true for all however they had sinned. Yet by degrees Lutheranism came to mean that certain blessings had been conferred on men who were more conscious of evil than others, and who therefore exercised more faith than others. The Consciousness and the faith, by whatever tests they were to be ascertained, cut *them* off from the rest of mankind. Loyola assuredly wished to raise a standard against sectarian divisions, to vindicate the existence of a Universal Society. Yet to be what he would have them be, men must lose all the individuality which appeared to be the very characteristic of men as distinguished from the animals. Calvin would arouse them to the intensest sense of individual existence. God's voice was going forth for the very purpose

Lect. XVIII.

The Problem.

The Sects abandon the search for any solution of it.

of arousing them. But since few seemed to recognise it, Calvin resolved that the majority of men must be in an outcast condition; those who were saved were exempted from the lot to which their *kind* was devoted. So long as the common Creed was adopted, there was a powerful counteraction to all these conclusions; those who were most earnest in their *convictions* were generally least embarrassed by the conclusions, least scrupulous about contradicting themselves to avoid them. For they believed in that which was above logic; grasping the premises, they could conceive that the deductions represented the feebleness of their intellects. But as sects and schools formed themselves, the deductions were found more manageable than the premises. They could be expressed much more distinctly in formulas; they were much more convenient for the rhetorician as well as the disputant. By degrees both of these had plentiful scope in maintaining or refuting different modifications of the conclusions which the experience of life seemed to suggest; modifications hard to justify by reasoning, but eagerly adopted by the affections, always shaking the stability of the general dogmas, always welcomed for the comfort which they afforded in individual cases. Men of strong hard understandings flung them aside with scorn and indignation; the feebler and more feminine clung to them in spite of all difficulties.

Such confusions and contradictions were to be

Marginal notes: Yet men and women feel themselves obliged to adopt one in the practice of life.

observed in all circles and schools where these questions were discussed; they could not escape the attention either of students or practical politicians. They must find some foundation for a common morality; one which should serve the wants of *men* irrespective of their schools and sects. They assumed on the authority of the sects and schools themselves, that their Creeds were not human, not meant for mankind. They would conduct their investigations therefore without reference to any theological maxims. What maxims should they substitute for these?

LECT. XVIII.

The Problem undertaken by Philosophers.

The name of Bacon stands before that of all Englishmen in the beginning of the seventeenth century. He had predecessors in Italy and Germany who may deserve honour greater than his for their actual discoveries in the world of Nature; who certainly endured persecutions for them from which he was exempt. But no one so deliberately undertook the task of explaining how investigations in Nature should be conducted; what in former days had hindered the success of them. No one having himself had a large political experience, being the most acute of writers on Morals, expressed so strong a conviction that there was a securer method of testing the facts of Nature than any which could be applied to the facts of human life. If he had been indifferent about these—if he had not employed immense diligence in fixing the relations of History, Ethics, Jurisprudence to each other, and in providing for

Bacon.

His Morality and his Physics.

the more effectual study of them—his manifest preference for the other kind of search—his greater hopefulness for it—would have made less impression on his readers. As the weight of the Lawyer's and Statesman's disappointments and errors was thrown into the physical scale, all that he had known, all that he had been, seemed to testify for the maxim which he asserted in the preface to his *Instauratio Magna*, that the ambition of finding a Moral Science had led to the fall of Man, that only Natural Science was innocent.

The form which this remark took shewed how familiar Bacon was with the modes of thinking which prevailed among theologians; he had more interest in Theology, more knowledge of it, than most who passed for learned divines; he never evinced the least dissent from the Creed of his country, rather a very firm allegiance to it. Yet no one spoke with greater warmth against the theological notions, especially as to final causes, which had disturbed the study of Nature; no one took such pains to warn divines that they must not bring their theories and preconceptions into the investigation of facts. Theories and preconceptions of *all* kinds must be sedulously banished from that investigation. Men must be continually on the watch against the mixture of the habits of their own mind, whether particular or general, belonging to them as individuals or as human beings, with the objects which they were contemplating. The main business of one who traced out an experimental method—a method for ascertaining the meaning of facts—was to explain where these habits were likely to intrude themselves, and how the errors to which they gave rise might be corrected.

That lessons so elaborate as these, proceeding from such a man, should have given a great impulse to the 'innocent' studies which he commended by precept and example, was surely to be expected. It might also have been expected that an age busy with a number of political experiments, occupied with many moral experiments, should not desert them, even if they were of the same character with those which produced the fall. Men would not be persuaded even by the ablest arguments that they ought to despair of knowing themselves, or even that such knowledge was not of primary importance to them. But might they not seek for *that* knowledge in the way which Bacon had declared to be most effectual for obtaining a knowledge of the external world? They had those reasons to which I have alluded for concluding that theologians who had been so troublesome in Physics would give no help in this region. To follow the teaching of the *Novum Organum* they must also detach themselves and their own modes of thinking from these investigations. How could that be done when they were the subjects of the investigation? There must be a *Human Nature;* a Nature belonging to all men, not to one as distinct from another, not

He promotes physical enquiries; he cannot deter men from moral enquiries.

But the moral enquiries begin to assume a physical character.

to Englishmen more than Frenchmen or Germans. This might be set apart and looked at, just as much as the nature of flowers or stones. Conclusions might be established respecting it and then applied to particular cases.

The students who were engaging in Bain's spirit and according to his method in physical investigation, would perhaps have wondered that the Moralists and Politicians who derived hints from the same source should apply them so differently. *They* had learnt to dread generalities; to fix their thoughts on particulars; to make their experiments on these; to discover laws in these. Their imitators were busy with what looked like a great abstraction—a very sublime generalisation. They were to start from the conception of a Nature; and from this fantastic entity to argue about the conditions and laws to which individuals must conform themselves. In general men who are engaged in different pursuits do not trouble themselves enough about each other's plans to make remarks of this kind. But they may have presented themselves to the eminent man whose works afford the first and most illustrious specimen of what I venture to call Natural Philosophy applied to the examination of Human Society.

I. Thomas Hobbes had been an amanuensis of Bacon. I do not know that he has confessed any special obligations to the great Chancellor. I should think they could have had little sympathy with each other. The habits of their minds, as well as their positive conclusions, were strangely unlike. Bacon was given to flights of fancy which Hobbes must have treated with much logical contempt. Yet the impression of one upon the other is unmistakeable. Hobbes always avowed a deep respect for the physical discoveries of his age; as great a scorn for the ethical and political theories of former ages. Nevertheless he felt that his vocation was to be an ethical and political student. Hating Plato and Aristotle and the Greek philosophers generally, he reverenced Thucydides. For he, so it seemed to Hobbes, had clearly prophesied of evils which were threatening England in the days of Charles I. Parliaments were raising their voice against Prerogative. Ecclesiastics were defending it by imagining some divine commission which the Monarch had received. Puritans were appealing from a visible to an invisible Ruler. What was coming? Such an anarchy as there had been in the Greek cities when they were fullest of dreams about liberty, when they were most impatient of dominion. All the evils of which Hellenic Democracies gave the examples would be tremendously aggravated by the Hebrew element which the religious men threw into the cauldron. How was the danger to be averted?

He comes from a physical school to investigate the political events of his time.

Throwing aside all conceptions which pseudo-philosophers or theologians have introduced into the enquiry, let us consider what Human Nature itself is. Hobbes is determined that the experiment shall be made fairly. The creature he is

Greek and Hebrew champions of liberty equally hateful.

considering must be stripped of all the wrappings with which we find him encircled. He must be pursued to his native woods. You will not find him in solitude there. Many savages are herding together. What is their business? Fighting. Every one has hold of something which the other wants. Every one wishes to get that something for himself. A brutal condition, you say. Well! but these creatures are like you in all respects. They are exhibiting your nature.

'Oh! impossible, my nature desires Society.' All in due time. The Society is to come. But first men must be weary of fighting. They must find out that fighting does not answer; that it does not bring each man what he craves for. Then they begin to perceive the worth of combination. They agree together not to rob and kill if they have some protection against the peril of being robbed and killed. They enter into contracts. They find the need of a supreme power which shall compel each party to observe the contract; which shall hinder A from cheating B, B from cheating A. It must be a *supreme* power; once established there must be no talk about the right of this man not to bow down to it, of that man to choose a governor whom he would like better, of a third to claim the help of some unseen Sovereign against what he fancies to be the injustice of his visible Sovereign. All such claims overthrow Society. They bring back the State of War; the savage State.

Society then is entirely *artificial;* no product of Nature at all. But it can only subsist if it is in conformity with the principles of that Nature which it seems to contradict. How can that be? Look at a stone. Its condition is to rest. But an outward force sets it in motion. Its nature obliges it to move when that force is applied to it. So is man subject to motives. If certain forces act upon him, let him be as naturally inert as he may, he must submit to those forces; he cannot help himself. The motives which dispose men to be at war with their neighbours may be so employed by the supreme power that they shall find themselves disposed or compelled—you may use either expression—to keep the peace with their neighbours. Peace may be accepted as their normal state. They may feel that it is each man's interest to keep war at a distance.

The arrangements of a Commonwealth fashioned upon these maxims form the subject of Hobbes' book *De Cive* and of his *Leviathan.* You must not call it an ideal Commonwealth. Hobbes wishes to have as little to do with ideas as possible. Those troublesome ideas of Right and Wrong— of what men ought to do and ought not to do— had confused the rulers and the ruled. The man who flings these aside that he may consider the motives by which men are swayed to one course of conduct or another, explains how Society actually is preserved from dissolution. Every scheme not grounded on these motives tends to its dissolution.

Irresistible Motives.

Is there nothing then which holds this fabric together besides the ruler who is subject to the accident of death? The answer has been practically given when it is proclaimed that men are subject to Motives which they cannot resist. Human Nature, like all nature, is under bands of Necessity. The man is as little able to break loose from that yoke as the smallest insect. He has dreamed of Choice. The sooner he gives up the dream the better, so far as it implies that he can in any wise determine to what forces he will yield, what he will resist. When you speak of his *Nature* you relinquish such demands for him. What his nature is he must be. What drives it this way or that must drive him.

Religion of Hobbes.

Such conclusions did not interfere with Hobbes' notions of a Religion. He declared himself a faithful member of the Church of England. He preferred it to other churches, because he thought it less aspired to set up its own claims against those of the civil Ruler. So long as men confined their belief to the unseen world he would allow them to entertain whatever they pleased. Whenever the belief came into contact with the visible world, or affected their behaviour as citizens, it was a nuisance which the magistrate must in one way or other abate.

Since I have told you that I believe we may learn something valuable from each of these seventeenth and eighteenth century teachers, you will ask me what specially I learn from this one who

FROM HOBBES TO KANT.

seems to contradict most of the positions which I have laid down in previous Lectures. I have derived these instructions from Hobbes for which I must always feel very grateful to him: (1) He has shewn me what men would certainly be if they came into the world as merely separate creatures without fathers or mothers, or any relations to their fellows. Then they would be the mere warring creatures which he has described. So I can appreciate better what the value of those facts is which make his account of mankind a fiction, though by no means a useless fiction. (2) Hobbes has made me understand more clearly than any one that I have a nature which inclines me to be at strife with my fellows, and that if I am the mere victim of that nature I *shall* be at strife with them. (3) He has convinced me that if Society is a merely artificial institution it must be what he supposed it to be, dependent altogether on Force, disturbed and shaken whenever the thought of Right mingles with that of Force. We might have gathered as much from the history of the Roman Empire before and after Constantine, as well as from some portions of more modern history; but we do not owe him less for drawing out the moral in his own clear and masterly manner. (4) No one I think has proved by such triumphant logic that to say we are governed by external motives is the same thing as saying that we are under a yoke of inevitable Necessity; that there is no Will in us, no Will over us. (5) Therefore I

LECT. XVIII.

Reasons for gratitude to Hobbes.

Relations.

Nature.

Force.

Necessity.

esteem Hobbes as a most effectual preacher of the doctrine, that if we really care to have a free Will in us we must acknowledge a Will over us which seeks to make us free. Hobbes, it seems to me, tears off more disguises from men's minds upon all these subjects than almost any teacher of any time; obliges rulers as well as subjects to give some account to themselves of their words and professions. Such services may warrant those who dissent most from his conclusions in ranking him high among their benefactors.

II. John Locke felt at least as much as Hobbes the influence of the physical enquiries which were occupying his age. Though a commentator on the Bible and a defender of Christianity he was quite as much resolved to consider Human Nature without reference to Theology. But he did not begin life with any dread of those who assailed Prerogative. He had suffered much from those who asserted it. He had heard from them a number of Scriptural arguments which appeared to him monstrous. He had been an exile during the reign of James II. He accepted the Prince of Orange as the defender of the Order on which his predecessors had trampled. The Jacobites exclaimed that the divinely appointed King had been set aside by a wilful and wicked insurrection of his subjects. Sir Robert Filmer produced a grand theory in support of that position. A patriarchal government over his descendants vested in Adam. The Kings of the earth derived it from him. To depose a Stuart was to set at nought the grant which had been made to the primeval ancestor of mankind. It was difficult to treat such an argument seriously. It must have been difficult for a believer in the Bible not to treat it as profane. Locke thought it worth while to use his vigorous intellect in refuting it; for it had, apparently, a certain hold on a portion of Englishmen disaffected to William's Government. The theory must be met by some counter theory. *The counter theory.* Locke was tempted to elaborate that theory of an original contract to which I referred in a former Lecture, the one which Mr Maine affirmed to be utterly 'unhistorical.' It deserves that reproach because Locke's contempt for Filmer's absurd caricature of patriarchal government led him to overlook the truth that lay behind it, and therefore to imagine as Hobbes had done what men might do and be if they chanced to come into existence without fathers. Once make that supposition, Hobbes's *Starting from the same hypothesis, that of Hobbes the more reasonable.* picture of the State of War and of the necessary submission to some ruler for the sake of terminating it has surely more consistency and probability than Locke's picture (far pleasanter to contemplate I own) of men deliberately meeting to choose a ruler under certain conditions, and affirming the right to cashier him if the conditions were broken.

But there is a sense in which Locke's conception was not 'unhistorical.' It bore very directly upon the history of his own time. Be- *Justification of Locke.*

cause he was practically busy about the acts and life of a Nation, he perceived the meaning of obligations; he could not resolve obligations into Force. Contemplating men as a set of naked units without kith or kindred, he ought to have arrived at the same conclusion with the philosopher of Malmesbury. But as he was not looking at England abstractedly, but was interested in its movements, was feeling and suffering with it, he was not able to forget the actual conditions of its inhabitants in a theory of what they might have been in some bygone mythical period. The Sovereign and the people in the year 1688 had bonds to each other—invisible, but most real bonds. They were made aware of their reality by a sudden convulsion; aware that they were under laws which neither Rulers nor people could set aside. The ancient Contract might be the dream of a shadow; there was a permanent contract involved in the very existence of a Nation, which was at that moment proving itself to be substantial. So the belief of a Justice and Injustice, of a Right and a Wrong, which Hobbes had blown to the winds with his triumphant Logic, were found somehow to exist practically— all Logic notwithstanding. Locke might express the belief in what words he pleased. It had hold of his heart: it came forth in his life. Like the Puritans, among whom he had grown up, he confessed that there was some righteous Being who had made a Covenant with the land. He translated the words into the Whig dialect and called it a Contract; for he was an honest man, and did not like to use phrases which in his lips and in the lips of his party would have been unreal.

He had another reason for the change. The Scotch Covenant into which English Puritans had entered was against Popery and Prelacy. It assumed the great calling of a Nation to be the extermination by all means of idolatry or of any opinions or forms of ecclesiastical Government which it supposed to favour Idolatry. Locke could not accept any such maxim as this for his Government. He was a Champion of Toleration. What did that word signify to him? If I read his Essay on the subject without knowing any of the circumstances which called it forth, I might suppose that he adopted the old doctrine of the Roman Empire; that regarding conclusions respecting the unseen world as uncertain, he would allow the subjects of a Nation to hold any which they liked, provided they did not interfere with the affairs of the visible world. But when I take his book with the commentary of his time, my view of it is greatly changed. The Covenanters and Puritans whom the Stuarts had tried to coerce did not the least confine themselves to speculations on the unseen. They affirmed a divine Government over the earth and its doings. The Quakers, whom both Episcopalians and Puritans had persecuted, avowedly proclaimed maxims which must affect all the acts of earthly rulers. Nevertheless William III. found himself compelled to pass an

LECT. XVIII.

The State confessing its impotence.

Act of Toleration, which either immediately or in its consequences affected all Sects. This Act Locke was called upon to defend against its impugners. They regarded it as an abdication of the duty which belongs to a State. He knew that it was a frank confession by Statesmen of their impotence to establish uniformity of opinion; however inconvenient diversities of opinion might be to them, however nearly many opinions might trench upon their own authority. In very deed the beliefs of men had proved too strong for any weapons that the State could employ against them. Toleration was simply an acceptance of this fact. There was one case in which it could not be accepted. Romanists were not tolerated. The Revolution was a declaration of war against all who would subject the crown of England to a foreign autho-

Locke's reason for making the fallibility of men's judgment his plea for Toleration.

rity. Locke must have felt it difficult to maintain a scheme of Toleration in face of so vast and notable an exception. He was therefore tempted to dwell much on the claim to Infallibility which the Roman Church had put forward for its head; to shew how much *this* assumption was the secret of persecution; how little right any State or Church had to imitate the pretension which it refused to the Pope. A most valuable warning surely; but one which involves no denial of an absolute ground for human belief, rather removes the most practical form of that denial. The notion that any mortal authority can prescribe belief is deduced from the uncertainty of it; from the doubt whether there is a Spirit of Truth who guides men into Truth. If Locke had foreseen a time when the English State would be obliged to confess its inability to restrain Romanism as much as any form of Protestantism by civil penalties, he would have seen that the imperial idea of Toleration was utterly inapplicable to the conditions of a Nation. An Empire desires to reduce the Belief of its subjects to a minimum; to make it as harmless, as insincere as possible, *therefore* it permits all varieties of opinion about divinities; only the actual confession of a living Ruler must be silenced. A Nation finds that the beliefs of its subjects constitute its strength. If their beliefs perished it would perish. Therefore it must avoid any meddling with opinions lest it should quench some of the life within them, which is its own life.

III. But I must pass from Locke to a pupil of his whose mind was cast in a very different mould from the master's, and who travelled far from his maxims. Lord Shaftesbury was a student of Human Nature like Hobbes. He disliked Puritans and religious teachers generally, as much as Hobbes. But he disliked them for what he considered their agreement with Hobbes on the subject of Human Nature. They regarded it as essentially corrupt and evil. Hobbes rejecting those terms, not accusing himself or his fellow-creatures of any sin, yet assumed that in a savage condition or in the most refined Society they were capable only of

392   *UNIVERSAL MORALITY.*

<small>LECT. XVIII.

Denounces Puritans and Hobbes for the same offence.</small>

being influenced by selfish motives. Against such a slander Shaftesbury lifted up his voice. You may no doubt, he said, present to our Nature degrading objects. You may make the object which you teach men to reverence most an object of Dislike and Dread. But our nature aspires after goodness and beauty, cannot be content unless it has an ideal of goodness and beauty before it. All great acts as well as noble conceptions have come from the contemplation of it. Men are rebels against their Nature, are deserting the true principles of it when they follow what Hobbes and the Divines would stigmatise as their natural instincts.

<small>His worship of an Ideal partly Greek, partly chivalrous.</small>

I need not repeat that Shaftesbury was even less inclined than either of the philosophers I have spoken of hitherto to introduce any theological element into his conception of human life. He believed that he was following the best of the Greek Philosophers in his worship of the Ideal; he felt also that he was asserting the dignity of an English Gentleman and Nobleman; that he was protesting against low and vulgar tendencies and the notions which justified them. Something of aristocratical hauteur there was no doubt in him; he might have a certain contempt for the profane herd; still it was man, not a particular class of men, that he desired to glorify.

<small>His use of the word Nature.</small>

As I have maintained that Hobbes made his point good, *if* we look merely at our natural tendencies or inclinations, you may ask me how I can sympathise with Shaftesbury. My answer is, I do sympathise with him thoroughly and heartily, because I do *not* identify Humanity with our natural tendencies and inclinations, because I believe as he did that any good deed and good thought in men has come from the aspiration after an ideal. The pursuit of the ideal, it seems to me, according to Shaftesbury's own shewing, raises a man above the inclinations and tendencies of his nature; above himself. Acknowledging the divine Humanity which Christendom in Shaftesbury's days professed, as it professes in our day, to believe, I am bound to accept his statements with this addition, which I should think must greatly strengthen them, that the Ideal has proved itself to be real, and that it has the power of attracting men to itself.

IV. The next thinker who presents himself to us was almost equally unlike Shaftesbury and Hobbes; indifferent to ideals; the profoundest of Sceptics, as Hobbes was the most vehement of Dogmatists. A hatred of Puritans and Covenanters, and of the zeal which those names represent, is the one point of common agreement between the three. David Hume despaired of metaphysics. Himself the most acute of speculators, his main effort was to shew that speculations about Causes and Principles could lead no whither, must end at last in vagueness and vacancy. But if we forsake these it is well, he said, to find some guide for practical life, to know how best we may steer our vessel so as not to be much disturbed by shoals and quicksands. When one considers Human

[margin: Hume. How he was led to seek for an ethical principle.]

Nature for this purpose, laying aside all dogmas about the ends which it ought to pursue, what does one perceive? Some men have this taste, some have that. Some prefer coarse animal indulgences, some have an appetite for intellectual gratifications; some desire solitude, some find their delight in refined Society. But all have an apprehension of what is useful for that end which they have set before them. A certain fitness in this or that act or course of action to give them the results which they wish for, every one is capable of recognizing; the more a man cultivates the faculties which he is endued with the clearer will be the recognition. We should have the best Morality, the least of friction and confusion, Hume thought, if this principle of Utility was felt to be the governing one in human Society. He carried his maxim into history and Politics. He might not himself care particularly for any scheme of Worship. But he believed that one should be sanctioned by the State in every country. It supplied common people with something which they wanted. An established Religion was useful in keeping down fanaticism; the citizens of a land being satisfied that every thing had been properly arranged with respect to the concerns of the invisible or future would not give their neighbours or themselves any extraordinary trouble about it.

After assenting to the doctrine of Shaftesbury, I should be very inconsistent if I adopted Hume's Utility as the exclusive, governing principle of human life. Hume might have expanded it to make it meet the taste of the philosophical Nobleman as well as of any one who preferred the turf and the gambling table to Plato; but that is practically to deny Shaftesbury's standard under pretence of tolerating it. Yet may we not be very thankful to Hume for fixing our thoughts upon the fact that there is this perception of the useful in human beings, that it is widely diffused among them, that it does curiously fit means to ends, and is awake to any disagreement between means and ends? If people had perceived this fact before— *Value of his doctrine.* if it could not be exactly new to any man—still the writer who compels us to take notice of it, to consider what we should be without it, how much in Nature would be lost to us, how impossible Art would be in its most mechanical or in its finest forms, assuredly renders us a great service. It is evident that in every region of action and thought this sense of utility was acting upon men during the eighteenth century. Hume shewed a remarkable insight into his time—the insight which comes from sympathy— when he gave it so much prominence. Paley, not only in his Moral Philosophy but in those of his works which were especially directed against Hume, did homage to it. Even the reactions against both Hume and Paley shewed how the principle which was the sacred one to each of them had mastered their contemporaries. Was Human Nature then the springhead of this *Utility the maxim of the 18th century.* Utility? Or did man's apprehension bear witness of some arrangements which he had not invented, of which he could only get partial glimpses? Apparently he did a number of very useless unprofitable things. How was it that in spite of these he was able to demand a kind of order in which means and ends should always be adjusted to each other? I do not give the answer to these questions: I do not maintain that Paley found the answer to them when he treated the Universe as a great workshop of ingenious contrivances; but I wish you to ponder them; you will appreciate Hume's contribution to Moral Philosophy better if you do.

V. A friend of Hume's made another contribution to it which seems at first to be utterly incompatible with the dogmas of Hobbes. Adam Smith thought that he found in Human Nature a principle of *Sympathy* which would explain some of the most remarkable facts and experiences of life. How strange it is that men should be able to throw themselves into the thoughts, feelings, interests of others! How marvellous is the common heart which pervades a crowd, composed of men who do not know each other, who have each his own cares and troubles! A play—tragedy or comedy with the tears and laughter that follow it— is not that indeed a mystery as it used to be called, a mystery in its effects if not in its subject? Adam Smith had thought of these things. They seemed to him not less worthy of investigation because they were common, because every one is aware of them. He was a practical man. His main occupation was not with Sentiments, but with the maxims of Trade and Commerce, with the material Wealth of Nations. In considering these, however, he was reminded of a certain sympathy between different countries which had been set at nought by legislation, while it aimed at promoting the good of one by injuring or weakening another. He was proving that antipathies between men of different lands did not favour the objects which they desired, but interfered with them. There was therefore a consistency in his thoughts, such as we may always trace in those of men who have exercised any considerable influence on the world, to whatever subject they have been directed.

<small>Commerce of Nations an illustration of the principle.</small>

The difficulty, as I said, is to reconcile his facts—for it is to facts that he called his reader's attention when he was writing on Morals as much as when he was writing on Political Economy—with those which Hobbes pointed out so clearly and forcibly. How can the self-seeking creature which he described to us be the same with the sympathetic creature of whose ways Adam Smith took notice? Yet facts must somehow harmonise with each other; if theories keep them apart, the theories must give way. Suppose it were true that human beings are not constituted separate atoms, that they cannot really be contemplated out of Society, that the attempt to sever themselves from each other—to set up separate interests—implies disorder and contradiction; and yet that each one of them is a distinct living

<small>How Smith and Hobbes can be reconciled.</small>

person and cannot lose his distinctness without injuring his Society. Sympathy such as Smith speaks of would then appear to be a necessary condition of Humanity, and yet the selfishness which Hobbes dwells upon may have made itself as fully manifest in all places and in all ages as he affirmed that it did; nay, he might be perfectly correct in saying, that the solitary nature of man out of all families and nations is this selfishness and nothing else. It would indeed in that case be a question of the most profound practical importance to which of these principles you should appeal for the support of Society, and how you may appeal to it effectually. If Hobbes detected not the bond of Society, but the secret of its dissolution, we may still be much his debtors for bringing that secret so distinctly and vigorously before us.

VI. A great enemy of Adam Smith's doctrine of Sympathy appeared in Jeremy Bentham. I alluded to him in my Lectures on National Morality as a young man at Oxford, who listened to Sir William Blackstone's exposition of the balance between our Monarchy, Aristocracy, and Democracy, and held it up to contempt in his *Fragment on Government*. Having satisfied himself with his work of destruction, he began to ask himself on what basis he could construct his social edifice. As he had been bred a Tory, and was specially impatient of the Whig dogmas respecting the Constitution, he naturally betook himself to Hume the defender of Charles I., the enemy of Whigs, yet free from any notion of a divine right, and from all theological prejudices. Hume's *Utility* at once commended itself to Bentham as the safe escape from the theories of both the English parties. What other foundation did Government want than this? The student of Human Nature throwing away traditions had perceived this to be the true rule of conduct for himself and his fellows. How absurd to suppose that a Government of human beings needed some fiction to sustain it! What was useful was alone good for private men or legislators.

Useful to *whom?* Bentham saw that he must answer this question. When he meditated on the answer he travelled very far indeed from his guide. To compare his Utility with Hume's is a most profitable study; we may discover into what delusions a Shibboleth may lead us, if we do not derive our interpretation of it from the habits and temper of those who adopt it. Hume did not like to be disturbed by men who had notions of some good to which Society might attain; who were tormenting themselves with certain supposed evils by which it was afflicted. 'My dear friends,' he said, 'be quiet; let good and evil alone; think only of what is useful; and do permit your neighbours to judge what is useful to them.' 'I demand,' said Bentham, 'the greatest happiness of the great-'est number. Governors chattering about good 'and evil have neglected what tends to promote

Hume and Bentham use the same word in the most different senses.

'that end; have done and are doing what produces 'advantage to themselves, mischief to the majority. 'We must work night and day to deprive them 'of their advantages, to save the majority from the 'mischiefs which they are inflicting on it.' Accordingly there was scarcely one practical conclusion deduced by Hume from his doctrine of Utility, that was not contradicted by one which Bentham traced legitimately from his. Were religious establishments the comfortable escape from enthusiasm in Hume's estimation? Down with them to the ground, they are the creation of the sinister interests of priests, they are sustained by those of lawyers, was the cry of his pupil. The ἦθος of the men, and therefore the ἦθος which they would respectively have cultivated in Society was more utterly opposed than that of almost any two whose biographies are preserved to us.

If therefore Bentham has some important lesson to teach us—I do not mean by his practical suggestions, which may be full of important lessons, but by the maxim which he announced as the all-satisfying and comprehensive one—it must be a lesson of an altogether different kind from any which the eminent Scotch Utilitarian has imparted to us. The words "Greatest Happiness of the greatest number," do convey to me a very profound lesson. I do not pretend that I can give them any definite sense. Happiness is to me an unknown quantity, of which I must learn the value by some process or other. The greatest number of Unity, as I have been trying to shew you throughout these Lectures, does not express mankind to me at all, seeing that I cannot contemplate mankind except in families or Nations, or as constituting a universal fellowship in some living Head. But I do not the less honour the man who set this Ideal before him, who steadily and manfully pursued it amidst all difficulties. The difficulties, indeed, seem to me stupendous, since they arose not only from the number of selfish interests which he felt were obstructing the path of every reformer, but even more, as I remarked in a former course of Lectures, from the doubt in Mr Bentham's own mind, whether the interest of the Community is composed of the interests of its separate members, or whether it is merely a fictitious entity assumed in order to explain what those interests are. Yet defying all these uncertainties he went right onward, sure that there was a common end for which private ends must be sacrificed, and actually sacrificing his private ends for the sake of it. However a man expresses that purpose—whatever phrases he may choose or may reject—he exhibits a faith which should be dear to those who reverence faith more than formulas of the intellect. If he assails any principle which we have realised, we may fight for it to the death; but we shall be sure that there is one which *he* has realised, and which it would be very dangerous for us to assail. It may be that in the ardour

The greatest number how composed.

Bentham's earnest faith.

of his practical labours, Mr Bentham did not feel how lofty an ideal had possessed him. Weaker men may be crushed under the thought of what it is which the greatest number require, and how they are ever to attain what they require. But if they are driven in their despair to think that there is One who knows this better than they do—if that is the only belief in which they are able to work for their fellow-men—they cannot be otherwise than most grateful to him for suggesting the aim which they own that they are quite unable to reach. It is not indeed in a comfortable Optimism that they can ever find refuge from the palpable evils which he has set before them, or from the sense of their own impotence. Those who have ever *wished* for the greatest happiness of a majority of their race or of the whole of it, cannot acquiesce in any pleasant dreams that somehow it will drop upon them from the skies. They know that it is better to be miserable than to take up with a lie; that nothing is so miserable as a lie. The service Mr Bentham will have done them is in leading them to ask themselves whether there is not a *Truth* in which the greatest number of men—in which all men—may trust, and whether that Truth will not make them free. If there is a Happiness without Freedom or beyond it, they may wait to learn what that is.

VII. There was no writer of the 18th century or of any century who was more resolute that theological speculations should not interfere with his Moral Creed than Immanuel Kant. There was no writer who opposed so sternly all the maxims of the school which made Utility its standard, Happiness its object. What have we to do with the consequences of our actions? There is a Command going forth to each man, not from without but from within, not from some power which enforces its decrees by promises of rewards or threats of punishment, but from a Reason which is higher and more binding than all calculations of profit and loss, saying 'Do this,' 'Abstain from that.' It speaks to each man. Yet there is a sign and test of its being meant for all men. You, A, trifle with the precept not to lie, not to slay yourself. How if B, C, and D, how if every one—did the same? Thus there is a Universal Imperative. If ninety-nine out of every hundred men set it at nought, it has not the less evidence of its Universality; every transgression of it is a confirmation of its reality.

LECT. XVIII.

An enemy of Theologians and Utilitarians.

I am sure I have no wish to accept this doctrine of Kant. It sounds to me very tremendous. It comes home to oneself. It is impossible to put it aside and treat it as a mere vague general proposition. But I frankly tell you that I cannot escape from it whether I wish to do so or not. Nor do I think that any one of you can. This voice is speaking in each of us. It has that awful authority which Kant ascribes to it. If one asks it, 'What shall I get by doing what I am told to do?' I believe there is no answer; a

His assertion forces itself on reluctant hearers.

<small>LECT. XVIII.</small>

<small>No help against it from the Benthamites.</small>

dreadful silence. When I refer to the lessons I have been taught in Bentham's school—though I cannot forget them, though they must have an application of their own—they do not seem to help me here. Perhaps they rather add to my alarm. Bentham himself, trained as he was in his own maxims, appears to have girded himself to his task of promoting the greatest happiness of the greatest number in deference to some internal monitor; how then can he give me any hints for avoiding one? Kant may have been unjust to Utilitarians—incapable of perceiving their truth—but they cannot confute for me the one which he perceived with such marvellous clearness.

<small>Yet terrific and withering to effort.</small>

But it is, as I said, a terrific truth if it stands alone. The Reason, or whatever it is which utters this command, can listen to no prayers or expostulations, will hear no confession of my failures, offers me no energy when I am weak that I may perform its behest. It merely decrees, 'This thou art bound to do;' 'this thou art bound not to do;' and if I am conscious of other and very sharp bonds which restrain me from compliance, it tells me not how I may break them, points to no door or chasm in the wall of my prison through which I may break loose from it. A very grand moralist is Kant; but some have thought a little cruel. And yet it is not his cruelty. The cruelty must be in the constitution of our own being, if he has told us all that we can know about it.

Now I do not the least complain of Kant for

his desire to put theology, according to his conception of it, aside. He took it to be a certain scheme of rewards and punishments, by which a power in the heavens induces His creatures on earth to do the things which He has ordered, not to do the things which He has forbidden. It was impossible to reconcile such a notion with the simple imperative which issues, as he believed and felt, from the deepest cavern of our being. I am rejoiced that he did not attempt to reconcile this religious philosophy, which was the current one in his day, with the principle which he enunciated. But supposing the divine voice not to be one thundering motives out of an unknown region to a set of creatures capable only of cringing to selfish fear or of being stimulated to selfish ambition—supposing there to be an actual divine Humanity such as Christians had confessed in their common Creed for a number of centuries— supposing, as their books affirmed, that the divine Head of Humanity had actually come among men that He might deliver them from their bondage to a selfish nature, and unite them to a Father who cared for them all — supposing these old sayings to be true, then the command would certainly come as Kant declared it did from within, from the secret depths of Humanity in each man and to all men—it would be more strictly a command to each man and to all men, than one could be which merely issued from what they might call their own Reason. Such an impera-

Lect. XVIII.

Kant's reasonable dislike to the Theology of the market.

Which was not the Theology of Christendom.

tive, however absolute, might be mistaken for the conclusion of a particular judgment which other and more mature judgments would set aside. Whereas on this hypothesis it would proceed from the common and Universal Reason, and yet from one who could enter into the weaknesses of those who were to obey it, one to whom confession of such weaknesses would be possible, who could impart the energies which convert wishes into purposes, and cause purposes to bear fruit in acts.

It would be very ungracious and unjust to complain of Kant, of Bentham, of Adam Smith, of Hume, of Shaftesbury, of Locke, or of Hobbes, for taking no account of a principle which though recognised by the people, was as habitually ignored by the divines of the 18th century as it could be by any philosophers. The divines also were greatly impressed by the physical teachers of the day. They were busy in constructing a Natural Theology; that is to say, in bringing evidences for the existence of *some* Author of the Universe; what kind of Author being *apparently* inferred from physical facts, *really* from certain moral beliefs which they brought with them to the investigation. Such arguments have proved very unsatisfactory to the students of Nature in later times. They proved very unsatisfactory to the hearts and consciences of ignorant men and women in those times. Our English Methodism with all its accompaniments was a protest against the inadequacy of a Natural Theology; was a demand by suffering men and women, conscious of evil, for a human and divine Helper. They might not more than dream of such a Helper for *mankind*. As in the 16th century the cravings of the religious *seemed* to be for some one who should exempt them from the condition of mankind. Still they resorted to the old Creed which expressed the larger belief; no other seemed to justify the narrower one.

And to the most unscientific.

Meantime there came from the cultivated men in France those expressions of scorn for all popular beliefs, which spread more and more through all the refined circles in Europe. It was emphatically and formally scorn for *popular* beliefs. Yet there was mixed with it so much just contempt and indignation for those who had oppressed the people and kept them in ignorance— so many pleas even for men who had been hindered from expressing their faith by persecutions civil or ecclesiastical, that the middle classes in France and elsewhere hailed the new teachers, even if they were over fond of Courts and great assemblies, as their champions. Rousseau indeed, who was so often at war with the scoffers, had a greater power than they had, and was looked upon as the real prophet of the coming time. But Rousseau, like them, believed that the Christian experiment had failed, that a Universal Family had as much ceased to be as a Universal Empire. How strong that persuasion was throughout Europe when the French Revolution began, it

The Esprits forts of France.

Accepted as leaders by the middle classes though attached to the upper.

<small>LECT. XVIII.
Cry for Fraternity.</small> is impossible to express in words. And yet the deepest cry of that Revolution was for a Universal Brotherhood. Whether that could exist without a Universal Fatherhood was to be the question for a future time. The Revolution only went thus far. It said distinctly, 'The Universal Brotherhood which we Frenchmen want cannot be based on such a Fatherhood as Christians have supposed to exist in the capital of Italy.'

LECTURE XIX.

THE MODERN CONCEPTION OF HUMANITY.

MANY writers on the French Revolution have maintained that the two cries for Liberty and Equality interfered with each other, that the destruction of Orders was the preparation for the Empire, and therefore for the loss of Freedom. It may be a question whether the Orders had not destroyed themselves before the voice of any popular assembly declared them to be no more; otherwise I can have no objection to a remark which is so much in accordance with those which I made respecting the dissolution of the Roman Republic. But for my present purpose it is of more importance to enquire how the third cry for Fraternity affected both the others. So far as Fraternity meant the union of all Nations, the first Napoleon might boast that he had accomplished what the Assemblies had only decreed. French, Spaniards, Austrians, Prussians, Swiss, all were compre-

LECT. XIX.

How the revolutionary cries were answered.

LECT. XIX.

The answer of the first Empire.

hended in his embrace; if Russia and England refused it, that was the fault of their exclusiveness; he would have cordially hugged them both. But Fraternity did not mean only or chiefly the removal of the barriers which Language or Customs or Laws had raised between the different portions of mankind. It meant first of all a union for Frenchmen. Other Nations might become brothers. France should set them the example, should shew them under what conditions Brotherhood was possible. These conditions it was evident were not exhibited by the Empire. If that had not quite satisfied the demand for Equality by putting down old distinctions to raise up others in their place, if it had met the appetite for liberty by establishing a marvellous and mysterious Police, it had certainly done nothing to make Citizens feel themselves members of a Family. Was the Conscription the sign of their adoption into it?

The philosophical answers.

But the craving which this word expressed was too deep a one to be extinguished because rulers, the most popular and triumphant, failed to provide any food for it. Philosophers, theoretical and practical, girded themselves to the task. It might have been foreseen that they would be most numerous and most accomplished in the country which had been giving birth to the Revolution. All those of whom I spoke in the last Lecture were brought up in a Protestant atmosphere, under the influence of its individualizing tendencies. Some, perhaps all of them, might be provoked to a reaction against these tendencies, might strive to throw them off. Hobbes and Hume both lived much in France, and for different reasons corresponding to the difference of their characters preferred French to English Society. Yet every one, from the philosopher of Malmesbury to the philosopher of Konigsberg, shewed that he could not begin from Society, that whether he talked of Motives or of Ideals or of Consequences or of pure Duty or even of Sympathy, he was still, consciously or unconsciously, contemplating each man in himself before he contemplated a body of men. The air which Frenchmen breathed was of a most different quality. They were social by instinct, social by tradition, social by the faith in which they had been educated, social by the influences of the Revolution which had cast off that faith. There had been a Calvinism in France which had added, I conceive, much to its health and vigour. The desertion of it by Henri IV., the persecution of it by Louis XIV., helped to destroy the moral fibre of the land. But it was an alien plant in the soil. The efforts of Kings to uproot it would have availed little if the heart of the people had cherished it. But unbelief and belief, the contempt of the *esprits forts*, the passionate zeal for Reform in the body of the Nation, seemed equally to stand apart from what we might suppose would have supplied some justification to the one, and have helped forward the other. The French love of Organization was impatient of any practice or any theory which did not promise first and above all things Combination and Fellowship.

Attempts of Ecclesiastics to use the revolutionary Symbol and in the reconstruction of Society.

Such a disposition offered a great encouragement to the champions of Catholicism who had seen it trampled down in the revolutionary fury. When that fury had spent itself there was sure to be a cry for some constructive power, some fusing principle, which might bind the fragments of Society together again. The more worldly Churchmen might accept the doubtful compliment of Napoleon, that the Papacy was an institution which it would be worth while to create if it did not exist; the religious would expect it to prove its unfailing vitality, to shew that no human hands could have created it. Jesuitism, as a protest against all tendencies to separation—for a mysterious unity—could not despair of being welcomed back from the banishment to which the last age had consigned it. The name of Brotherhood was itself mediæval. The Church had called religious Brotherhoods into existence, which had ministered in many ways to order and civilization. Trade Brotherhoods had been produced by the same impulse, had borne the same stamp. Might not the watchword of the Revolution be reclaimed by ecclesiastical wisdom, be consecrated to an ecclesiastical use?

Though such thoughts might hover about a number of minds, might penetrate into some hearts, the Papacy was evidently too much terrified by the destructive symbol—too much inclined to suspect mischief in all who gave it even an half spiritual sense—to seek help from popular sympathy, when the old Governments were restored. Its simple policy was to ally itself with them; to discourage all associations which savoured of freemasonry; to treat the protection and preservation of property as the supreme interest of the Church no less than of particular States. If the States felt that it was performing this function for them, they might be willing to keep down heretics within their borders; to enforce, as far as they could, reverence for the Priesthood.

The Papacy rejects this Policy.

But a higher interest than this it was felt must be vindicated by some Society, whether it was called the Church or by any other name. The idea of a Brotherhood for men as men which had taken hold of men at the Revolution, could not be realised by institutions which merely contemplated Possessors, and sought to secure them in their possessions. Wherever there had been the conception of a Universal Society by the most exalted Philosophers, by the simplest peasants, a certain Communism had mingled with it. States might regard the word and that which it represented with dread; might resolve to keep it at a distance. But were they not narrow in their objects; tied by traditions and genealogies and class distinctions? Were they for ever to divide the world?

No institutions based on Property or aiming at the protection of it can satisfy the craving for a Universal Brotherhood.

If I tried to notice in this Lecture even a few

LECT. XIX.

Schemes more or less communistic.

of the schemes to which this prolific thought has given rise I should do both them and you injustice. I might lead you to think of them merely as visionary when they were the result of much practical observation and experience. I might exhibit some of their weak points when it would do us much more good to perceive where they were strong. I might connect them with titles which have become opprobrious when the objects of their propounders were benevolent, when they desired to promote Order, not Confusion. I would only make these two remarks, which you may find useful. The first is that for the reasons I have given already the most carefully elaborated of these schemes will be found to have French authors, though no doubt opportunities have been afforded by the freer life of Great Britain for practical experiments limited in extent, but of great interest and value—*e.g.* that of Mr Owen at Lanark. The second is that beneath all the schemes, great or small, however diverse in character and design, lies the conviction that somehow or other there must be, or there must be formed, a Human Family. If only a few compose it, still it must in virtue of its principles be capable of embracing all men.

The idea of a Human Family underlies them all.

I am thus drawn on to consider what I have called in the title of this Lecture the modern conception of *Humanity*. Inattention to the nomenclature of different periods or, what means the same, to the nomenclature of the most eminent thinkers in different periods, often leads us into

THE MODERN CONCEPTION OF HUMANITY. 415

fatal misapprehensions respecting their distinctive qualities. We may easily confound the *Human Nature* which was the favourite and common subject of study in the last age with the *Humanity* which has begun to be so much spoken of in ours. If we do, I suspect we shall not appreciate the step which we have taken in advance of our immediate predecessors; we shall understand even less where we stand in relation to those who were before them. We shall be embarrassed with schools, each of great historical and even present importance, but partial and contradictory; when we might ascend through them to a living and practical moral ground.

<small>Lect. XIX.</small>

<small>Human Nature giving place to Humanity in our speech.</small>

The disciples of M. Comte maintain that it is he who has brought us to this higher ground, that he has interpreted the earlier experiments of this century, and has embodied them all in a comprehensive system. I am not at all anxious to dispute these claims, or to set up any rival who can challenge a share of them for himself. I assume that his philosophy does represent the modern conception of Humanity. Probably it is nowhere so completely expressed as in his writings. He has explained to our generation the desire of former teachers to build up a Universal Society, and a Morality which should be adapted to it; their eagerness to associate this Human Society and Human Morality with physical studies; their impatience of Theology and its traditions and associations; their resolution that whether or not it was necessary in other days it should be

<small>Auguste Comte.</small>

<small>His services to previous philosophers.</small>

banished from the new age. It seems to me that he has brought these questions to a more distinct and intelligible issue than any previous thinker. As a Clergyman and a Professor of Moral Theology, I feel myself under unspeakable obligations to him. For he has cleared the ground of much rubbish which hindered us from knowing where we were standing; he has compelled us to abandon all apologies for our faith, and simply to ask ourselves what we mean by it, and what we suppose it can do for mankind. If it can do nothing, if what we have called the Kingdom of Heaven is not concerned about the Reformation or Regeneration of the earth, we must confess that we have been walking in a dream, or have been deliberately imposing a lie upon our fellow-creatures.

1. M. Comte has dwelt much upon the fact that since the time of Bacon[1], Moral Philosophy has been more and more inclined to assume a physical, and to discard a theological foundation. The truth and importance of this remark I fully recognised in my last Lecture. I did not

[1] M. Comte joins the name of Descartes to that of Bacon. I am not competent to estimate the kind of impression which that illustrious thinker has made on his own countrymen. If I am not mistaken, his influence on England, where his physical speculations are little prized and where his search for a ground of his own thoughts has affected the most earnest students at some stage of their lives, has been rather to counteract than to promote the tendency which I spoke of in my last Lecture.

THE MODERN CONCEPTION OF HUMANITY. 417

merely accept it as a general proposition; I endeavoured to illustrate in a number of particular cases taken from the representatives of schools utterly opposed to each other. The period between our Civil Wars and the French Revolution presented a series of experiments all conducted upon the maxim which M. Comte supposes to have established itself for ever as the only reasonable or possible one. I recognised the great value of each of these experiments; the undoubted result to which it conducted us. But upon that maxim which each of these students assumed, they could not be reconciled, each must be at war with the one that preceded it. Introduce the maxim which they agreed to cast out and which yet continued to subsist as the acknowledged basis of the people's faith in all countries of Europe, and we could do justice to each of these results; it was impossible to part with any one of them.

LECT. XIX.

Reference to the previous Lecture as to this method of the last century.

2. The agreement of such remarkable men—so different as those I have enumerated—in the most advanced period of European Civilization, that Theology had been used up—at least for moral and political purposes—that a physical age had set in—offers surely a great excuse for M. Comte's grand generalization, which Mr Mill reckons his most characteristical one. The study of Physical facts, he says, must be taken as the sign of the world's maturity; the study of Theology of its infancy; a middle period of Metaphysical speculation being the transition from one

The Infancy, Boyhood and Manhood of the world.

27

LECT. XIX.

to the other. No man who has heard such a proposition enunciated can forget it, or can fail to find instances in history which seem to esta-

Personal experiences have done more than history to make this conception popular.

blish it. What will have really far greater weight with most men than these instances, what will give *them* weight will be their own personal experiences. 'Were not we,' they ask, 'theo-
'logians in our nurseries? Did we not stum-
'ble about in strange metaphysical puzzles of
'which we could find no solution, when we first
'became capable of exercising our thoughts? Do
'we not discover as we become men that our busi-
'ness is with "positive" things; with the outward
'world, of which in the earlier periods we knew
'nothing?' There is a force in reflections of this kind which those who submit to it are not aware of. And it is a force which affects ordinary men of the world even more than students. For the

Ambiguity in the word "positive."

name 'positive' covers much ground. It may be taken loosely to express the processes or the results of scientific enquiries. But that is not its obvious or natural signification. It denotes rather the material on which these processes are exercised, that with which men are concerned who buy and sell if they never trouble themselves about science.

Positivism of the Stock Exchange and the Clubs.

In this sense practical men may exclaim that they have been talking Comtism all their lives without knowing it, because they have said to each other: 'It is very good for children to say prayers with 'their mammas in the nurseries. It does not much 'signify what nonsense they talk about their minds

'and souls at College. When they become law-
'yers or merchants or Members of Parliament,
'they soon tame down into common sense. Then
'what they care about is the prices which things or
'men will fetch in the market.' Discourse no doubt
denoting a high civilization, but one which cannot
be appropriated to the 19th century. Opinions
similar to it in all essentials are attributed to citizens of London in Ben Jonson's Comedies, to
citizens of Rome in the Epistles of Horace.

<small>This Positivism not new.</small>

But this assuredly is not orthodox Positivism,
not what M. Comte meant by the third or mature
stage of human existence. That Experimental
Philosophy, in Bacon's sense of that word, has been
reserved for this last stage and has been one of the
greatest gifts to mankind, I take to be his doctrine; surely a very sound one. I do not feel less
gratitude to him for this announcement that he
has expressed it in terms which are open to the
other construction. The ambiguity will be useful to us if it teaches us that there are two possibilities; one of ascent from our infantine wisdom,
one of descent. We may rise to a scientific apprehension of the meaning of facts, we may sink into
the habit of considering them only as they affect
our private interests. We may become human,
we may drop into a positive money-worship which
is merely brutal. That we should avoid the degradation and attain the elevation would have
been surely M. Comte's desire.

<small>M. Comte evidently desired an opposite one; a growth into Science through experiment.</small>

What I maintain is that the hindrances to

Experimental Philosophy were also the great hinderances to theological belief. As long as men are counted infallible the investigation into the meaning of facts will be checked, precisely because the belief in a God of Truth, in a God who stirs men to pursue Truth and leads them on in the pursuit of it, is checked. The practical denial of God, not faith in Him, makes us afraid that if we seek we shall not find, if we knock it will not be opened to us. Those nursery prayers which the Club sage thinks were so good for the child, so inappropriate to the man, ought to be so regarded if the man's ultimate vocation is to get all he can for himself. But in that ripest period he will look back upon his childhood, and fancy it must have been the sunniest and most blessed moment of his existence because he cherished delusions which have passed for ever away. Whereas, if his vocation is to know Truth and to be true, he may have then had his first glimpse of the vista which through ages upon ages he is to explore. He may have been shewn who would be his guide through the bewildering, but most needful and precious questionings respecting himself and his fellows into which he enters as he grows older; he may feel that he first knows the full need of his mother's lessons when he grapples with the mysteries either of the outward Universe or of Human Society.

3. So I come to that great development of the doctrine that Physical or Positive studies should be the induction to Human studies in which

M. Comte supposed the glory of his System to consist. Here I feel myself in a difficulty which I must state frankly, and about which I greatly desire light from those who can give it. M. Comte supposes that there is an order or hierarchy of studies, that Humanity is at the summit, but that Mathematics, Chemistry, Biology and others lead up to it. Now I am utterly unable to ascend this scale. I do not affect to be a Mathematician, a Chemist, or a Biologist. It would be the greatest quackery to pretend that I can judge whether M. Comte's arrangement of these subjects is right, or how well or ill he has treated any one of them. Am I therefore unfit to understand his doctrine so far as it bears on Humanity? Is it impossible for me without this qualification to become a Comtist? Or can I only acquire that qualification by taking for granted all that is said in M. Comte's course on topics about which I am ignorant? In the first case it strikes me that the limits of the school must be drawn very closely; that the conditions under which it is entered are severer than those which any sect in the world has laid down. But I open a book written in a popular style and addressed to all Europeans and Americans; there I find people of every class and tongue urged at once to become proselytes of the new faith. That book sometimes leaves a painful impression upon the mind that the second alternative—that of implicit faith—is demanded of us. Much is said to have been done by 'Positivism'

The Hierarchy of Studies.

Must we know them all before we become Comtists? or accept the whole course of them as articles of faith?

LECT. XIX.

The School apparently invites us to consider their human teaching without this preparation.

behind the scenes; we seem sometimes to be told that we *must* receive its lessons on Humanity, they being inevitable deductions from doctrines previously established respecting Mathematics, Chemistry, Biology. When, however, I meet with Comtists, men of the highest worth and honesty, who do not profess any deep acquaintance with these subjects—who, at the same time, would never submit to the infallibility in a Philosopher which they deny to a Pope—I feel that I must have misunderstood them on these points; that they do not mean to exclude us from the benefit of their lessons upon what they deem the highest of all topics, because we are not competent to pass an examination in the lower. Although therefore I should like some more confident assurance that I am not venturing on sacred ground without the proper initiation; I shall assume that it is lawful to claim my portion, ignorant as I am, in the Humanity of which the Comtists speak. I think they will find hereafter that men will not care as they ought to care for Mathematics or Chemistry or Biology, if they are not first induced to assert their rights as

Humanity may be the last of Studies; is it not also the first?

men. I may fully accept M. Comte's doctrine that Humanity is the climax of these studies. I must also believe that it lies beneath them, and must in some way be the preparation for them.

4. If this point is settled we can do much greater justice to the comprehensive Humanity of this teacher. That he refuses to confine it by any sectarian limits, that he would recognize of all kindreds

and nations as sharers in it is a valuable and necessary protest, it seems to me, against opinions which have prevailed in all parts of Christendom. What the humanity of the Eastern Empire was I have tried to shew you. How the West became more and more Latin in all its thoughts and conceptions; how Protestants rebelling against this limitation introduced others still narrower, so that the rejection of what is common to man seemed to be the badge of their circles, I have also been compelled to explain. We may not have learnt these facts from the Comtists' preaching; yet we may be heartily thankful to it for not allowing us to forget them or explain them away. As little can we deny the service it has done us by declaring that the mere Roman Virility must not be confounded with Humanity; that we cannot feel the length and breadth of that word till we acknowledge the grandeur of the woman's position. Once more we must rejoice that they have not permitted these to be barren maxims, that they have insisted upon them as truths which must affect the Politics of the world; which must be tested by the circumstances, not of other times, but of our own. Such hints are most salutary and bracing; they speak not of compromises but of battle; if we are to be swept away in the battle, as they threaten that we shall be, we must nevertheless prepare ourselves for it.

LECT. XIX.

The comprehensiveness of the Comtist Humanity to be highly prized; as well as the claim that it should be tested in practice.

5. If I recognise the worth of this conception because it protests against the attempt to exclude

any portion of the race from the circle of Humanity, I honour it quite as much because it treats Humanity not as degraded, but as glorious. On this point also I have been forced to own that it is at war with the lessons which different portions of Christendom have derived from their teachers, with those which prevail in Protestant sects, as well as among Romish Orders. It is at variance also with the doctrines of Philosophers so little in sympathy with either as Thomas Hobbes. The difficulty indeed of combining a view of Humanity which is inclusive with one which is elevating has been felt in all ages and by all thinkers to be enormous. Is it not a truth that a majority—a vast majority—of our species are gross and animal; nearer—to use a phrase which an illustrious statesman has made classical—the ape than the angel? Does not every new investigation bring this truth more home to us? Is not Science endorsing it? The consequence is that from whatever point theorists start, they commonly end with adopting under some form or other, the doctrine which they complain of when it assumes its Calvinistical form. They hold whatever is good among men to be exceptional. The Comtists bravely resist this conclusion. They will pay the highest honour to Humanity as such. If they contemplate it in particular specimens, that is, if I do not mistake, because they suppose the characteristics of it to be most fully exhibited in those specimens.

6. And they suppose the human characteristic,

that which all are to strive for because it is human, to be not Selfishness but Love; only when each man seeks not his own interest, but the interest of the whole Society, is he truly human. That is the goal we are to seek; not the obtaining of rewards, not the escape from punishment, but this sublime and perfect Charity. Great as the Intellect is, it must bow to the heart; all efforts after knowledge, even if pursued according to that wonderful system which M. Comte elaborated, are still conducing to this higher end; only when that is attained has Positivism fulfilled its mission.

LECT. XIX.
Acknowledgment of Love to others not ourselves as the true end of Humanity.

Portions of this language may sound not altogether new to us. Do you think we can safely dismiss them on that plea? Have we understood them so well—have they penetrated so far into our practice—that we can afford to part with any one who sings them afresh to us, mingled possibly with some sharp notes of denunciation and contempt? If Comtists know the secret of combining reverence for all mankind with resistance to the selfishness to which we feel that each of us has continually yielded, surely we should listen earnestly while they impart it. If they do nothing but cause us some shame, that may be the very good we want; those who stir us to that may be our highest benefactors.

Benefit of this lesson even though we may have heard it before.

What is the secret then? It is this: 'Part 'with your Theology. Exalt Humanity into the 'place which it has occupied.' The words have a most tempting sound. There are numbers who

The way to the goal.

are eager to accept them. I think I have partly shewn you why. If I gave you different passages from M. Comte's books which shew what he supposed Theology to be, you would be still better acquainted with his reasons. He often compliments the Theology of the Catholic Church for vindicating the feelings against the mere glorification of the intellect by Philosophers. But Positivism, he says, does that more perfectly; it exalts the heart to its right place, to its highest honour. Theology has worshipped a woman in the person of the Virgin. How much better does Comtism fulfil the same object! Theology has kept up a certain notion of a Society not confined to one nation with a Supreme Dogmatist over it. That was very well for the Middle Ages; it was better than the anarchy which the brutal conflicts of the different States might have produced. It suggested the thought that there is an educational power as well as a merely governing one. But Positivism has adopted all that is good in this doctrine into itself. A supreme Dogmatist must give place to a perfect System; a wider Humanity must displace what was merely the preservation and development of certain maxims originating with a set of Hebrew teachers. Then Theology has its direct mischiefs. It encourages Selfishness. It leads men to abandon the interests of the earth and mankind for the sake of rewards which are to be obtained in some future world. It is also adverse to fixed principles such as Science craves for. It introduces uncertainty and fluctuation by promising continual interferences on behalf of particular favourites.

The Creed and the Lord's Prayer passed over as insignificant.

Now you will perceive how much excuse there is for these charges; how little right any one of us may have to say, 'They do not apply to me.' But did it not occur to M. Comte that there was another way of judging what the Theology of Christendom is besides an examination, which must be somewhat loose and hasty of the tenets and practices of its particular teachers? Might he not, just for a moment, have looked at those very short documents to which I have referred so often, seeing that they are recognised by all the teachers, and also are the language of the people? If he had done so he would have discovered exactly what is the difference between his conception of Humanity and the theological one; he would *not* have discovered any one of those characteristics which, either for praise or blame, he has imputed to Theology.

The Humanity of the Creed.

He would not have found that the Creed of the West speaks either of the feelings or the Intellect. He would have read in it of God a Father who is the Creator of Heaven and Earth, that He is emphatically *not* a capricious Being who interferes on behalf of a few favourites, but One who had made Himself known to men through a Son— that Son entering into the nature of men, dying the death of men, rising for men, exalting His manhood at the right hand of God, being the

> LECT. XIX.
>
> *A Head of Humanity unites all the elements of it.*

Head and Judge of men. Here is the common Humanity of men; here is that Humanity exhibited not in some partial examples, but in a Central Object to whom all may turn, in whom all may see their own perfection. And that Perfection is emphatically the Perfection of Unselfishness, of One who sacrifices Himself for the good of the kind, for the pure Love which M. Comte deems the supreme good of man. M. Comte, if he had continued the perusal of this simple manual of Theology, would have heard of a Uniting Spirit who builds up a Society of men, who sets them free from sins, who promises to raise up their bodies out of death, who gives them the Life of the Eternal God which has been shewn to be the Life of the Eternal Charity. Certainly not a limited Latin or Greek Society, not one held in subjection to any Supreme Dogmatist or to the rules of any Sect.

A Headless Humanity reproduces all the different idolatries that have divided it.

What is it that M. Comte calls upon us to exchange for this obsolete infantine Theology? We are still to believe in Humanity, only in a headless Humanity. It is a Humanity which has no deeper root than our own nature, which can only be understood and adored in ourselves and in our fellow-creatures. It is no metaphysical abstraction. Positivism abhors Metaphysics. It must therefore take concrete forms; it must be reverenced and adored in those. Every one who reads history, who knows anything of himself, must perceive how plausible such a doctrine is, how highly probable it is that it should bring forth practical fruits. M. Comte has produced the most clear and complete Philosophy of Idolatry that exists in the world; the fullest justification and apology for all the worships that have divided Humanity. The only question is whether such a Philosophy is the way to a United and Universal Humanity.

I think it may be, if it has the effect which it ought to have, of leading us to see how much we have, one and all, been acting on the maxims of this Philosophy, how much we have been deifying our own partial tastes and conceptions, how little we have been confessing a Centre from which the life of all human creatures is derived, in which they may find a fellowship amidst all their diversities. What honour do not Comtists deserve of us—what columns and statues can be too magnificent for their high priest—if they bring us back to the belief that the Love which they say is the sublimest quality of men is indeed, as St John said, the very being of God; that which was manifested to men in His Son; if in the bitter despair of becoming by any effort of ours what they tell us that we ought to be, in the full consciousness of all the selfishness which Hobbes imputes to our Nature, we are led to confess a Spirit who can raise us to a participation of the divine Nature? For my own part I do not profess the least skill in confuting Comtists. I am glad to be confuted by them, since their exposure of my Theology compels me to

How Comtism may lead us back to the uniting Humanity; away from the idolatries which it seems to endorse.

understand how little I have appreciated it, and what the worth of it is.

Practical suggestions of Comtistson questions of national Policy.

I am anxious to distinguish between any Social arrangements which Comtists may recommend and their fundamental principles. Their dogmas about the relations of Labourers to Capitalists are entitled to the same respectful consideration as all others that have been propounded by Frenchmen or Englishmen who have devoted thought to that subject. If they seem to contradict others which have commended themselves to our judgments, we need not be in a hurry to reject either. Still less ought we to despair of a solution of the most difficult problems, because our assent is demanded to so many different solutions; every student, every practical man may contribute some hint which we cannot afford to lose; in action we may discover the use of one and another that we have slighted. If Comtists sometimes appear as decisive in their conclusions upon those points which must be open to the influence of varying circumstances as upon the most universal principles, that is the ordinary infirmity of young and vigorous schools bent upon shewing that they are not content with figures in ivory or pasteboard, but must have actual pawns and bishops and kings to play with. And surely it is well for us to be reminded that all our principles must be tested at last by what they can do for our own characters and for mankind.

From those applications of this System which

concern the intercourse of Nations with each other, we may all I think derive much instruction; many grave warnings as to immoral notions and habits which we have tolerated in public men, and have perhaps cherished in ourselves. As long as they adhere to the word 'international,' I can listen to them gratefully; for that word recognises the distinctness of the bodies which hold fellowship with each other; it excludes the imperialism in which Nations are lost. But there is in this system such a dread of the individuality which I believe is involved in the existence of Nations; such an evident hankering after the 'death' of Jesuitism if it could be secured without the name which Loyola adopted, and (as I hold) dishonoured; the founder and disciples of this school have such an admiration for Charlemagne's doings in the West, such a liking for the civilization of China even though the 'Progress' which they admire is not quite compatible with its 'Order'; that one cannot but perceive an Empire looming through all their speculations, however much it may at present be kept out of their own sight as well as ours.

LECT. XIX.

And on international questions.

Importance of that phrase.

Tendency to Imperialism in Comtists.

If that vision did come in its fulness upon some of the disciples of this school, if they saw that they must in deed as well as in name renounce the Liberty which was once dear to them—I suspect they would begin to reconsider with great seriousness the steps by which they had arrived at such a result. I should be very sorry if their reflections led them into an angry reaction against

Danger of a Reaction in men awakening to the worth of Liberty.

their teacher or his lessons. Those who have known most of these reactions in themselves or seen them in others would be guilty of a crime if they tried to produce them in any one. I hope that instead of revolting against M. Comte, his disciples may always remember him as the discoverer to them of the great truth that there must be some Universal Society for men. That Society, as I have tried to shew you, may take the form of an Empire; then it will be but a repetition of the experiments against which the cry in men for a Brotherhood has ascended to heaven. It may take the form of a Family; then it may satisfy that cry, if indeed there is a Father in Heaven who adopts men of all Nations and Kindreds into His Family, and teaches them what are their places in it.

LECTURE XX.

DEMAND IN THE NEWEST CIRCUMSTANCES FOR A DIVINE GROUND OF HUMAN LIFE AND HUMAN MORALITY.

WHEN I spoke to you in the last Lecture of that which I called the Modern Conception of Humanity, I did not intimate any purpose of adding to that conception some theological tenets modern or ancient. If I undertook such a task, I should not only be forsaking my proper province as a Moralist, I should be making all that I have said to you about Morality unintelligible. I have not tried to shew you that something is desirable besides the Universal or Human Morality which has been the subject of this course; I have wished to ascertain what is the foundation of that Morality; how it can be in very deed a Morality for men as men, a Morality for you and me. I believe, as I have said, that all the partial conceptions of Humanity and of Human Morality which the enquirers of the 18th century be-

<small>LECT. XX.

Purpose of this Lecture.</small>

434　　　　　*UNIVERSAL MORALITY.*

LECT. XX.　queathed to us, as well as that more comprehensive one which has been elaborated in our own day, afford us the greatest help in understanding the lessons of those periods which we had examined previously. But I fully admit that the test of all principles affecting to be moral and human must be their application to the circumstances in which we are placed. What signifies it to us if they were adapted to Palestine in the first century, or to Constantinople or Rome in the middle ages, or to the Teutonic nations at the Reformation, if they do not explain our lives, if they cannot direct our practice in this year 1869? We may respect them as fragments of antiquity, we may deposit them in museums, but we must have something else for our common daily business. Because I can find no other which is adequate to our emergencies, I go back to the principle of a Universal Family which was announced eighteen centuries ago, and which has been subject to so many contractions and mutilations in subsequent periods. I accept the principle in that primitive form which has been preserved among the people of Christendom, whatever may have been the opinions of its different doctors.

The real test of a Principle.

The Root of Humanity.

I. That a Fatherly Will is at the root of Humanity and upholds the Universe was the announcement which shook the dominion of capricious demons and the throne of an inexorable fate in the Roman Empire. The circumstances in which it was first proclaimed shew how much the

Universality of the announcement was involved in its essence. The resistance to it came from the Jews, because they said they were the chosen people of God, the only favourites of Heaven. The Apostle of the Gentiles—whom it is the most modern fashion to credit with the characteristic peculiarities of Christian Theology—affirmed his privilege as a Jew only to be this, that he might proclaim his Gospel concerning God to all Nations. His cause would have been lost, every argument which he used would have been stultified, his sufferings would have been wasted, his influence on mankind would have been nothing, if he had not delivered this as a message to men just as he found them, not after they had entered the Church, but as the reason why they should enter it. Every attempt that was made afterwards by any Church or any school to make the truth of the announcement dependent on the acceptance of it by one set of men or another was a defiance of his express words; must deprive the morality which he deduced from it of all reality for them or for their race.

Universality of St Paul.

Now the circumstances which are at this time creating the greatest suspicion of Christian Morality are these. We know that an immense world has been discovered of which the Palestine fishermen and the tentmaker of Tarsus knew nothing. 'While it was possible to contemplate Christen-
'dom as constituting the world, or at least all that
'is sacred in it, the morality of these teachers,' it

Modern objection to Christian Morality.

it is said, 'might be accepted as sufficient. It
'led to great crimes and brutalities when new
'regions of men were revealed to the sailors of
'Spain or Holland or England. Those who lay
'outside the fold might be treated with unbridled
'ferocity, or be compelled by such ferocity to come
'within it. Afterwards when along with com-
'mercial intercourse and civilization some notion
'of a common Humanity began to prevail, the
'Churches caught a little of it, talked with pity of
'the poor exiles from God's mercy, and when no
'longer able to persecute them, made considerable
'efforts to persuade them that the European faith
'in some one of its forms was better than their
'own. But though in these efforts some gentle-
'ness towards people of other religions may
'have been called forth—though that may have
'been found on the whole the most useful policy
'for the proselytisers—what fellowship can they
'have felt with those whom they warned under
'the most terrible penalties to become like them;
'how can they have confessed that there was any
'common moral standard to which they might
'appeal?'

I am not careful to consider the numerous exceptions to this charge which the records of every
sect and Nation might offer, because I wish you
to observe, that if it was true absolutely and
without any exception against all Christians, it
would only shew what had been the effect of neglecting the maxim from which they started. It

is equally true that every instance of the behaviour towards men of other races and faiths which is the opposite to this has been an adherence, whether intentionally or not, to that maxim. Suppose a man to hold it fast, he must trace all sense of Justice, Veracity, Equity, Kindliness in himself to that which he affirms to be the perfectly good Will; he must acknowledge every unjust, untruthful, unfair, unkind act of his as a rebellion against it. He must attribute all the imperfection of his acts either to a confused apprehension of this Will, or to some perverse influence which hinders him from giving effect to his apprehension of it. And this judgment of himself must be also the one which he forms of all with whom he is brought into contact. Whatever sense of Justice, Veracity, Equity, Kindliness is found in them must have its source in that same Will, cannot have any other source. Whatsoever in them is unjust, untrue, unfair, unkind, must come from a confused apprehension of this Will, or from some false influence which prevents them from giving effect to their apprehension of it. The principle in both cases is precisely the same. And the treatment of the cases must be in all essentials the same. To set up a Western standard of morals against an Eastern is to deny our principle—to exalt ourselves in any degree, either on the plea that our civilization is better, or that our religion is better, is to confute the claims of each. The man who boasts of *his* peculiar

Deduction from the apostolic maxim.

What it prohibits.

LECT. XX.

Boasting self-contradictory.

civilization boasts of his narrowness, of his incapacity to recognise the distinctions and varieties which are found in the society of men as in the natural Cosmos. The man who boasts of his religion, boasts that he has some special God who is not the Father of all the Families of the Earth, who is not the root of all that is right and true in himself and all men, who does not abhor what is wrong or false in him as much as in all other men.

There can be no doubt that any one who is uniformly just, fair, kindly in his dealings with those of another faith, still more that any one who deliberately exerts himself to improve their condition, to elevate their thoughts, to make them partakers of all that he finds most precious to himself whatever it be, does undermine the worship of separate local gods, still more the worship of unjust and cruel gods, even though he never speaks a word against them, though he enters into no argument to withdraw any one from them.

Influences which undermine or sustain immoral divinities.

On the other hand, if, under any pretext, we assume a right to insult or bully or corrupt or cheat any man in any country whom the chances of dominion or diplomacy or trade throw in our way, we do what in us lies to confirm that man in the belief of insulting, bullying, corrupting, cheating gods; we lead him to pay them homage as the best means of securing their connivance or support, and of counteracting our violence or our tricks. This effect we shall produce, because we are, in our inmost hearts, doing homage to these gods ourselves, because we are invoking them, if not at public altars and temples, yet in our daily transactions, in our secret thoughts. It is well that we should thoroughly understand this. Comtists or others may talk to us about getting rid of theology. We can very easily get rid of that theology of which I have spoken to you in these Lectures—of that theology which recognises a Righteous Will, a Fatherly Will, as the ground of us and of the Universe. We do get rid of that continually; we shake it off as a most inconvenient burthen. But we cannot get rid of *some* theology. When we have rejected the name or names that men have worshipped, the substance, the character which the names represent, cleave to us as closely as ever. The more we feel that there is no object above our nature —no ground beneath our nature—the more will those tendencies, appetites, antipathies, which we find *in* our nature, present themselves to us as irresistible powers which we must obey. They will associate themselves, as they have done in all mythology, with the powers of the outward world; then in spite of all our knowledge of that world, these powers will combine with those which we feel characteristic of ourselves to terrify and enslave us.

I believe the circumstances of our time are compelling us to take notice of these facts, that men in all directions are taking notice of them.

> LECT. XX.
>
> *Recognition of a common Standard by opposing thinkers.*

Those who speak most of the moral corruptions which are to be discovered in Hindostan, Japan, in any Eastern land; those who complain that we will not recognise the nobler qualities which are to be found in the natives of all these countries; those who ask whether the same evils which Christians have denounced as the results of Heathen worship are not to be seen in their own actions—all alike, however they may wish to fix our attention upon one set of facts, and to make us incredulous of others which rest upon evidence as strong and decisive, are leading us to the same result. They all point to a standard of which they are conscious, of which they discover a consciousness not only in particular men, but in whole Societies of men; they recognise in each particular man, in every Society of men a departure more or less violent from that standard. The

> *The peculiar standard less elevated than the common one.*

question how if that is so we are to account for the dissimilar maxims which men have proposed to themselves, and by which they have tried to regulate their conduct, may seem to become more difficult as our experiences become more manifold. In fact those manifold experiences are driving us to a practical solution of the difficulty—are interpreting the old solution of it. Not that which is peculiar, not that which is exceptional, is most elevated; but that which has the largest, most comprehensive sympathy, which can most enter into the conditions of those who are lowest and most degraded. Whence can such a Sympathy have issued, whence can the desire of it have issued? If its source is in our circumstances it must soon be exhausted; those circumstances, by their varieties and contradictions, are exhausting it. If the source is in ourselves, the Self of each man must extinguish it. The circumstances have given rise to those partial conceptions of worth which men in different regions have formed, which they have exalted into gods. The selfish instincts have made these conceptions incapable of reconciliation. Suppose the sympathy to have sprung from a Will which has called Man into being, which is the origin of Life and Order to the Universe, there is at least the dawn of light upon this great paradox, the promise that all our acts, thoughts, and habits may not for ever be entangled in the meshes of it.

<small>Lect. XX.</small>

<small>Those which separate men can be explained; whence has come that which unites them?</small>

II. But a Fatherly Will always must seem a monstrous and incredible dream to human beings living in a world such as we live in, if they have been left to destroy themselves and each other according to their whims and fancies. If that is the Will or the Fate which governs the Universe, there must be some Deliverer from that Will or Fate; some Prometheus who shall steal the fire that is to hinder human creatures from being utterly wretched, utterly at the mercy of the Tyrant. Such redemptions every mythology is full of—full in proportion to the experiences which there were of human misery in the land that produced it. There must be some friendly demon,

<small>Redemption:</small>

<small>from what?</small>

some co-operator with the poor victims of mortal oppression or of Death, the common oppressor—one who shall at least alleviate the wretchedness of some district or family or time if he cannot remove it. To secure such aid and co-operation what prayers must not be poured forth, what sacrifices offered! If a child will secure the help of the intercessor, if it will buy off the wrath of the enemy, can that be grudged? More and more the enemy is contemplated as absolute and supreme; the helpers as temporary and accidental. And supposing they are habitually well disposed—supposing they have not been alienated by any offences of their votaries, what do they know about the wants of their votaries? There may be pity; what participation in woe can there be? A modern poet has given admirable expression to the sense of hopeless separation between the inhabitants of the earth and its supposed rulers and to the cry which it suggests. He may or may not be right artistically in attributing such sentiments to a Greek Chorus, but they are in themselves most striking and true.

Lect. XX.

The cry for a Prometheus.

Swinburne's Atalanta, pp. 50, 51.

"But up in heaven the high gods one by one
    Lay hands upon the draught that quickeneth,
Fulfilled with all tears shed and all things done,
    And stir with soft imperishable breath
    The bubbling bitterness of life and death,
And hold it to our lips and laugh; but they
Preserve their lips from tasting night or day,
    Lest they too change and sleep, the fates that spun,

> The lips that made us and the hands that slay;
> Lest all these change, and heaven bow down to none,
> Change and be subject to the secular sway
> And terrene revolution of the sun.
> Therefore they thrust it from them, putting time away.
>
> "I would the wine of time, made sharp and sweet
> With multitudinous days and nights and tears
> And many mixing savours of strange years,
> Were no more trodden of them under feet,
> Cast out and spilt about their holy places:
> That life were given them as a fruit to eat
> And death to drink as water; that the light
> Might ebb, drawn backward from their eyes, and night
> Hide for one hour the imperishable faces.
> That they might rise up sad in heaven, and know
> Sorrow and sleep, one paler than young snow,
> One cold as blight of dew and ruinous rain;
> Rise up and rest and suffer a little, and be
> Awhile as all things born with us and we,
> And grieve as men, and like slain men be slain."

[Sidenote: Why should not the gods suffer with men?]

The answer to this passionate demand according to the Christian Theology has been given once and completely. He whom it recognises as the Creator and Life-giver of the Universe 'has grieved as men, and like slain men been slain.' He endures the tyranny which is triumphant over man's nature that He may redeem the Will of men from subjection to their nature and to all the accidents which befall their nature; that He may ultimately raise their bodies as well as their wills out of the death to which He submits.

[Sidenote: The Christian answer.]

If you fancy that you can trace in modern Europe—in any of those who have accepted the Christian Revelation—that very confusion which has mingled with the mythologies of the old world, and with those which Oriental scholars bring under our notice—if you see among the people of Christendom and even among their teachers a disposition to think of a Redemption from the Creator instead of by Him, of a Sacrifice to change His Will rather than to accomplish it—that is only a proof how little we can trust the opinions or notions of men in one region or another—how common a gravitation there is in all these notions and opinions towards narrowness and self-seeking— how habitually, if we think as the Apostles thought and spoke as they spoke, we must look not to men but to Him of whose Will they testified, whose redemption they proclaimed, to sustain our confidence in either. And all modern circumstances, it seems to me, by bringing into clearer light the feebleness and insecurity of our judgments and, at the same time, the needs of Humanity in every region of the earth, are urging us to adopt the original language, undiluted by the least Sectarian mixture, which declared that a Redemption had been accomplished for Mankind by the obedience of the Son of God, by the sacrifice of the Son of Man.

III. The announcement of a Fatherly Will as redeeming human creatures from their bondage to evil and death by this Sacrifice has been felt in all ages to be characteristic of the New Testament, however it may have been reduced and explained away by those who have undertaken to interpret the New Testament. If we accept its language in the simplest and obvious sense, another announcement was at least as distinctive of it, and was no less closely connected with its claim to be intended for all Nations. The commonest, vulgarest people were told that the Spirit of the Father in Heaven would be with them to raise, reform, and educate their spirits, to emancipate them from their animal and sensual nature, to deliver them from the suspicion, malice and vanity which set them at enmity with each other and made the pursuit of selfish ends the business of their lives. No words can be more distinct than those which contain this assurance. The presence of such a Spirit is declared to be the very bond of the Universal Society which was to be composed of such heterogeneous elements, that which alone could prevent them from breaking loose from each other, and becoming more hostile than ever. These statements lie on the surface of the record, so that the man who runs may read them. Yet they evidently belong to its inmost essence. If there is a Society for men as men, they, according to the teaching of the Apostles, explain the possibility of it. Accordingly the *people* of Christendom, when they have felt the social impulse strongly, when they have become impatient of class divisions, have turned to this language, have recognised in it a message addressed to them. On the other hand, the learned men have been anxious to construe it in some other than its apparent sense, to explain that it could not interfere with the authority of teachers

A message to the People.

Accepted by them.

who had better means than wayfarers of judging what was true in belief and right in action. Whether these advantages were derived from some external advantages of position or culture, or from divine gifts and the inspiration of the Apostles descending upon them, might be disputed. There was an agreement to this extent, though one not precluding the bitterest controversies between those who entered into it, that the popular belief is a dangerous one, sure to issue in an outbreak of enthusiasm which must be dangerous to all organization, civil or ecclesiastical. This was the feeling of the divines as well as of the philosophers in England during the last century. Enthusiasm was their horror. That must in all ways be checked. Hume's method of checking it by establishing a religion in which he did not believe I have referred to before; it was accepted by numbers who denounced his scepticism, as a desirable and judicious expedient. For they had evidence—clear evidence—from the facts of their own days, as well as from the testimonies of history, that very wild incoherent acts were perpetuated by individuals and sects who supposed that they had possession of this divine gift; to that persuasion might be traced the contempt of learning which had characterised the followers of Ziska in Bohemia, the contempt of Law and its restraints which had characterised the Anabaptists in Munster. These appeared sufficient reasons for making efforts—desperate efforts—to prove that the Apostles did not mean that this was a gift for men in all ages; that it was in fact exhausted, for all practical and important purposes, in the miracles which they were enabled to perform. To shew how necessary these were for their work—how strong the evidence was that they were performed in that age—how little any subsequent age could assert the same privilege—was a chief object of those who aspired to connect scholarship with Christianity. Protestants indeed were obliged to combat the traditions of the Latin Church in favour of the continuance of miraculous powers; but as against what were called the enthusiastical delusions, they might generally calculate on the co-operation of their opponents.

<small>LECT. XX.

The gift of the Spirit absorbed in miracles.</small>

So it was in the 18th century. A great change has taken place in ours. As in the 13th century, the popular conviction has sensibly modified if not overpowered the opinions of the learned. Our fashionable language is in many respects the very reverse of that which was adopted by our forefathers. We do not denounce enthusiasm. We are wont to speak of it as a great power, indispensable for the study of any subject, for energy to fulfil any task. The reaction has been so vehement that, as was sure to be the case, another is setting in. There is seen to be much affectation in the talk about enthusiasm, that the talk cannot promote energy either in study or action. Motives, it is supposed such as Hobbes deemed the only powerful ones, are necessary to

<small>A revolution and counter-revolution.</small>

LECT. XX. stimulate both. Rewards and Punishments of some kind are said to be the only securities for diligence in one kind of work or another.

The demand for a Society of human beings.

But however fashions of speech may alter among the wise or the unwise, the great movements of the world go on. There is in every land a people demanding to be recognised under that name, not as a set of castes; there is a demand for a fellowship which shall not be confined by boundaries of space or even of time, which shall unite us to men in the most distant regions of earth, which shall unite us to our ancestors and to our posterity. States may do their utmost to assert their authority; but can they satisfy these requirements? Ecclesiastics may put forth their highest pretensions. Can they control these aspirations?

States, Churches, Sects.

Both confess their inability. They say, 'We are rent asunder by Sects.' These, cry the Statesmen, make it most difficult to educate the people of a country; these, cry the Churchmen, destroy the Unity which we declare to be the special characteristic of Christian life. Yet what deliverance is there from these Sects? The States have tried persecution and have failed, have tried toleration and have failed. The Latin and Greek Churches have tried Excommunication, and Sects have been the result of it. Protestants have followed in their wake, behold what they have accomplished. There remain two courses. One is to ignore all that the Sects have been inculcating; to cultivate indifference; to decide that we can know nothing of the invisible world. I have not denied before—I shall not deny—the many pleas which there appear to be for this course, or the number of philosophical men who recommend it, or the attraction which it may well have for the body of citizens in every country weary with the contentions of its religious parties. I would only ask whether it is possible; whether what you have disposed of under one name is not certain to appear under another; whether as we become acquainted with different lands and seek for living intercourse with the inhabitants of them, we are not obliged to perceive how thoughts of the invisible world have mingled with all their thoughts of the visible, so that you cannot extinguish one except at the risk of extinguishing the other? In an age which demands the freest scope for thinking there must be a broader, deeper line of demarcation drawn between the subjects which it may approach and those which it must avoid than the most dogmatical priest or ruler of consciences was ever able to draw. We may confidently affirm that if it were drawn in this day as in former days hosts of new sects would spring up to efface it, and would obtain power over the hearts of the people everywhere just *because* they effaced it.

<small>Lect. XX.

Scheme of banishing the invisible, how far feasible.</small>

The other alternative is that which I have just spoken of. We may believe actually, as we have professed in words to believe, that there is a

<small>The other method.</small>

LECT. XX.
The Spirit who teaches Fishermen and Sages.

Spirit guiding and educating the thoughts of us and of all men, awakening us to activity when we are most inclined to be slothful, keeping us at one when we are most inclined to be divided. Instead of shrinking from this assertion as one that is likely to exalt the vulgar against the cultivated, we may announce it to the most vulgar because we desire for them the highest culture; to the learned because we wish them to know what Humanity really is, and how they may be instruments in bringing forth that which is latent in the most brutal. So the first may feel all arrogance, self-conceit, refusal to learn, all unsocial tempers, a rebellion against a divine Teacher who would make them capable of receiving illumination and diffusing it; so the second, when their zeal in study and discovery is flagging, may recognise an inspirer, may perceive that he is a detecter of the frauds which they practise on themselves, of the excuses which they make for not fairly grappling with facts and giving all weight to evidence. Then as to common morality. It was a great blunder in the teachers of the last century, first to tell poor men that they must not rob and cheat, and that they ought to be good husbands and fathers; and when they said they had found a counseller nearer

And keeps them from vile acts.

to themselves who resisted their inclination to rob and cheat, who inspired them with a desire to be good husbands and fathers, then to reply, 'There 'is no such counseller for you; there was One who 'enabled the Apostles to do strange acts, but He 'has left the earth long ago.' It was a fearful blunder, for it led these poor men to rejoin, 'Well, 'and why should not we perform strange acts 'too? We did prize the Helper who enabled us 'to do common acts, to care for our neighbours, 'to be honest and just in our dealings, but since 'you say that there is no other sign of His pre-'sence but the doing of that which is uncommon, 'we will try to work wonders.' So the enemies of spiritual guidance became the abettors of the impostures and insincerities which they intended to put down.

<small>LECT. XX. The results of denying His presence with common men.</small>

But whatever may have been the case then, the circumstances of our time shew how certain it is that Society in the most civilised lands will perish through the frauds of rich men as well as poor men—of the most refined and the most outwardly religious—if there is not some power which can create a habit of honesty, which can resist the secret temptations to flagrant dishonesty in men whom neither the terrors of law nor of public opinion can hinder from bringing disgrace on themselves and ruin on their fellow-citizens. Such discoveries give us stronger reasons for asking whether the news of such a Power which came to men centuries ago must be discarded as false, whether they may not be accepted in a more complete sense than they have ever been?

<small>Commercial knavery.</small>

There are other facts which the sight of the streets in every civilized capital bring home to us, which are brought much more vividly home to

<small>The Streets and Homes of London and Paris.</small>

those earnest men who have penetrated into the dwellings within those streets. Much, very much has been done — much more might be done — for the improvement of those streets and dwellings by mechanical contrivances, by medical knowledge, by wise legislation. But there are habits in men and women which may set at nought the effects of all mechanical contrivances, of all medical knowledge, of the wisest legislation. They cannot be reformed by any of these; till they are reformed they will produce ever more crimes, ever fresh misery. Who can work this reformation? Threats of punishment cannot, promises of reward cannot. Is there not some demand for the old faith in a Spirit to regenerate social life as well as individual life, to overcome the sources of death, ultimately to raise men out of death itself?

We want — I cannot say how much we want — the labours of physiologists, of statesmen, of men with every kind of gift, to co-operate for the removal of the plagues that torment Humanity. We want them; most thankful we shall be that so many of them are ready to meet the want. Who has inspired them? Who has taught them to labour for an end which is not a selfish one? I wish they would ask themselves that question. I have tried to find an answer to it in this Lecture. I have sought for the source of that Humanity, of that human Morality, which I see and admire in one man or another. I have sought for the source of the habit, the temper, the character which I believe is struggling in every man with those impulses to self-indulgence and self-aggrandisement which I find in myself, which the wisest observers have detected in our nature. I cannot discover any defence of this Morality, any security for the permanence of it or the development of it, any power of combating that which is opposed to it, except in that Spirit to whom the Apostles attributed every gift which they possessed, but to which they traced as habitually the consistency and harmony of the Society that was meant for all men. The phrases which confess this presence cannot be the power that we want if those phrases are true. They speak of that which is not measured by our notions or apprehensions of it, they promise that clearer revelation of it by which we hope to see the weakness of our apprehensions detected, all that is strong in them expanded.

LECT. XX.

Opinions about such a Spirit must be false if the power is in them.

There is however a notion current among men of letters and men of business—not unsanctioned by divines—that the portion of the New Testament which has been supposed to contain its Canon of Morality is wholly unsuited to the conditions of Modern Society, though it may be accepted as a respectable and venerable document if it is reduced into figures and denied all connection with ordinary practice. 'The Sermon on the Mount speaks,' it is said, 'of those 'to whom it is addressed being perfect as the 'Father in Heaven is perfect. Of course, therefore, it only suggests what are technically called

The Sermon on the Mount.

Counsels of Perfection.

'*counsels of perfection* to men who are disposed 'to quit the business of the earth and devote them-'selves to the contemplation of a future world. It 'leaves ordinary crimes which men are prone to 'commit in order to warn the select class against 'purely internal evils. It bids that class abs-'tain as much from seeking the protection of law 'as from self-defence by arms. It teaches them to 'depend on divine help such as is afforded to 'ravens, not to work for their bread. It encou-'rages indiscriminate almsgiving which we know 'to be so mischievous. It forbids us to exercise 'any criticism on the acts and opinions of our 'fellow-men. In every particular it sets at nought 'the most established maxims of modern civili-'zation, all that has been proved to be most 'important for the well-being of our community.' If these statements are true, the doctrine which I have endeavoured to establish in the Lecture is overthrown. I am therefore very anxious to examine whether they are true.

1. That the command—*Be ye perfect as your Father in Heaven is perfect*—taken in connection with the previous words—*He maketh the sun to shine upon the just and the unjust and the good and the evil*, instead of recognising a class of devotees was the first complete proclamation of a Universal Morality, I have maintained already. All dreams of such ' counsels of Perfection' as lead to the separation of men into classes, of just and unjust, of good and evil, are shattered by that

sentence. Unless there is some way in which the disciples of Christ can care for the just and the unjust, for the good and evil—can care for men as men—they are declared to be not like their Father in Heaven. Accordingly the strongest denunciations of the sermon are directed against the Pharisaical sect of Jews which was following *these* counsels of perfection. Such were the counsels of the Scribes and Pharisees—schemes for cultivating a righteousness which should make them eligible for higher rewards than other men. Those rewards, so the sermon everywhere declares, could not be the rewards which the Father who seeth in secret bestows. His reward is that likeness to Himself, the unselfish Being, which such self-seeking makes impossible. *Denunciation of Pharisaical righteousness.*

2. Instead of such crimes as Adultery or Murder being spoken of as if they belonged only to the outside world, the disciples are expressly reminded that they are just as liable to fall into them as any men; that the propensities which lead to them exist in every human being and may at any time be developed into acts. The acts are subject to the cognisance of the Law. If it meddles with any thing besides acts it becomes mischievous and cruel. Yet the Lawgiver feels that there is something behind which is producing the acts: if there was any power which could reach that something, which could prevent the commission of the acts, what trouble he would be saved, how thankful he would be! Christ tells men the good news that they may have a will in accordance with the Law, *Laws against overt acts.* *Christ deals with the source of the acts in the man.*

LECT. XX. that they may overcome that in themselves which leads them to violate it. An esoteric Morality surely in the strict sense of that adjective; but universal *because* esoteric—applying to the inner life of all men, to the man himself. To talk of this as a superfine morality, a morality for the specially religious, is to pervert language grossly. It is only a morality for them so far as they acknowledge themselves to be like all other men. It is a message to all men that they may be right and true, for God would make them so.

The internal Morality the universal.

3. "If any man ask thy cloak, let him have thy coat also" is supposed to interfere with the principles of Justice. I apprehend that we interfere with the principles of justice when we take other men's coats or cloaks, not when we give up our own. A man of great genius in our day, Victor Hugo, has perceived the immense power which a literal compliance with this command might exercise in the reformation of a criminal. The hero of the *Miserables* is changed from a ruffian into one of the noblest of men precisely by this kind of conduct in the Bishop from whom he stole a pair of candlesticks. A beautiful illustration surely of the way in which the interests of Law and of Social Order may be promoted by one who does not consider that they exist to promote *his* advantage or secure *his* property; that a man is worth more than these. He benefits the individual and the Community equally because he does not prefer himself to both.

The Bishop in the Miserables.

4. There is however one great exaggeration and perversion of the words "If he compel thee to go with him one mile, go with him twain," which this excellent Bishop sanctioned in his practice. He seems to have read, "If a criminal tell thee one lie, tell him two." So his virtue confirmed the offender in one of his most characteristic vices. Apply that doctrine to the passage in which the disciples of Christ are told not to turn away from him that asks. The whole principle of the Sermon being that the man is to be like his Father in Heaven, we must learn what this precept means from the sentence. 'Your Father in Heaven will not give those who ask Him a stone for bread, a serpent for a fish.' He will not do men an injury merely to please them. If I regard a beggar as a fellow-man, as a brother, I shall conform to the same rule. I shall not give him what would make him idle and brutal. I do turn away from him if to get rid of him or to please myself I degrade him. What then if it has been proved by criminal statistics or by Political Economy that indiscriminate almsgiving is most mischievous? That proof determines this application of the principle in the Sermon on the Mount; it shews what would be an unbrotherly act. It does not alter the principle unless Statistics and Political Economy have proved that all men are *not* brothers. No National Morality rises to *that* principle. But its own principle of neighbourhood, needs the deeper and more universal one to sustain it. Maintain the *meum* and

Lect. XX.
How the Bishop extended and perverted the principle.

The case of Beggars.

The national Morality of neighbourhood demands a Universal Brotherhood to sustain it.

tuum if you can; but the *tuum* will be effaced by the *meum* if there is not some principle which is capable of defending humanity against selfishness. In that case, Political Economy will never be able to defend itself against the natural instinct of monopoly, let its maxims be as much accepted as they may.

Work not better when the workman is restless.

5. Christ's disciples, it is supposed, were told that they need not work because they were commanded not to be anxious and restless about the results of their work. If I wanted evidence that this Sermon belongs to the circumstances of our time this passage and the objections to it would supply the evidence. We have fallen into the notion that we shall work more energetically with our hands and with our brains, because we are continually fretting ourselves about what will come of our work, what pence or praises we shall get by it. And yet every one of us knows in his inmost heart that this fretting destroys the honesty of his work and the effects of the work. If we could be free from this perpetual fever, if we could work from an internal impulse, not under

The modern incentives to labour of the hands and brain.

the pressure of external motives,—if we could work as freemen not as galley slaves—what a difference it would make to the health of our bodies and of our spirits and to all our influence upon Society! If it were not a falsehood to tell the student of a University, or the tiller of the ground, or the woman in a factory, You have a Father in Heaven who cares for *you* at least as much as for the sparrows, who will sustain your life—your human and your animal life—no less than that which He has given them, what a new spring of hope there would be for them in their most solitary hours, what a sense of fellowship! Is it wonderful that this part of the discourse should be more out of harmony with the temper of a restless excited age than any other, and yet that none should be so necessary for such an age? And what a curious illustration it is of our current notions that we should be supposed to need this kind of inward help and strength less than a former age, because our occupations are so multiplied, because we have so many new mechanical aids which earlier times had not for fulfilling them.

marginalia: Lect. XX. How they confirm the lesson which is said to be obsolete.

6. Precisely the same twofold remark is applied to the command not *to judge lest ye be judged*, not *to take the mote out of other men's eyes while a beam is in our own*. None can be so tormenting to all of us of every school and sect and profession; none seems so necessary if Society—human Society—is not to be extinguished by the jealousies and enmities of schools, sects and professions. If there is a Social Morality this must be its leading maxim. If there is a Personal Morality this must be its leading maxim. Here they coincide. The distinctions of the just and the unjust, of the good and the evil, which are as much recognised in fact by those who reject the words as by those who attach the most importance to them, cannot be discovered by the study of other men's lives, by

marginalia: The command not to judge. Its application to our day.

prying into their acts and their motives. I can only be a true critic when I am my own critic; when I distinguish between the powers which are fighting in me for ascendency, which are claiming me for their servant. And when I enter into this criticism I perceive how treacherous it will be if there is not a Judge over me who detects what I cannot detect, who shews me my evil that He may lead me out of it. When I ask who this Judge is, the old words come back to me. I find that the internal teacher, who appears to take me apart from my kind, is in very deed that Spirit of the Father in Heaven who unites me to my kind, who shews me that the highest blessings are those which I share with it, that the worst curse is to lose fellowship with it and therefore with Him.

The need of a Judge of our thoughts and purposes.

I shall have more to say on this subject in my final Lecture. I will conclude the present with two remarks. The first has reference to the passive or feminine character which has often been ascribed to the Sermon on the Mount. It has been thought to discourage all the qualities which have been most conspicuous in heroes who have struggled for freedom; to commend the submission which is sought for by tyrants and paid by slaves. Since I have spoken to you of the message concerning a Father in Heaven as being exactly that which encountered the image of a Man God upon earth, you will understand how far I can accept this statement. The Sermon on the Mount was expressly designed to prepare those who heard it for

The morality of the Sermon said to be feminine, and unheroic.

opposition and persecution, for the courage which could defy both and endure to the end. That object is manifest upon the surface of it. The notion that it is hostile to courage springs from the opinion that what sustains courage is a sense of self-importance, and therefore that whatever undermines this sense weakens courage. That unquestionably is a favourite tenet in this day. The incapacity of this self-seeking, bragging spirit to resist any great oppressor will, I believe, be made manifest by the circumstances of our time. When Imperialism comes forth in its full force to demand our homage, we may find that *we* demand something to oppose it which we have lost. And then we may understand as we never did before, that the free and brave Spirit is the Spirit of Charity and Truth, the Spirit who fights in us with our selfishness; a Spirit which makes men feminine, if feminine means courteous, deferential, free from brutal and insolent pretensions; but which also gives women manliness, if manliness means the vigour to live for the cause of Humanity and die for it.

The other remark has reference to what I said in a former Lecture about Cardinal Virtues. I said I believed there might be such virtues, and I quoted the words of the Apostle concerning Faith, Hope and Charity. I did not say more lest I should mislead you. There is in some a notion that Cardinal Virtues mean certain specially grand and exceptional virtues which entitle certain men

[marginal notes: LECT. XX. The courage of the braggart not that of the hero. Cardinal Virtues.]

LECT. XX. to specially grand and exceptional rewards hereafter. Cardinal Virtues in this sense are identical with those Counsels of Perfection to which I have just referred. You will judge therefore how little I can admire them or associate them with Universal Morality. But a Cardinal Virtue may signify just what its etymology would suggest. It may be the hinge on which other Virtues turn, without which they would have no coherence, no vitality. If that force is given to the phrase, there can be no doubt that the Sermon on the Mount does set forth the Cardinal Virtue. Self-Sacrifice is that upon which all its precepts hinge. Without this the Faith, Hope and Charity of the Apostle would be mere idle names, they would have no relation to the practice of Life. But Sacrifice leads us again to the original principle of the Discourse— 'Be like your Father in Heaven.' Men are only bidden to exhibit this grand principle of Morality in their acts—they are only able to exhibit it because He has given the example of it. The Paradox is amazing, but it is the Christian Paradox, the Human Paradox. The fuller illustration of it must be reserved for the last Lecture of this course.

<small>Self-Sacrifice the cardinal principle of Human Morality.</small>

<small>Its divine foundation.</small>

LECTURE XXI.

HUMAN WORSHIP.

I CONCLUDED my course on Domestic Morality with a Lecture on Domestic Worship. In all classical Mythology—in all Mythology we could hear of— divinities were spoken of as parents, children, brothers, husbands, wives. To deduce these thoughts from the phænomena of Nature was impossible; to connect them with the conditions of earthly families was obvious. The question was forced upon us, *What* is the connection? The Mythologies contemplated it under two contradictory aspects. There was a continual tendency to impute all the corruptions of Family Life which are found on earth to the unseen rulers of the world. There was an acknowledgment not less clearly manifest of a domestic Order from which these were departures, there was a feeling that the Gods must be the preservers of that Order. This conflict of opinions could not be adjusted, though in different places and times either might be pre-

<small>LECT. XXI.

Domestic Worship.

Its two aspects.</small>

dominant. When a Society is clearly sinking into disorder and baseness—when it is becoming untenable—its tastes and appetites are eagerly transferred to the rulers above; they exhibit the same in a more aggravated form because they are credited with greater power to indulge them. On the other hand, whenever any cry begins for the reformation of a Society, for some escape from its domestic confusions, there arises a suspicion that the conception of Worship has been a false one, that the Gods cannot be the images of those whom they are supposed to govern and direct; that if they exist at all it must be as the models and protectors of Order, not as the examples and patrons of what is disorderly. If that is so, cannot they shew that it is so; cannot they come forth to vindicate and establish the Order? to cure the disorders?

<small>Lect. XXI.
Moments of decay.
Moments of renovation.
The Nation and its worship.</small>

That thought of an Order, if not wanting before, acquires quite a new vigour when a *Nation* emerges out of a horde of Families. By whatever revolution that change is effected, it seems always to be preceded by the sense of oppression from some visible power, sustaining itself by an appeal to invisible powers; with the belief in a Deliverer from the oppression of both. The conviction becomes mighty that He has in some way made Himself manifest in that character; has proved Himself to be a Ruler as well as a Deliverer. So *National* Worship begins. It is in its deepest root the recognition of the ruler of all as Righteous, not capricious, as a Deliverer not as an Enemy. He is the Author and Vindicator of Law, the Defender of Boundaries, the Head of the Host, the Source of Speech and Government. There blends inseparably with this the old sense of Domestic Authority. He is the Avenger of all outrages upon domestic life and peace. He upholds the right of the Father and the Child. He binds the Husband to Wife. He is the detecter and the foe of the Adulterer.

LECT. XXI.

Recapitulation of its characteristics as described in a former Lecture.

In all national worship therefore is implied a continual cry for help against oppression, for the defence of Right when it is most crushed under Might. A King of Kings is always judging the visible King—when he is thoroughly given up to self-seeking and arrogance, putting him down. There is a prayer to one who is on the side of the poor and the helpless. But there is also a prayer from the man against himself, against his own inclinations to break the law under which he is living and to become an oppressor. There is the same tendency to corruption in this Worship as in that which is more strictly domestic. The Statesman may discover a great charm in the notion of a Religion which by arts that he does not possess can keep the people quiet. Could he not turn it to his account? Could he not bring the object or objects of the people's worship into his service? might not the thunders above echo the decrees which go forth from his lips on earth? It is a wonderfully clever fancy. He finds priests and augurs who thoroughly enter into it. The impres-

Its degeneracy.

sion of their power on the multitude will be much deepened if the lords of the earth shew that they are dependent upon it. By degrees these priests actually persuade themselves that they can command those gods whom they profess to obey. The fraud creeps unawares into their souls till it possesses them wholly. Then they and the statesmen cheat and overreach each other; the people are the victims of both. They may pray for luck in their traffic or their robberies; they can scarcely hope for deliverance from any oppression; for are not the powers above the agents of those below? To this state was the Worship of Rome sinking just at the time when its most enlightened citizens were learning from Greeks to treat it as an open question whether Gods existed at all—or whether if they did, they must not be simply enjoying their own felicity without any concern about the happiness and misery of mortals.

Imperialism was the inevitable outcome of this highly civilised morality, this religious Unbelief. I shewed you that there was no novelty in the Empire or in its worship. Families could not be abolished, therefore the old names of divinities which pointed to the existence of families could not be abolished. It was convenient to retain the old names which spoke of laws and orders; therefore it was convenient to retain the worship of Gods who upheld laws and orders. But Domestic life, national life, were crushed under the hoof of the Cæsar, therefore the Cæsar must be *the* God of the

World, whatever other Gods there were in earth or heaven. {LECT. XXI.}

Family Worship, National Worship had both been mingled with the idea of Sacrifice. It was felt that Sacrifice must for some reason or other be the essential of both. It seemed to be the bond of Society, to be strangely interwoven with the fears and hopes of individuals. Yet it seemed also to be the dissolution of the bonds of Society, to involve frightful violations of domestic affection, to enable the individual offender if he was rich to rise above the law and the gods who enforced the law whilst the poor man became at once a hater of the law, and a victim of the priest who taught him by what offerings he might escape from the greatest terrors of it. Everywhere legislators felt that Law was imperilled by the notion of Sacrifice, everywhere that it was a notion rooted in the hearts of men which must, if possible, be converted into an ally. Imperialism cut the knot. 'Let there be sacrifices to as many gods, or to what gods you please; but there must be Sacrifice to the Image of the Emperor.' That was the true crisis of the principle. For so it was shewn that the first of all questions in Universal or Human Worship is not 'Shall there be sacrifice?' but to what kind of Will shall the Sacrifice be made? and the second, What shall be the chief oblation? {The practice of Sacrifice involved in all worship.} {Sacrifice: to whom?}

The Christian Martyrs amidst many confusions of speech and of thought made very distinct answers to both these questions. We must not sacrifice, they said, to this image, but to the Image of One who is in contrast of this Cæsar; to One who is not bribed by the sacrifices of His creatures, but who has made the great Sacrifice for them that He may reconcile them to Himself. And the oblation which He enables us to make that we may be like Him, is the oblation of ourselves. They thus proclaimed to their generation and to the generations which should come after them and should have any honour for their memories, that Christian Worship is a protest against all self-willed, self-seeking power in Heaven or Earth, is an acknowledgment of a Fatherly Will—a Will to redeem and restore Humanity, a Will which is expressed in Sacrifice; that it is an offering to that Will of the men themselves that they may be what He would have them be, may do what He would have them do. That I understand to be the idea of Christian Worship which has been floating in the minds of all Churches and Schools in Christendom, however little they may have realised it. My object is to shew you how that idea the more it is realised exhibits the principles and sustains the practice of a Universal Morality.

I. The announcement of a Will, such as I have supposed to be at once the ground and the object of our Worship, obviously presumes a Revelation. In the last Lecture but one I spoke of what seemed to be the entire inefficiency for any moral purpose of what is called a Natural Theology. I did not deny that those who have elaborated that Theology have imported into it many conceptions of Justice, Mercy, Benevolence. But it seems to me that these conceptions *are* imported into that region. They are not found in the stars, or in the wings of insects or amidst geological strata. To demand of a Natural Philosopher that he should detect them seems to me a gross injustice. I rejoice when he rises up against it. I think it is honesty in him to say, 'We cannot pick up divinity or morality on the sea shore, they do not grow amidst any flowers that we have examined.' I think they are honest also in pointing out all the contradictions of the natural world, all the signs of death and destruction that are found in it; all the reasons which might excusably lead men and have led them to suspect malevolence as well as benevolence in the construction of it. Nothing of this kind ought to be suppressed; to hide facts or try not to look at them is a great rebellion against such a Will as I confess.

<small>LECT. XXI.
Meaning of the word.</small>

And how then can I know anything of such a Will? When I answer, as I have answered so often, I can only know a Being who is above me if He reveals Himself, I do not mean if He tells me in some laws or letters what He is. Accepting the New Testament I believe that He cannot shew me in laws what He is, that He can only shew me in a Person and in the acts of a Person what He is. The older records took that principle for granted. In acts of deliverance and judgments done for a Nation and explaining in some

<small>Discovery of a Will to those who are its subjects.</small>

LECT. XXI.

The Old Testament speaks of such a Revelation.

measure the government which was exercised over other Nations the Jewish lawgivers and Prophets say that He declared His mind which is the same throughout all ages. The words of wise and true men who believed in the Divine Order and sought not to mix their own confusions with it, illustrated and expounded these acts to their countrymen; they disclaimed the vanity of being themselves the authors of any wisdom they might impart; they traced it all to the Source of Wisdom. So they became, I conceive, instruments of the Divine Revelation; so they taught all in all ages what Discovery is, who it is that enables them to know whatever they do know. But since they testified of an everliving Teacher and Discoverer, they could not be satisfied with any Revelation of Himself which had yet been made. They believed that He would shew fully in some Man what He is.

What was needful to complete it.

What we call the New Testament Revelation is the unveiling of such a Being—of such a Will, to men; that is to say, of a perfectly Moral Being—of the Will in which all the Justice, Sincerity, Fidelity which exist partially in any Nations or Men have their fulfilment and their root, a Will which cannot be satisfied except in delivering men from their Injustice, Insincerity, Infidelity; except in imparting to them His own character, His own Image. That I take to be the first part of a Human or Universal Worship, the acknowledgment in whatever forms of speech, by whatever signs—the most simple and universal having most evidence of a divine origin—of a Will that is absolutely good, of a Will that has sought and is seeking to make men good. In Mr James Mill's *History of British India* there is a powerful exposure of what he calls the flattery of Worship; of the attempt to conciliate the power which is supposed to be supreme by bestowing upon it grand titles and giving it credit for sublime virtues. That must undoubtedly be the way in which divinities are honoured who are regarded as answering in the unseen world to Emperors in the visible world; as liable to their changes of temper and open to the motives which affect them. But there is a delight in Truth and Goodness which must find an expression that is compatible with awe and reverence; which as it shrinks from flattering the dearest of earthly objects must be horrified at any approach to insincerity towards Him from whom their excellence is derived. To be made true is above all other things that which you ask of the living and true Being.

Flattery of the powers above.

II. That which you *ask;* for that is the difference between the subject of the last Lecture and the one with which we are occupied now. Then I was considering what a demand the newest circumstances of our time, the newest philosophies of our time, make for a divine ground of Society and Social Morality. The circumstances are overwhelming in their multitude, in their variety, in the temptations which they offer to ambition,

How the demands spoken of in the last Lecture suggest the need of Prayers.

self-seeking, fraud. The philosophers are tremendously severe and exacting. We must seek the greatest happiness of the greatest number, we must acknowledge the imperative of Duty, we must have a love for others in which the love for ourselves is lost. The first two forms of philosophical Dogmatism stand apart from Worship; when the last dawned upon M. Comte he felt that there must be a worship of some kind. It was a great discovery. But it has seemed to many of his disciples that he was merely placing a Corinthian capital upon an edifice already very firm and compact, a capital which though it struck him as a very beautiful and artistic completion of his design, had in their eyes a rather incongruous appearance. I confess that if I looked upon Worship as having this ornamental character I should not care much about it. I might introduce it into a discussion upon Social Morality along with Stage-Plays and Cricket Matches, but I should not expect it to command the same attention as either.

It is because having learnt the demands which the time and the philosophers make upon me, and the exceeding difficulty from my own selfish tendencies of satisfying the demands, that I turn to Worship, adopting what M. Comte would call the infantine conception of it. If it is possible to have communication with a Will such as I have been speaking of—one which is good, and is seeking to make us all like itself—then I must suppose that we may singly and unitedly ask that this

HUMAN WORSHIP. 473

Will may be accomplished in us all, and so that we may become reasonable members of a Society —in the real sense of the word, fellow-creatures.

When I speak of the Will which I own as being the highest of all 'seeking' to make us right, I am not indifferent to the question which has tormented you and me and all human beings— 'Why does it not make us right without seeking?' Having known what this doubt is I certainly should not dispose of it by saying, 'How can we know?' For such an answer would at once throw us back on a mere Power which may be dreaded but cannot be worshipped. I believe we *can* know because we can ask to know. The asking shews us what sort of rightness that would be which comes apart from communication with any higher Will, what that rightness is which is the effect of communication with it. However little or feeble our apprehension of that communication may be, it is enough to make us aware of the difference between the rightness of a stone which rolls down a hill because an impulse has been given to it, and the rightness of a Will which struggles with obstacles and overcomes them because a higher Will is inspiring it. And the effort at all hazards, and in spite of all resistance external and internal, to grasp that higher Will and to claim its energy when our own is least, may shew us all in some degree what the wonder of our human life is. I do not know in what way Physiologists may ultimately determine the difference between it and the life of brutes.

LECT. XXI.

The paradox of a Supreme Will seeking to make men right.

How it is solved in practice.

474 UNIVERSAL MORALITY.

LECT. XXI.

In the struggle with a something in us which is assuredly brutal, in seeking for a divine strength against it, the most degraded men have realised—I know no other way in which the most intellectual can fully realise—this difference.

Visions of the Past, how to escape from them.

In that struggle we become aware of one human distinction which some might be glad to part with. The past rises again, links itself to the present, as if they were one, forbids us to separate the future from either. In vain philosophers teach us that it is foolish and childish to occupy ourselves with the recollection of that which has been, that remorse is unnecessary. The past occupies itself with us; the spectre appears without being summoned; like Cæsar's it says, 'I will meet thee again.' When any philosopher offers us a charm for laying the ghost, how rejoiced we are to try it! to adopt a new one when the last has failed! There has been a trade in these charms wherever human beings have dwelt; every superstition has been an attempt to disengage men from their bygone acts and thoughts, from their own past existence; those dark sacrifices to which I alluded before have seemed to promise most.

The deliverance from Self.

And surely the expectation had a right ground. Through Sacrifice—through the giving up of a man's self—must come his escape from the ghastly visions of the past as well as of the present and the future. Only if he can acquire a portion in that Humanity which, as M. Comte perceived, cannot be selfish—does he obtain what he craves for, that freedom from the torment of the individual Conscience which enables him to be truly a social being. Such a giving up of Self Christians have affirmed to be possible since the Head of their race has made it first, since He has shewn forth a perfectly filial submission in doing it. If that is so a Worship which turns upon the confession of this Sacrifice, which claims for each human being the right to accept it for himself, cannot be a mere supplement to Morality, should be the most effectual instrument of removing all that interferes with the daily practice of it.

LECT. XXI.
The Sacrifice.

III. When first the belief in such a Sacrifice, not for one nation or class, but for mankind, dawned upon a little band of men speaking the most uncouth dialect of Palestine—scarcely aspiring to be reckoned genuine Jews—they may well have been staggered. But they could not doubt that the Worship which had such a principle for its ground must be emphatically a Eucharist, a thanksgiving for a transcendant gift making all common things look beautiful and amazing, giving a divine character to the earth which they trod, to the food which they ate. It could not have been so if they had not believed that He who 'like slain men was slain,' had overthrown the Empire of Death, had vindicated Life, human life, animal life, from the destruction which in every man seemed to have overpowered it, and yet to which no man could willingly submit. The supremacy of Death is that which has everywhere

The belief in a Conquest of Death.

been the plea for superstitions in those who have sought for a while to baffle it, the plea for slavish surrender to a necessity in those who have despaired of any effect from these superstitions. Yet every one who devises plans for the future which he can never see completed, every Physician setting the devotion to fate at defiance, every scientific man waiting for unknown results, not suffering himself to be checked by Christian or Comtist who tells him they may be worth nothing—men of letters, students of all classes who do not work to please their own age and meet its fancies—bears witness that the works of man and the thoughts of man are not 'rounded with a sleep;' that there is an unlimited future before him. It is easy to say that the expectation of such a future must be selfish if it is personal; that if it is anything but a vague dream of some benefit to posterity it must be inconsistent with an enlarged and enlightened humanity: to say this is easy; to feel it is easy. For since selfishness dogs us at every step, since it mingles with every feeling that is most adverse to it, since it checks every aspiration that springs up in contradiction of it, can we wonder that popular writers represent all good if we claim to be sharers in it, all truth if we say to be without it is to be in Hell, as so much property which we are wishing to enjoy by excluding others from it?

It is so natural, so obvious, that when we read of the Son of God, 'that for the joy which was set before Him He endured the Cross and despised

HUMAN WORSHIP. 477

the shame,' such writers scream with delight, 'See His own disciples confess that His aims were selfish,' though they affirm that He gave up Himself to redeem and restore the Universe. And how can any one answer the charge in his own case who is conscious of a continual disposition to seek his own interest at the cost of the interests of other men? He cannot answer it except by saying that he feels his selfishness to be the curse and misery of his existence; that it is his privilege as a human being to seek fellowship with one who did sacrifice Himself for the sake of mankind; that he can, whilst he aims at that fellowship, confess the self-seeking habits which separate him from it; that he can look forward to a resurrection and renovation of Humanity, to its deliverance from that which is destroying it; such he conceives the highest reward he can desire for himself or for any of his fellow creatures. But he will not pretend that he does not look upon all minor rewards as included in this; the renovation of all intellectual energies which are dwarfed and impaired by the low and grovelling aims to which they were directed; the renovation of physical health in Societies which, as the most recent evidence demonstrates, have been and are suffering in unspeakable ways and through unknown channels from their moral corruptions. Believing that all in their different walks and vocations may contribute to the restoration of health and the removal of the corruptions which lead to disease and sickness, he counts it a

Lect. XXI.

The victory over Self the great reward.

All other rewards involved in this.

grand comfort that all may in a common Worship seek for the common inspiration which shall make these ends dear to them, and which shall call forth the wisdom that may devise means suitable to such ends. Unless there has been a Resurrection, a permanent vindication of the glory of Life, a contempt put upon Death in all its aspects and forms, I cannot think that any theories or speculations—least of all any sentimental expressions of tenderness for death as if it were not an Enemy—can avail to free men from the terrors of it, and from all the slavery to which those terrors have led. For Death will assuredly express to men the ultimate purpose of the Universe—attribute the origin of it to Nature, Necessity, or molecules or demons as you please—if there has been no conquest of it. And that purpose once admitted there must be a drying up of the human energy and hope which have risen up against it; a drying up of this energy and hope as much in those who have supposed them to be their own as in those who have traced them to a Father in Heaven.

IV. Those who do trace them to that Author must, I conceive, see in all Worship at once the profoundest confession of their own impotence and nothingness, and the profoundest assurance of a good to Humanity which they cannot in the least conceive of, but which neither their selfishness nor the selfishness of all men can obstruct. The highest, the most celestial contemplation they can imagine is that of the purposes and movements of the

Will which has called them into existence; of the methods by which it has worked, and is working, to bring all things, and especially all human Wills, in subjection to itself. But such a contemplation cannot be separated from a hope for the renovation of the Earth; for a destruction of all that has caused its degeneracy and decay; for a discovery of every one of its vital powers and principles. To all men who are busy in searching for those powers and principles, under whatever difficulties, amidst whatever confusions, the true worshipper must, in the strictest and solemnest sense of that language, wish God speed. He must be sure that God is speeding such enquiries and will bring them to their full result. There has been a notion amongst moralists and divines, that the physical student is seeking for certainties, that they are to be content with probabilities. Hence all communion between them is destroyed; they seem to have a different starting point and to be pursuing different objects. A Worshipper can only rest upon One who is absolute Truth, who guides into Truth. He begins therefore from certainty. But since it is not *his* certainty, since he may have only a feeble grasp of it, he looks for a guide to himself and to all, in whatever directions their intellects and their affections may move, through all the mazes in which they may be lost, to the rock which lies beneath them, beneath the Universe.

Worship then I conceive becomes the link

Lect. XXI.

Worship the bond between Moral and Physical Studies.

between Physical and Moral Studies. It vindicates a common ground for both; it asserts Science not Probability to be the aim of both. All restraints upon the freest exercises of human thought by any mortal power it leads us to regard as a defiance of God; all checks upon discovery as indicating an unbelief that He is or that He is such a Being as Christ has revealed to us. But the severe restraints which Science imposes upon the self-conceit and arrogance which are the enemies of clear free thought, upon the haste which substitutes our judgments and notions for discovery, have their best protection and security in the humility and awe which Worship cultivates, or rather which He to whom the Worship is directed cultivates in us. The moral demands of physical Science are, if we may trust its most earnest defenders, those who are most jealous of our interference, quite amazing; we wonder when we think of the patience, self-denial, continual surrender of the most cherished notions which they exhibit, and without which they say no progress can be made, no victories achieved. Just so far then as Sacrifice which is the principle and the end of Worship is sought for and obtained, just so far may we look for fresh vigour, for new successes in physical enquiries, because for a deeper and more complete Social Morality.

We do not want the pursuers of physical science or their great teacher to remind us that there may be an innocence in their studies which stands in great contrast to all that the Social Moralist encounters in his proper sphere. He finds himself amidst the disorders of Families, the calamities of Nations, the more terrible contradictions of the Society which professes to be Universal. To believe that there is a harmony amidst all these discords, to believe that the Harmony will at last prevail over the discords is most hard. It becomes harder the more closely we look into particulars, the more the actual details of domestic life, of civic life, of ecclesiastical life discover themselves to us. They must be faced in our every day's experiences; they pursue us into our solitude if we fly from them; there we find the source of the confusions which torment us in the world. But if there is at the root of all human Society, of Humanity itself, that divine Sacrifice which our Worship sets before us, the Spirit of which it teaches may go with us wherever we go, whatever we are doing or thinking or purposing; there must be a light penetrating the gloom. When I have spoken of Human Worship, I have not meant some grand Cosmopolitan worship to be hereafter evolved out of the modes of particular races and nations, when all those are blotted out. I have endeavoured to shew you how much mischief has proceeded from every effort to constitute a Universal divine Society which shall swallow up these distinctions into itself. We want for the establishment and

The Social Moralist obliged to encounter evils of which the Physical Student takes no account, and therefore to seek a deliverance from them.

rectification of our Social Morality not to dream ourselves into some imaginary past or some imaginary future, but to use that which we have, to believe our own professions, to live as if all we utter when we seem to be most in earnest were not a lie. Then we may find that the principle and habit of Self-sacrifice which is expressed in the most comprehensive human Worship supplies the underground for national Equity, Freedom, Courage; for the courtesies of common intercourse, the homely virtues and graces which can be brought under no rules, but which constitute the chief charm of life, and tend most to abate its miseries. Then every tremendous struggle with ourselves whether we shall degrade our fellow-creatures, men or women, or live to raise them—struggles to which God is not indifferent if we are—may issue in a real belief that we are members one of another, and that every injury to one is an injury to the whole body. Then it will be found that refinement and grace are the property of no class, that they may be the inheritance of those who are as poor as Christ and His Apostles were; because they are human. So there will be discovered beneath all the politics of the Earth, sustaining the order of each country, upholding the charity of each household, a City which has foundations, whose builder and maker is God. It must be for all kindreds and races; therefore with the sectarianism which rends Humanity asunder, with the Imperialism which would substitute for Universal fellowship a Universal death, must it wage implacable war. Against these we pray as often as we ask that God's will may be done in Earth as it is in Heaven.

NOTE.

It may be as well to mention that the reference in a note to p. 66 of this volume is not to the Essay of Mrs Butler which introduces the deeply interesting series of Essays on Woman's Work and Woman's Culture; but to an earlier pamphlet which had excited much attention in Cambridge and elsewhere. The volume of Essays had not appeared when the Lectures on Domestic Morality were delivered. In connexion with the subject of this final Lecture, I would commend to the attention of my readers the eloquent and fervent protest of Miss Cobbe on behalf of her sex against the worship which the Comtists claim for it. Miss Cobbe expresses, with much greater power, the conviction to which I have given utterance, that if we set up idols for ourselves to worship, the idols will suffer as much degradation as those who bow down to them.

www.ingramcontent.com/pod-product-compliance
Lightning Source LLC
Chambersburg PA
CBHW052132010526
44113CB00034B/1908